TROUBLED MEMORIES

SUNY series, Genders in the Global South

Debra A. Castillo and Shelley Feldman, editors

TROUBLED MEMORIES

Iconic Mexican Women and the Traps of Representation

Oswaldo Estrada

SUNY
PRESS

Cover illustration: *Inundación Castálida*, by Perla Estrada. Courtesy of Perla Estrada.

Published by State University of New York Press, Albany

Printed in the United States of America

For information, contact State University of New York Press, Albany, NY
www.sunypress.edu

Library of Congress Cataloging-in-Publication Data

Names: Estrada, Oswaldo, author.
Title: Troubled memories : iconic Mexican women and the traps of representation / Oswaldo Estrada.
Other titles: Mexican women and the traps of representation
Description: Albany : State University of New York Press, [2018] | Series: SUNY series, genders in the global south | Includes bibliographical references.
Identifiers: LCCN 2017058956 | ISBN 9781438471891 (hardcover : alk. paper) | ISBN 9781438471907 (pbk. : alk. paper) | ISBN 9781438471914 (ebook)
Subjects: LCSH: Mexican literature—21st century—History and criticism. | Women—Mexico—History. | Women in literature. | Sex role in literature. | Archetypes in literature. | Women in popular culture.
Classification: LCC PQ7123.W6 E88 2018 | DDC 860.9/35220972—dc23
LC record available at https://lccn.loc.gov/2017058956

10 9 8 7 6 5 4 3 2 1

To my daughter, Elena Alegría,
whose life inspires me beyond words.

Sobre el cadáver de una mujer estoy creciendo,
en sus huesos se enroscan mis raíces
y de su corazón desfigurado
emerge un tallo vertical y duro.

(Upon the corpse of a woman I am growing,
among her bones my roots are entwined,
and from her disfigured heart
emerges a strong and vertical stalk.)

—Rosario Castellanos, *Poesía no eres tú* (*Poetry Is Not You*)

Contents

Illustrations

Acknowledgments

I began working on this book several years ago, and although other projects came along, I always returned to this one with the love one feels for those dreams that take longer to achieve.

On two different occasions, I have been a faculty fellow at UNC's Institute for the Arts and Humanities, first in 2011 and again in 2016, when I received a Chapman Family Distinguished Teaching Award. Thanks to my conversations with other fellows whose work and feedback have inspired me in many ways, I studied these iconic women from an interdisciplinary perspective, surrounded by a community of engaged scholars. Thanks to an Academic Excellence Award from the Institute for the Arts and Humanities, I was able to do research in Mexico in 2014.

Having the opportunity to present some of this research at various scholarly gatherings has been invaluable, and for that I thank Oswaldo Zavala (Graduate Center, City University of New York), Susan Antebi (University of Toronto), Encarnación Cruz Jiménez and Grant Gearhart (Georgia Southern University), Francie Chassen-López (University of Kentucky), Liliana Wendorff (Queens University of Charlotte), Tamara Williams (Pacific Lutheran University), José Ramón Ruisánchez (University of Houston), Louis Pérez (University of North Carolina at Chapel Hill), and Vinodh Venkatesh and María del Carmen Caña Jiménez (Virginia Tech). I also thank Carlos Roberto Gómez Beras, editor of *Cuadrivium*, for inviting me to submit an article on Elena Poniatowska's *soldaderas*, which comes in part from the fourth chapter of this book.

Several friends have given generous comments and thoughtful suggestions for improvement after reading some of my chapters: Mónica Díaz on Malinche, Patricia Saldarriaga on Sor Juana, John C. Chasteen on Leona Vicario, and Francie Chassen-López on the *soldaderas* of the

Mexican Revolution. Having this input throughout the writing process was vital. I am deeply indebted to Debra A. Castillo, coeditor of the SUNY series Genders in the Global South, for welcoming my project from the beginning and for all of her suggestions. I am also thankful to Rebecca Colesworthy, acquisitions editor at State University of New York Press, and Chelsea Miller, her assistant, for their professionalism, dedication, and constant help throughout this process. Dana Foote has been an amazing production editor. Two anonymous evaluators gave great suggestions for improvement, and I thank them sincerely. I also thank Perla Estrada for giving me permission to reproduce her paintings of Sor Juana and Frida Kahlo, Cecilia Hinton for her collage *Si Adelita se fuera con otro*, and Janet Kelo for her drawing of Leona Vicario. Special thanks to Perla Estrada for giving permission to use her wonderful painting of Sor Juana for the book cover.

Many other friends have been supportive while I was writing this book: Corinne Pubill, Julia Medina, Clare Counihan, Pablo Brescia, Ignacio Sánchez Prado, Ariana Vigil, Irma Cantú, Sarah Pollack, Anna M. Nogar, Verónica Grossi, and Anca Koczkas. As always, my UC-Mexicanistas family has been there for me at all times, especially Sara Poot Herrera, Linda Egan, Norma Klahn, Jacobo Sefamí, Beatriz Mariscal Hay, Alicia Rueda Acedo, Ignacio Ruiz Pérez, Ricardo Vivancos, Brian L. Price, Cheyla Samuelson, Judith Farré, Yasmin Temelli, Vittoria Borsò, and Adela Pineda. I am also thankful to Carmen Alemany Bay, Eva Valero Juan, Francisco José López Alfonso, Dianna Niebylski, Luz Elena Zamudio, Maricruz Castro Ricalde, Elizabeth Martínez, Rocío Ferreira, Anadeli Bencomo, and Rose Mary Salum for conversations, collaborations, and a shared love for this profession. Along these lines, I have greatly benefited from a fruitful exchange of ideas with writers Elena Poniatowska, Pedro Ángel Palou, Rosa Beltrán, Cristina Rivera Garza, Sandra Lorenzano, and Adriana González Mateos, whose exceptional generosity and knowledge of these women have greatly affected my work.

I am grateful for an amazing group of graduate students at the University of North Carolina (UNC) at Chapel Hill, with whom I have discussed my work on numerous occasions. Many thanks to Alejandra Márquez, Wesley Costa de Moraes, Adrienne Erazo, Etna Ávalos, Jhonn Guerra Banda, and Carlos Vázquez Cruz. Special thanks go to Sarah Booker for editing and improving my translations from the original sources. Many thanks to Teresa Chapa, UNC's librarian for Latin American, Iberian, and Latina/o studies, for getting me so many books so I could write this one. My colleagues from Romance Studies have been very supportive, especially Rosa Perelmuter, Juan Carlos González Espitia, Jessica Tanner, Monica Rector, María A. Salgado, Irene Gómez Castellano, Hélèle de Fays, Abel Muñoz-Hermoso, Glynis Cowell, Emilio del Valle Escalante, Federico Luisetti, and Sam Amago.

I thank my family on both sides of the Atlantic for believing in me, for standing by my side through thick and thin, especially my wife, Cristina Carrasco, whose optimism, strength, and unparalleled love for life have saved us, time and again, from sinking into deep waters. Home is where you are, our daughter's laughter and smiles, her first words, her scribbles on a piece of paper that mean the world to us.

Introduction

Iconic Mexican Women at the Threshold of a New Century

On April 17, 2015, after more than three decades of forensic anthropological research, Sor Juana's attributed remains returned to Mexico City's Convent of San Jerónimo, where the prodigy of New Spain lived and produced the vast majority of her literature over the course of twenty-six years. During the mournful ceremony marking the 320th anniversary of her death, her remains were carried in a wooden casket crowned with the nine-foot rosary found with her body to the church choir, where she will stay "until the Day of Judgment," as several reporters announced on national television, social media, and various online sites. Many visitors, faculty, and students carrying red roses filled the Universidad del Claustro de Sor Juana (University of the Cloister of Sor Juana) to attend the solemn procession. Round tables featuring new publications on Sor Juana and readings by specialists on the nun's literary production took place over the course of two days. The jewel in the crown was a reading of the "Oración fúnebre" (Funeral oration) that Octavio Paz, winner of the 1990 Nobel Prize in Literature, wrote for the 300th anniversary of her death in 1995. The event, followed by a recital of Baroque music, included the presentation of an official Mexican postage stamp featuring a portrait of Sor Juana, painted a few years earlier by Carmen Beatriz López-Portillo Romano, rector of the university. The event was a total success. The ceremony was immediately covered by *La Jornada*, *Milenio*, *Excelsior*, *El Universal*, *Proceso*, and other important papers throughout the country with impressive headlines and pictures of people in mourning around the coffin as if someone had just passed away.

Only an iconic figure like Sor Juana Inés de la Cruz would have the power to do this three centuries after her death, even if there is a chance those remains are not hers. After all, icons behave in this way. They have the capacity to convey a relatively fixed meaning or value to a community that knows how to read their signs and symbols in situations that include veneration, admiration, and other complex emotional responses (O'Connor and Niebylski, "Reflections" 1). Icons re-create particular prototypes or models; they are regarded as cultural artifacts; and they are, indeed, the vehicles by which societies project themselves. Because of these intrinsic qualities, icons are able to communicate their encoded messages to a given community that, for better or worse, sees them as constant cultural companions (Onasch and Schnieper 17, 31, 209). In addition, they signify differently in multiple contexts; they may incorporate legend or myth but extend far beyond the limits of a single story. Ultimately, they stand the test of time because they are malleable, elastic, and adaptable to changing circumstances and historical contexts (Irwin xix).

Precisely because of their transformative power, the women that I study in this book—from Malinche and Sor Juana to Leona Vicario, the *soldaderas* of the Mexican Revolution, and Frida Kahlo—have become, like other cultural icons, objects of consumerism (Miller, "Contesting" 62). Not coincidentally, all of them have appeared on Mexican currency: Malinche on a banknote from the Banco de Tabasco in 1901 (5 pesos); Sor Juana on the 1,000-peso bills of 1985, the 1,000-peso coins of 1988, and the 200-peso bills in circulation since 1994; Leona Vicario and the anonymous *soldaderas* on the 100-peso coins of 2010; and Frida Kahlo on the 500-peso bills of 2010. Even though some of them are "worth" more than others, these banknotes and coins, as well as the postage stamps in which Vicario, Kahlo, and Sor Juana have appeared in or outside Mexico, highlight their cultural significance and their overall monetary value. This market value, I would add, has increased in a globalized era that sells their images as autochthonous or genuine Mexican products in a great number of postcards, logos, T-shirts, hats, and posters.

As true objects of consumerism, these iconic women symbolize a set of historical values, cultural desires, social tensions, and specific gender confrontations, debates, and transgressions within Mexico's patriarchal society. Historically, Malinche has been considered a traitor to her nation for helping the Spaniards during the Conquest of Mexico, even though we have many reasons to believe she was an astute messenger, diplomatic ambassador, and effective interpreter. As a lettered nun, Sor Juana has been depicted not only as Mexico's greatest intellectual of the Baroque era but also as an anomaly. Surrounded by her books and writing utensils, sitting at her desk instead of kneeling in front of a religious image, she is the highest expression of colonial knowledge, a *rara avis* who uses words as a weapon in a world made for men. Along with other female patriots of Mexico's independence, Leona Vicario is remembered for sacrificing her personal fortune and social status to help the insurgents. If Malinche is the mother that Mexicans reject, history and popular legend have turned Leona into the beloved mother of a new nation. The *soldaderas* of the Mexican Revolution, regardless of their multiple roles as nurses, soldiers, messengers, and spies, have entered history as passive camp followers; they are commonly known as *Adelitas*, as if they all shared the same identity. Frida Kahlo is the tormented artist of the twentieth century whose disabled body defies normalcy and validates otherness and transgression. Her bizarre self in pain, mutilated and perpetually in disguise, represents a challenge to heteronormativity and a blow to calcified beauty ideals.

As icons, all of them have become symbols of national identity—associated with the Conquest of Mexico, the colonial era, the birth of the nation, the Mexican Revolution, and the postrevolutionary era.[1] What makes them unique is the fact that they have transcended their historical specificities to symbolize cultural values associated with certain female archetypes and signs that have been appropriated by high and low culture in countless ways. They exist because Mexican culture needs an indigenous woman to carry the heavy weight of the Conquest; a criolla prodigy whose intellect defies coloniality; an altruistic patriot who fights to free her nation from the Spanish Crown; a loyal *Adelita* who follows her *Juan*, unconditionally, to build a better Mexico; and a controversial artist whose difference, otherness, and disabilities fuel stories of empowerment and success. As mythical figures, these women communicate something, a particular message, a type of language; they signify and transmit specific concepts; they represent a system of signs and symbols (Barthes, *Mythologies* 217). Their iconic status allows them to adjust to new historical contexts, different cultural circumstances, political agendas, aesthetic demands, and ideological struggles.

Since the early twentieth century, several of these women have been reimagined in novels, essays, poems, and chronicles that reveal how history and gender politics, popular tradition, coloniality at large, nationalism, and religion have placed them on a reduced spectrum in which women are either good or bad and rarely occupy intermediate zones. The North American Free Trade Agreement (NAFTA) of 1994—"the linchpin of Mexican neoliberalism in the 1990s" that promotes privatization, deregulation, and free trade to allow mostly middle-class people to "shop the world," while the poor majority is left behind (Chasteen, *Born* 332–35)[2]—also affects literature production and the rearticulation of historical figures of the colonial era, national icons of Mexican independence, and revolutionary heroes. At the turn of the twenty-first century, as a growing number of social institutions embraced neoliberalism and increasingly became personalized and privatized, Mexican literature overtly explores the uniqueness of the individual, intimate emotions, personal experiences, and the world of the private. After all, in the context of neoliberalism, emotions—in art, in the self, or in other people—do not always challenge market-oriented thinking. Instead, feelings and emotions are acquired, invested, traded, or speculated on (Smith 6). Not coincidentally, the novels, plays, chronicles, short stories, and essays I analyze herein were produced and marketed at the same time that Mexico celebrated the 200th anniversary of its independence and the 100th anniversary of its revolution. Their content reveals neoliberal trends found in a number of sitcoms, TV series, films, soap operas, and talk shows of the same period: the overt exploration of privacy and explicit sexual confessions in tune with the experiences of a middle class trapped in a matrix of consumption and globalization (Monsiváis, *Aires* 237; Sánchez Prado 71).

I analyze the literary representation of these iconic women because I believe that literature is socially significant: it captures social ideals and tensions, cultural problems, and beliefs. Literature, as Beatriz Sarlo argues, is a high-impact discourse whose constant state of conflict between aesthetics and ideology "stays in the text and can be re-activated once the text has exhausted its other social functions" (29). Literature represents a plurality and multiplicity of knowledge. It transports the essence of human conscience, along with doubts, fears, hopes, and spiritual intensity. It reminds us especially that the world is full of contradictions, unresolved cultural conflicts, abject realities, and dissident voices that reject simplification (Sontag, *Al mismo* 156–61). In the best scenarios, literature can also be subversive: it communicates personal opinions, social criticism, political postures, and hegemonic or counterhegemonic ideals that invite us to think critically of the world we inhabit (Vargas Llosa, *La tentación* 221). Even bestsellers produced for fast and easy consumption project the anxieties of a community at a given historical time, regardless of their literary quality, superficiality, ephemeral reception, and poor aesthetic value. The fact that many people buy them not for their literary quality but for their attractive covers—to decorate their homes, to give away as presents—expresses a contemporary reality: that societies do not always privilege reading but cannot live without certain icons and cultural products representing a set of values attached to fame and popularity (Zaid 58).

Inevitably, the literary works I analyze here raise controversial issues in regard to "high" and "low" culture, especially if we consider that some of them will stand the test of time and others will not. Although bestsellers certainly make profit for the publishing industry, the vast majority of them, in this neoliberal era, will not generate rereadings and rewritings, even though our world propitiates constant dialogues between "high" and "popular" culture (Gutiérrez Mouat 72–75). The issues at stake here are not the boundaries between high art and mass culture or the fact that they are becoming increasingly blurred and reveal new discursive configurations (Huyssen ix–x). Literature, after all, exists within the market industry. What we tend to see in contemporary times, however, is that the market influences certain literary products from their initial conception, as if they were only written in order to sell, or to entertain, and not necessarily to promote in-depth reflections (Rodríguez Freire 122–24). These new literary principles reflect numerous societal changes in a neoliberal era that promotes the massive consumption of "easy" and/or "light" literary works that will hardly survive their own time.

Thus, focusing on a wide range of men and women Mexican authors born throughout the twentieth century, over the course of four chapters and an epilogue I discuss the challenges involved in the representation of affect and emotions, authenticity, verisimilitude, and the logical or unbelievable creation of possible worlds. In view of this literature, I explore the central place of historical women and female archetypes in contemporary Mexican culture, as well as the innovative or troublesome ways contemporary authors either contest or perpetuate a series of bad habits and tendencies attached to the historical and literary representation of a woman's life. Consequently, this book addresses the role of memory and discourse, the perpetuation of otherness, textual experimentation, and the long-lasting effects of gender violence, among other themes and topics.

In many ways, *Troubled Memories* creates a dialogue with the pioneering work of Seymour Menton (1993), Noé Jitrik (1995), Karl Kohut (1997), Juan José Barrientos (2001), and Fernando Aínsa (2003), whose critical and theoretical postulates are key to understanding Latin America's historical narratives produced in the 1970s, 1980s, and 1990s. Invaluable to the development of this book has been the work of critics Kimberle S. López (2002), Ute Seydel (2007), Magdalena Perkowska (2008), Elisabeth Guerrero (2008), and Brian L. Price (2012), whose studies highlight the political quality of numerous rewritings of history of the late twentieth century. Unlike these works, my book focuses exclusively on the representation of iconic Mexican women and mainly on the literary production of the twenty-first century. My approach to recent rewritings of Mexico's history, grounded in feminist and gender theory (produced in Latin America, Europe, and the United States) addresses Mexican writers who either transgress women's silence and misrepresentation or re-create misogynist perspectives, hegemonic gender constructions, and solidified gender archetypes.

Troubled Memories follows the line of research that Anna M. Nogar and I developed in the volume *Colonial Itineraries of Contemporary Mexico: Literary and Cultural Inquiries* (2014), in which fourteen critics reflect on several "rewritings" of the Mexican *colonia*, taking into account a representative sample of novels, films, poetry, and chronicles produced in and outside Mexico since 2000. I mention this book as a precedent because the contributions in it extend beyond the limits of the novel as a re-creative genre and produce innovative interpretations and alternative readings that challenge orthodox theorizations on the so-called new historical narratives of the 1980s and 1990s. Fine examples of this type of work focused on recent rearticulations of the Mexican colonial past are the volumes edited by Cecilia Eudave, Alberto Ortiz, and José Carlos Rovira, *Mujeres novohispanas en la narrativa mexicana contemporánea* (*New Spanish Women in Contemporary Mexican Narrative*) (2014), and *Personajes históricos y controversias en la narrativa mexicana contemporánea* (*Historical

Characters and Controversies in Contemporary Mexican Narrative) (2014). *Troubled Memories*, however, extends beyond the colonial experience to analyze the vicissitudes of several iconic women representative of the independence period, the Mexican Revolution, and its aftermath. Furthermore, each chapter takes into account a wide range of literary genres, in constant dialogue with other cultural expressions, such as films, soap operas, theater productions, and popular *corridos* (ballads).

Even though some of the writers I discuss here raise universal questions that speak for the postmodern self and the creation of gendered subjectivities in a neoliberal era,[3] some contemporary works insist on returning Mexico to its deterministic roots and cycles of oppression. To address both ends of this spectrum, I analyze how contemporary literature responds to the feminist denouncement of women's marginal state and historical invisibility. I explore how recent literary rearticulations of history combat or reproduce reductive representations of Mexican women and an entire Mexican society trapped in labyrinths of private and public conduct. Affect, after all, is deeply involved in the production and consumption of books and the commercialization of iconic figures, especially now that feelings and emotions previously relegated to private spheres have a material and symbolic value in the public space. The multiple manifestations of affect present in today's historical literature inevitably reflect ethical and political postures; their combined aesthetic impulse problematizes the production and propagation of certain knowledge, mirrors social conduct, and allows us to enter a simultaneous world of real and symbolic experiences (Moraña, "El afecto" 323).

Troubled Memories deals directly with the production of conflicted historical narratives in an age of globalization and neoliberalism. As we read through numerous texts that re-create the lives of iconic Mexican women from a contemporary perspective we analyze how recollections of the past are organized from a particular gendered perspective and how they are constructed—like historical monuments—with relentless omissions, calculated absences, and imposed amnesia (Achugar 156–57, 164). The hybrid nature of historical narratives, those that emerge from the fusion of history and literary creation, allows us to do this. Historical narratives, as Fernando Aínsa argues, revolve around Latin American identity, history's official and unofficial discourses, and national myths. The authors who dig into history for primary sources of inspiration articulate a retroactive agenda to understand the problems of the present with hints and clues from the past (Aínsa, *Reescribir* 27–28, 77). The ultimate goal is to dynamite previously established values and restructure historical foundations within a coherent and sensible fictional world. Dealing with these collective memories is of course the major challenge inasmuch as they constitute the foundation of a particular society or social group; they represent not just the heart of a nation but the compass that allows their people to orient themselves in the present to imagine a possible future (Lienhard 13–16).

Memories, however, are not just copies of the past or mere representations of it. They are flexible and malleable. They can adapt to new historical circumstances precisely because they are built with a flash-forward attitude that makes them current and indispensable. They are inventive acts built and rebuilt from incongruent pieces, silence, oblivion, and constant discoveries (Portella 5). Fictionalizations of the past carried out in the last two decades of the twentieth century already show that historical characters tend to be portrayed behind the scenes, often from the perspective of a privileged witness, and with the explicit intention of revealing intimate details that would have never been included in official records. To a great extent, this tendency to craft the past from an intimate point of view is still present in numerous historical rewritings that work with history's rumors, ambivalences, untold subjectivities, and irreverent passages (Barrientos 15–19). The articulation of marginal voices to confront the legitimacy of hegemonic historical discourse, a persistent trait throughout the 1980s and 1990s, is still present in today's historical narratives (Perkowska 33). Most historical novels, plays, short stories, and chronicles of the twenty-first century, however, are less interested in rearticulating the past, resorting to the heteroglossic, carnivalesque, and polyphonic strategies that Menton observed in many historical fictions of the late twentieth century (24–25).

Ultimately, the literary texts that revise history today, particularly through famous historical characters, prove not only the vitality of such narratives in contemporary societies but, perhaps more important, the fact that present-day societies are anxious to disintegrate the conclusiveness of the past. Concurrently, the proliferation of so much historical literature commemorating 200 years of Mexican Independence and the 100th anniversary of the Mexican Revolution has proven that only those texts that emerge from an in-depth process of historical documentation and research are able to properly and convincingly question, recontextualize, and transgress history (Rivera Garza, *Los muertos* 114). Yet all of the iconic women discussed in this book, whether they come from the distant period of the conquest and the colonial era or from more recent times, such as the revolutionary and postrevolutionary years, present themselves as true "border crossers." As genuine signs and symbols of Mexican culture, these women are simultaneously an intrinsic part of their own historical worlds and of contemporary Mexico. They act as mediators between the past, the present, and the future. They contribute substantially to the self-image and identity of individuals belonging to a particular culture, deal with a world of emotions, retain mystery, and are capable of being analyzed intellectually (Onasch and Schnieper 22).

Studying these memories through the lens of gender allows us to see that Mexican society continues to organize itself as a binary, because of the historical normalization of inequality between men and women and the unbalanced distribution of male and female roles, social practices, and behaviors (Castro Ricalde 112–13). If gender is culturally constructed through a set of regulatory practices, and if identity is indeed a normative ideal (Butler 9–23), my study traces how gender and identity are portrayed, problematized, or contested in contemporary literature. The gendered identities I discuss here are, as Marta Lamas would argue, cultural expressions of how the female body is interpreted as a physical and symbolic artifact capable of conveying an ample range of emotions under the limitations of society (159). The explicit gender divisions reproduce current patterns of domination and subordination, sexual discrimination, determinism, limited acts of empowerment, and prevalent inequality. Socially constructed, the female bodies I study reflect the impact of male privilege or, more precisely, the ways women are culturally converted into symbolic objects, almost always dependent on others, pulled by masculine expectations, and moved by supposedly feminine feelings and emotions (Bourdieu 83–86). Most of them are torn between their real and ideal(ized) bodies, opposing labels, complacency, and rebellion.

The literary analysis of Malinche, Sor Juana, Leona Vicario, the *soldaderas*, and Frida Kahlo, as they are depicted in Mexican literature today, reflects that sexism is a prevalent condition, an imperial practice that dominates at least half of humankind or an ideological system that continues to situate women in a subordinated position in relation to men. Sexism divides the world between men and women, masculine and feminine, aggressive and passive, and it also denies people belonging to a particular gender the possibility of action, agency, and autonomy. Sexism in fact reveals why a considerable proportion of Mexican women—and female icons, of course—continue to be represented in the literary production of the twenty-first century as myths that follow previously designed patterns (Monsiváis, *Misógino* 22–28). A gendered reading of this literature seeks to unveil the discursive strategies used by Mexican culture to describe and constrain the female body; it also wants to highlight the ruptures and discontinuities of female subjectivities in a misogynous world that for the most part tends to reduce their multiple and contradictory experiences, their fragmentary nature, ambivalences, and variations (Richard, "La crítica" 77–80).

Several other historical, mythical, or iconic women could have been included in this book, such as Isabel Moctezuma, Catarina de San Juan (La China Poblana), Josefa Ortiz de Domínguez (La Corregidora), or María Ignacia Rodríguez de Velasco y Osorio Barba (La Güera Rodríguez). I chose Malinche, Sor Juana, Vicario, and the anonymous *soldaderas* as representative icons of different historical periods because they have been depicted in numerous literary texts and mass media in the early twenty-first century. Each one is the main protagonist of at least three or four novels, a few soap operas, TV series, films, cartoons, children's books, plays, songs, and graphic literature. They transport specific meanings in and outside literature, perhaps more than others. Malinche carries the heavy burden of *mestizaje* and therefore a fatal destiny. She represents the anonymous women of the conquest whose bodies were used by the Spanish conquistadors for sexual pleasure and were denied a discourse of their own (Glantz, "Doña Marina" 126). In perfect agreement with her colonial labels as the Tenth Muse and Phoenix of America, Sor Juana is idealized as an exceptional phenomenon of the Baroque era. She is a secular madonna who tends to be portrayed as a *rara avis*, cerebral and virginal, almost like a superhuman (Hind, "Official" 249). Leona Vicario symbolizes female patriotism at a historical moment when the country needs foundational heroes. She is the sign of altruistic ideals, unthinkable without her husband, Andrés Quintana Roo. Her iconic figure tells people throughout the twentieth century and well into the twenty-first that the heroine is the hero's lover, regardless of her personal commitments and political engagements (Monsiváis, *Misógino* 107). The *soldaderas* are remembered as the self-sacrificing women of the Mexican Revolution who carry their children on their backs and follow their men like loyal companions. As mythical figures, they are depicted with saintly sweetness and condemned to a destiny of invisibility (Leal, *Aztlán* 185; Monsiváis, *Mexican* 6). Frida Kahlo, studied in the epilogue, is seen as the icon of the twentieth century who uses her own body as an artistic object. Her popularized image evokes an aching body that presents itself as an artifact in the making, in a constant process of definition, evolution, and presentation (De Toro 67).

Regardless of their intrinsic differences as iconic figures, most of these women are trapped in puzzling, challenging, or thought-provoking literary representations that reveal the following characteristics:

1. The construction of a portrait that must be approached as a composite idea. Made up by blocks of meaning, in a Barthesian sense, the portrait is presented in the text not as a copy of the original but as a Cubist representation that seeks to supplement meaning.

2. The overt exploration of the icon's intimacy and sexuality. Insistently, they are depicted in private, in the midst of their sexual acts. Stripped of their clothes, these iconic women emphasize their physicality and highlight their humanity, paying a great deal of attention to their gender orientation and sexual desires. Thanks to this literary striptease, readers become accidental voyeurs.

3. The development of a love story. Several iconic women display a lover's discourse of their own, marked by anguish, longing, eroticism, and passion.

4. The articulation of the icon's religious and/or political beliefs.

5. A persistent tendency to depict these women as important agents of history, capable of carrying out transgressions, acts of empowerment, and heroic deeds. For the most part, they are portrayed as virtuous models of exemplary behavior.

6. The perpetuation of extremes or stereotypes historically attributed to women and femininity with recurrent fictionalizations of the domestic space, particularly the kitchen.

7. The successful or ineffective attribution of feminist ideals to a female icon trapped in gender struggles.
8. An alternative story of their lives, either written by the women, found in lost manuscripts or letters, or told by a female eyewitness. This characteristic places some of these iconic women at the center of a lettered culture.

Because of these traits, the women studied in this book are often tainted by exoticism or condemned to misrepresentation and invisibility. Yet some rearticulations undoubtedly craft metaphorical certificates of citizenship within convincing scenarios that validate a plurality of experiences and create gender incisions in the discourses of hegemony. The differences in the representation of these iconic women have more to do with each author's poetics and personal engagement with gender politics than with their gender identities. Misrepresentations and genuine acts of empowerment can be found in literary texts written by both women and men, who belong to different literary generations and have had various literary influences. Not all texts written by women promote gender equality, and not all texts written by men misrepresent women. While some texts, especially those crafted from an autobiographical perspective, challenge domination and represent acts of political and narrative resistance (Beard 2), not all of them work well as possible worlds of fiction.

Considering a wide range of historical interpretations, ideological rewritings, political rearticulations, and feminist reframings of Malinche, produced primarily over the course of the twentieth century, in the first chapter I analyze four literary works: the play *La Malinche* (2000) by Víctor Hugo Rascón Banda, and the novels *Amor y conquista: La novela de Malinalli mal llamada la Malinche* (*Love and Conquest: The Novel of Malinalli Mistakenly Called Malinche*) (1999) by Marisol Martín del Campo, *Malinche* (2006) by Laura Esquivel, and *La verdadera historia de Malinche* (*The True History of Malinche*) (2009) by Fanny del Río. Together, these works invite us to see Malinche behind the scenes of official history and understand her fears and desires, her inner self, her motivations for siding with the Spanish conquistadors or for staying true to her own culture. As we internalize her dilemmas as an interpreter, her religious beliefs, or her existential crisis and personal contradictions as a divided and hybrid subject, we revisit her cultural heritage and the aftermath of a sexual, social, ethnic, and political conquest.

Although the Sor Juana archetype is a constant in recent works by Mexican women writers, in the second chapter I analyze four Mexican novels published between 2007 and 2010 that explicitly re-create Sor Juana's life: Héctor Zagal's *La venganza de Sor Juana* (*Sor Juana's Revenge*) (2007), José Luis Gómez's *El beso de la virreina* (*The Vicereine's Kiss*) (2008), Mónica Lavín's *Yo, la peor* (*I, the Worst*) (2009), and Kyra Galván's *Los indecibles pecados de Sor Juana* (*The Unspeakable Sins of Sor Juana*) (2010). In reaction to an orthodox Sor Juana, who is usually portrayed as a sexually inactive intellectual, these novels pluralize our conceptions of her. As we corroborate with these novels that historical truth is fragmented and dispersed, that memory elaborates its own palimpsests, and that our relationship with the past is never neutral, we face unresolved issues of gender construction and sexual differentiation that originate in the colonial era. The challenges of representing an iconic female intellectual who has been obscured by centuries of hagiographic accounts are counterbalanced by the present need to adjust a historical role model to Mexico's social, political, and cultural dilemmas.

The third chapter is devoted to the study of Leona Vicario, named by President Antonio López de Santa Anna in 1842 as the "Sweet Mother of the Fatherland." Taking into account her mythification, thanks in part to the biographical work of Genaro García (1910), I study how Leona Vicario is depicted in three contemporary novels published in celebration of the 200th anniversary of Mexico's independence from Spain. In Celia del Palacio's *Leona* (2010), Carlos Pascual's *La insurgenta* (*The Insurgent*) (2010), and Eugenio Aguirre's *Leona Vicario: La insurgente* (*Leona Vicario: The Insurgent*) (2010), this iconic woman is treated like a romantic heroine in love with Andrés Quintana Roo or as a model patriot who sacrifices her life to liberate her nation. Although Leona is simultaneously portrayed as a wife, lover, mother, and rebel, often her political participation is diminished and her domestic existence is highlighted. Therefore, I discuss the masculine gaze against a feminist perspective, the impossibility of alternative histories of female empowerment, and ongoing challenges of individualistic and intimate narratives that sacrifice a woman's intellect, her potential to subvert an established order, and her abilities to resignify a marginal space.

Trapped in a misogynist society, most of the women who participated in the Mexican Revolution, even those who were involved in important battles as soldiers or as their partner's assistants, have remained nameless and have been referred to as cockroaches, sloppy workers, gossips, sluts, robbers, and *Adelitas*. To analyze the mythification or disappearance of female corporality in the midst of the turbulent movement and in contemporary rewritings of history, in the fourth chapter I study several works that reinforce a long chain of female archetypes that, from Malinche onward, instead of representing a historical truth, personify an anxiety generated by the active participation of women in crucial moments of Mexican history. To highlight their current invisibility and mythification, I analyze several works that mention them in passing or without interior development, such as Rosa Helia Villa's biographical novel *Itinerario de una pasión: Los amores de mi general* (*Itinerary of Passion: My General's Lovers*) (1999) or Paco Ignacio Taibo's biography *Pancho Villa* (2006). To counterbalance some of these rearticulations, I also read Elena Poniatowska's chronicle *Las soldaderas* (1999), Estela Leñero's play *Soles en la sombra: Mujeres en la Revolución* (*Suns in the Dark: Women in the Revolution*) (2011), and Mónica Lavín's novel *Las rebeldes* (*The Rebels*) (2011), on the women of the Cruz Blanca Constitucionalista who played a vital role in the Mexican Revolution. The chapter concludes with a reading of Fernando Zamora's queer novel *Por debajo del agua* (*Under the Water*) (2001).

I end with an epilogue on Frida Kahlo to show that her iconization and contemporary rewriting in Mexican literature reflect similar cultural anxieties present in the representation of other legendary women. Taking into account several works by Carlos Fuentes, Elena Poniatowska and Margo Glantz, or Carlos Monsiváis, F. G. Haghenbeck, and Ana Clavel, I conclude that Frida Kahlo is depicted as an eccentric broken body because the world needs her as a symbol of Mexicanness and marginality. She suffers from the exoticism that affects the other women studied here and assures us that icons have afterlives, which does not necessarily mean we will find them within cohesive fictional worlds.

Several decades ago, in one of her poignant reflections on women and their image, Rosario Castellanos concluded that history has mythified them, placing them in a faraway kingdom where it is difficult to recognize their humanity and intellectual capacity (*Mujer* 9). The literature I discuss in this book attempts to shatter the monolithic composition of some of Mexico's historical women. But working with history's icons is a challenging endeavor, as I will show, more so if they resist contemporary rearticulations and ideological projects that do not always capture their essence and historical context, ambivalence, multiplicity, and troubled memories.

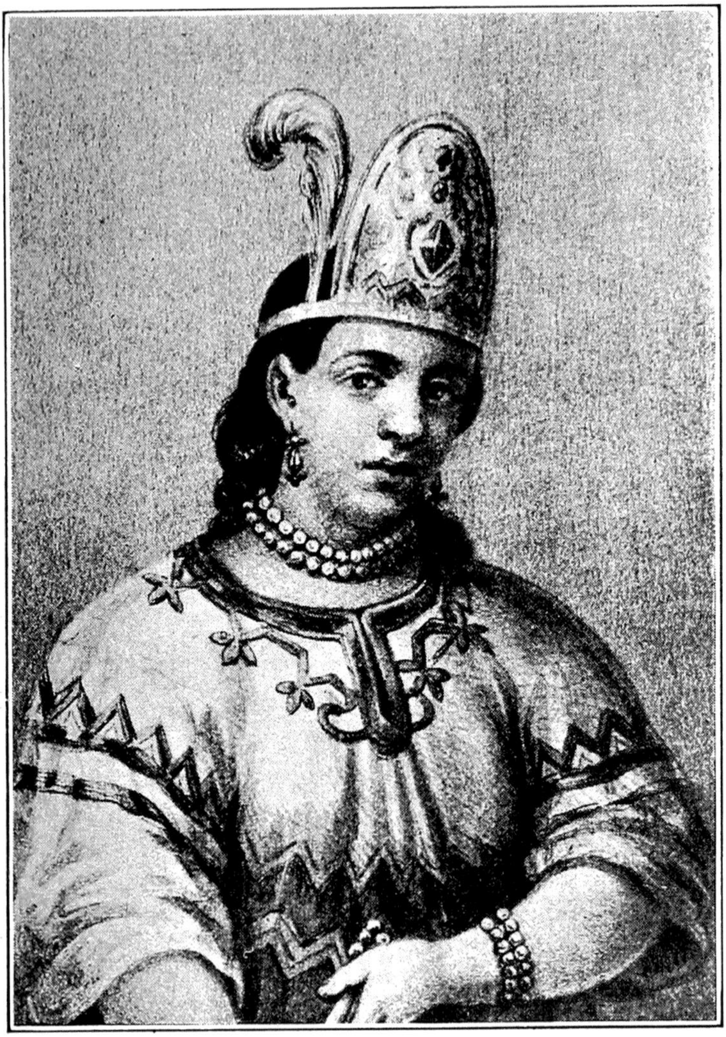

La Malinche as depicted in *The Mastering of Mexico: Told After One of the Conquistadores and Various of His Interpreters*, ed. Kate Stephens (New York: Macmillan, 1916). Wikimedia Commons.

1

Forget Me Not

Malinche's Struggles in Twenty-First-Century Mexico

> Era de buen parecer y entremetida y desenvuelta . . .
> y como doña Marina en todas las guerras de la Nueva España
> y Tlaxcala y México fue tan excelente mujer y buena lengua,
> como adelante diré, a esta causa la traía siempre Cortés consigo.
>
> ([She was] good-looking, intelligent, and self-assured . . .
> As Doña Marina had proved such an excellent person, and
> a good interpreter in all the wars of New Spain, Tlascala, and Mexico
> —as I shall relate hereafter—Cortés always took her with him)
>
> —Bernal Díaz del Castillo (XXXVI, 58, 59/82, 85)

Bernal Díaz del Castillo's *Historia verdadera de la conquista de la Nueva España* (*The Conquest of New Spain*) (completed around 1568 and published for the first time in 1632) may not be a true account of the Conquest of Mexico (1519–1521). But his detailed portrait of Doña Marina, the converted Nahua woman who became Hernán Cortés's lover and interpreter, has certainly stood the test of time, seducing countless chroniclers, historians, novelists, dramaturges, and poets from the colonial era to the present. Unlike Cortés, who refers to her in his *Cartas de relación* (*Letters from Mexico*) as "la lengua"—literally "the tongue," the interpreter—Bernal Díaz highlights her fundamental role in the conquest, grants her a noble lineage, and presents her as an exemplary Christian woman. Thanks to his literary rendition of Doña Marina, we can imagine that she was an important woman whose parents were caciques of a town called Paynala, situated about twenty-four miles from Coatzacoalcos. With the wisdom of an old storyteller, the chronicler writes that after Doña Marina's father passed away, her mother sold her into slavery to prevent her from inheriting his estate. After her tragic enslavement in Xicalango and Tabasco, the tale continues, she was passed on to the Spaniards along with nineteen other women as a gift. Although at first she was Alonso Hernández de Puertocarrero's servant and mistress, within a short time she became the most important woman of the conquest as Cortés's companion, mediator, and interpreter. This, of course, is the story of a woman who would make history as an iconic figure of Mexican culture, the legendary and irreplaceable Malinche.

To enhance his story, Bernal Díaz writes that when her mother and brother miraculously found her during one of her travels with Cortés, on her way to Las Hibueras (present-day Honduras), Doña Marina forgave them for selling her into slavery. A master of characterization, he records the encounter with a verbal picture that has been used on many occasions to depict her as a traitor to her people:

> Y como así los vio llorar la doña Marina, les consoló y dijo que no hubiesen miedo, que cuando la traspusieron con los de Xicalango que no supieron lo que hacían, y se los perdonaba, y les dio muchas joyas de oro y ropa, y que se volviesen a su pueblo; y que Dios la había hecho mucha merced en quitarla de adorar ídolos ahora y ser cristiana, y tener un hijo de su amo y señor Cortés, y ser casada con un caballero como era su marido Juan Jaramillo; que aunque la hicieran cacica de todas cuantas provincias había en la Nueva España, no lo sería, que en más tenía servir a su marido y a Cortés que cuanto en el mundo hay.

> (When Doña Marina saw her mother and half-brother in tears, she comforted them, saying that they need have no fear. She told her mother that when they had handed her over to the men from Xicalango, they had not known what they were doing. She pardoned the old woman, and gave them many golden jewels and some clothes. Then she sent them back to their town, saying that God had been very gracious to her

> in freeing her from the worship of idols and making her a Christian, and giving her a son by her lord and master Cortés, also in marrying her to such a gentleman as her husband Juan Jaramillo. Even if they were to make her mistress of all the provinces of New Spain, she said, she would refuse the honour, for she would rather serve her husband and Cortes than anything else in the world.) (XXXVII, 62/86)[1]

We will never know whether Doña Marina actually said these words; if, thanks to her process of transculturation, she was transformed into a new Christian woman; or if she was truly enamored with the Spanish conquistadors, their cultural values, and beliefs. Obviously, Bernal Díaz wants to present her as a God-sent miracle of the New World, well aware that his portrayal is close to a biblical model: "Y todo esto que digo sélo yo muy certificadamente, y esto me parece que quiere remedar lo que le acaeció con sus hermanos en Egipto a Josef, que vinieron en su poder cuando lo del trigo" (What I have related here I know for certain and swear to. The whole story seems very much like that of Joseph and his brethren in Egypt, when the Egyptians came into his power over the wheat) (XXXVII, 62/86). Precisely because Bernal Díaz grants her an honorable past of epical undertones, in his chronicle she is destined to become Cortés's loyal companion, accomplice, and ambassador.[2]

Regardless of how accurate he is, what ultimately matters is that the story of this excellent and well-mannered woman of good looks, confident character, fluid discourse, and noble origins, the same one who assisted Cortés in the conquest of Moctezuma's throne, propitiates the creation of a negative female archetype and symbol. This composite "sign," as Sandra Messinger Cypess eloquently argues in *La Malinche in Mexican Literature*, "functions as a continually enlarging palimpsest of Mexican cultural identity whose layers of meaning have accrued through the years" (5).

All historical details about Malinche's life remain uncertain. We do not know her date of birth or death, although most researchers propose that she was born either in 1502 or 1505 on the day called Malinal (or Malinalli) and passed away as early as 1527 or 1529, or perhaps between 1531 and 1532. Some sources confirm that she was still alive in 1539 and was dead by 1541 (Baudot 73; Cypess 33; Karttunen 352; Townsend 11, 171). Even though several historians have proposed that the Spaniards named her Marina because it was close to her original name, supposedly

Malinalli, all we know for certain is that she was called Malintzin in Nahuatl (pronounced "Malinche" by the Spaniards) and Marina in Spanish after her Christian conversion in 1519.[3] We know that she had a child with Cortés in 1522, she accompanied him in the expedition to Las Hibueras in 1524, and during that voyage, she married Juan Jaramillo; apparently, she had his daughter and remained married to him until her death. Only Bernal Díaz del Castillo, unlike Hernán Cortés or Francisco López de Gómara, respectfully calls her "Doña Marina" in his voluminous chronicle (Brotherston 20). Bernal highlights that she was a woman of extraordinary courage and manly strength, that the Indians obeyed her, and that without her the conquistadors could not have understood Moctezuma's language. Malinche's importance as interpreter and warrior is immortalized in several indigenous pictograms and hybrid books, such as the *Florentine Codex*, the *History of Tlaxcala* (in which she appears as *dea ex machina*), the *Codex Azcatitlan*, the *Relación de Michoacán*, the *Tepetlan Codex*, the *Coyoacán Codex*, and the *Libro de los gobernadores de Cuauhtinchan* (Brotherston 34–37; Wood 67).

Taking into account these scattered historical facts from various Spanish and indigenous sources, Mexicans have created a number of national myths and legends around Malinche, saving her a preferential seat right next to other female archetypes, such as "the bad one" and "the good one," "the virgin," "the whore," "the exemplary mother," "the dedicated wife," "the untouchable nun," "the *solterona*" (old maid), "the schoolteacher," and "the *beata*" (overly religious woman) (Leal, *Reader* 285–97). Obviously history and popular tradition (influenced by nationalism) have placed Malinche closer to "the bad ones" on a reduced Manichean spectrum where women never occupy the center and are kept away from any intermediate zones. Octavio Paz reproduces this negative portrayal in *El laberinto de la soledad* (*The Labyrinth of Solitude* [1950]), where Malinche is represented as a raped mother who is fascinated by the Spanish conquistador. In his writing, as is well known, she is depicted as popular culture perceives her: as a traitor to her nation, as the Mexican Eve, as the woman who sells her world's knowledge to the Spanish invaders, or as the ultimate reincarnation of "La Chingada" (83–87). Other authors and scholars like Carlos Fuentes, Margo Glantz, Jean Franco, Blanca López de Mariscal, and Marissa Belásteguigoitia, have presented Malinche in a more positive light. Collectively, they redeem her agency in the Conquest of Mexico, her work as a trustworthy messenger, her metaphorical role as the mother of American hybridity, and her vital function as the interpreter of two different worlds. Unlike them, cultural critic Carlos Monsiváis observes that without the ideological weight that holds her responsible for the conquest of her people and the traumatic birth of the nation, Malinche has become a useless legend, unfit for the postnational state, awkward in a neoliberal era, anachronistic and outdated ("La Malinche" 183, 193).

We may or may not share Monsiváis's views, but as I discuss in this chapter, Mexican literature continues to reactivate Malinche's story well into the twenty-first century in several novels, plays, and histories of all sorts. These recent rearticulations of Malinche come from a long line of literary projects where she appears as an openly fictional character or as a female archetype. After her debut in the nineteenth century, in the anonymous novel *Xicoténcatl* (1826), in the novels *Los mártires del Anáhuac* (*The Martyrs of Anahuac*) (1852) by Eligio Ancona, *Amor y suplicio* (*Love and Torture*) (1873) and *Doña Marina* (1883) by Ireneo Paz, or *Eva* (1885) by Manuel Castro, La Malinche entered the twentieth century in a number of fictional works. We find her archetypical profile, for instance, in several novels of the mid-twentieth century, such as Francisco Rojas González's *La negra Angustias* (*The Black Angustias*) (1944), Margarita López Portillo's *Toña Machetes* (1956), Rosario Castellanos's *Balún Canán* (1957), and Elena Garro's *Los recuerdos del porvenir* (*Recollections of Things to Come*) (1963). She has appeared in such plays as Celestino Gorostiza's *La Malinche o La leña está verde* (*Malinche or the Firewood Is Green*) (1958), Rodolfo Usigli's *Corona de fuego* (*Crown of Fire*) (1960), Salvador Novo's *Cuauhtémoc* (1962), Carlos Fuentes's *Todos los gatos son pardos* (*All Cats Are Gray*) (1971), and Rosario Castellanos's *El eterno femenino* (*The Eternal Feminine*) (1975).[4]

In view of these and other works that have reactivated Malinche's struggles, accomplishments, broken history, and permanent stigmas, more than three decades ago Beth Miller rightly concluded:

> Everyone who touches on the subject of Marina reveals an evocation of a historical being. Marina escapes description and categorization because of the centuries which separate us from her and the paucity of evidence about her which has survived. She also escapes us perhaps, because, though she lived by language, for us she has no language and no words. Or it may be because she is a woman, and therefore she is Other to the men who, by trying to capture her essence, have succeeded

> only in defining themselves. She has been exploited without apology by writers of all disciplines and ideologies—historians, sociologists, novelists, dramatists, imperialists, rightists and leftists, all of whom have thought of her as an empty vessel ready to be filled by their formulations. (98–99)

Some works produced in the 1990s seek to correct part of this problem. In Carlos Fuentes's *El naranjo* (*The Orange Tree* [1993]), for example, specifically in the story "Las dos orillas" ("The Two Shores"), Malinche is presented as a bridge between Spain and the New World. She is called, on one hand, a treacherous woman and a whore, but almost immediately Fuentes's narrator points out that she is the only one who understands "el secreto que unía a nuestras dos tierras, el odio fratricida, la división" (the secret uniting our two lands: fratricidal hatred, division) (159/21). Malinche is depicted here as she appears in Jean Franco's analysis: as a complex human being who shortens the distance between two different cultures to construct a modern world (*Las conspiradoras* 204). A strong promoter of uniting Spain and the Americas, Fuentes had previously fictionalized Malinche in his play *Todos los gatos son pardos*, highlighting her role as a mediator between Moctezuma and Cortés. Taking her agency a step further, in "Las dos orillas" Marina decides the course of the conquest, advises opposing parties, interprets only what she considers appropriate, leaves her past behind, and looks forward to a promising future of inevitable uncertainties. Still attached to her historical stigma, in the end she appears triumphant as the woman whose hybrid child represents the promise of a new world (43).

Also in the 1990s, other Mexican writers like Ignacio Solares and Carmen Boullosa positively revive the Malinche archetype in the novels *Nen, la inútil* (*Nen, the Useless*) (1994), *Llanto: Novelas imposibles* (*Llanto: Impossible Novels*) (1992), and *Duerme* (*Sleep*) (1994). No less contestatory and revisionist of Malinche and her negative archetype are several works penned around the same time by some Chicana writers, like the poem "Malinchista, a Myth Revised" (1989, 1993) and the essay "Malinche's Revenge" (1999) by Alicia Gaspar de Alba, or *The Hungry Woman, a Mexican Medea* (1995) by Cherríe Moraga. This is understandable. After all, as Debra A. Castillo argues, "Chicano, and specially Chicana, critics and writers including Norma Alarcón, Gloria Anzaldúa, María Herrera Sobek, and Ana Castillo have turned this negative image of the indigenous woman on its head, rewriting her story as that of an empowered woman" ("Coagulated" 68). Well aware of this situation, in her book *[Un]framing the Bad Woman*, Gaspar de Alba recognizes that Chicana (particularly lesbian) feminists have transformed Malinche's story so that she now represents resistance and affirmation: "of a woman's freedom to use her mind, her tongue, and her body in the way that she chooses and to cultivate her intellectual skills for her own survival and empowerment" (78).

Given this wide range of conflicting historical interpretations, ideological rewritings, political rearticulations, and feminist reframings of Malinche, produced primarily over the course of the twentieth century, here I analyze four literary works that reveal a number of unresolved cultural anxieties and bad habits associated with the representation of legendary women in contemporary Mexico. I refer to the play *La Malinche* (2000) by Víctor Hugo Rascón Banda and to the novels *Amor y conquista: La novela de Malinalli mal llamada la Malinche* (*Love and Conquest: The Novel of Malinalli, Mistakenly Called Malinche*) (1999) by Marisol Martín del Campo, *Malinche* (2006) by Laura Esquivel, and *La verdadera historia de Malinche* (*The True History of Malinche*) (2010) by Fanny del Río.

Although some of these works invariably construct an intimate portrait of Malinche, including her fears and desires, her gendered point of view, her motivations for siding with the Spanish conquistadors, or, alternatively, for staying true to her own culture, others redeem her job as an interpreter and attempt to remove the historical stains that cloud her name.[5] Other works explore Malinche's religious beliefs, her existential crisis, or her personal contradictions as a divided and hybrid subject, as well as her cultural heritage and the aftermath of a sexual, social, ethnic, and political conquest. Together, these literary texts validate Malinche's prevalence in contemporary Mexico, not just as a malleable historical icon but as an integral part of today's culture. In one way or another, all of them do what much literature does in a neoliberal era: they reflect the behavior and mentality of a particular society involved in numerous market transactions, including the commercialization of interiority and the accumulation of untold, private, and unique experiences or desires (Ruisánchez, "Introducción 7–8).

Hasta en las mejores Malinches

In one of his lucid reflections, Roger Bartra reminds us that at least since the beginning of the nineteenth century and thanks to several waves of nationalism, Malinche's alleged love for Cortés has been associated with betrayal, dishonor, and illegitimacy. Representing other Indian lovers who supposedly "fall in love" with the Spanish conquistadors and have illegitimate mestizo children, Malinche suddenly becomes "la Chingada Madre," the raped Indian woman who betrays her nation and consequently merits immediate displacement by a virginal and pure mother, the Virgin of Guadalupe (196–99). Bartra's appreciation is absolutely right. Indeed, five decades earlier Octavio Paz had observed that because Malinche represents the Indian women who were fascinated and seduced by the Spanish conquistadors, she will never be forgiven by the Mexican people (*El laberinto* 90). We will never know whether Malinche fell in love with Cortés, much less if she enjoyed her sexual encounters with him. We can only imagine that he used her sexually—just as other women were used by the Spanish soldiers—and as his personal interpreter and diplomatic ambassador. Likewise, we may assume that Malinche used Cortés to transgress her marginal situation as a slave, and thus become an indispensable woman in the Conquest of Mexico (Manrique 247–48). Yet several women writers of the twenty-first century insist on depicting Malinche in love and as an overly sexualized character, in sync with a neoliberal attitude that seeks to liberate sexuality from its mysterious aura through copious descriptions of sexual practices and desires (Monsiváis, *Aires* 44). This tendency to reveal the intimacy of certain people with morbid details has colonized a good number of talk shows in Mexico since the early 1990s—such as the famous *El Show de Cristina* (*The Cristina Show*), or *Hasta en las mejores familias* (*Even in the Best Families*), *Laura*, and *La rosa de Guadalupe* (*The Rose of Guadalupe*)—and a significant portion of contemporary literature.

In her 1999 novel *Amor y conquista*, Marisol Martín del Campo shows Malinche as completely bewitched by the Spanish conquistadors. Although she is passed on to the soldier Alonso Hernández de Puertocarrero to serve him as a sexual partner and personal slave, she quickly falls in love with him. From the beginning, their relationship is depicted as love at first sight to the point that Malinche, forgetting her renewed condition as a slave, appears to have fallen head over heels for him. Instead of a brutal sexual encounter between the Spanish conquistador and his Indian mistress, Martín del Campo creates an initial love scene with unfortunate romantic undertones: "él le quitó la cáscara a mi corazón para dejarlo en carne viva; vivía de puras sensaciones agradables, ensimismada, sensible. Todo me hacía reír, el sol de Alonso me había insolado" (he peeled the skin off of my heart and left it naked; I lived in a state of happiness, absorption, and sensitivity. Everything made me laugh. Alonso's sun had burned me) (68). Apparently, Malinche gives Alonso her virginity, which is hard to believe if we take into account that she had been a slave since she was a child. Her love for Alonso is so strong that she loves him unconditionally long after Cortés sends him away to keep her by his side as his mistress and interpreter.

Similarly, even though Cortés takes her by force and makes her feel dirty and used, soon Malinche desires him beyond words. She describes herself shivering with love because she is away from Alonso and, concurrently, remains attached to a new sentimental and sexual relationship that consumes her: "Me odio por depender del capitán Hernán, de sus iras, besos, indiferencia, de su sudor" (I hate myself for being dependent on Captain Hernán and his rage, kisses, indifference, and his sweat) (136). Unfortunately, Malinche's discourse loses credibility from the moment that she speaks like a passionate soap opera character who has little to do with her historical context, her personal struggles as a slave in the hands of new masters, and her overall agency as a woman of action. Her participation in the conquest is, as Blanca López de Mariscal argues, a complex endeavor and not the result of her infatuation with the Spanish conquistadors. Even though she is depicted in Mexican culture as an object in the midst of numerous transactions, because she has the power of language—or, more precisely, the tools and weapons of the interpreter—it is safe to assume that her active participation is most likely an option, an act of self-determination (López de Mariscal 71).

We certainly perceive this idea in Bernal Díaz's *Historia verdadera*. The gossipy chronicler could have developed in his lengthy *relación* Doña Marina's sexual advances or her love relationship with the conquistador. After all, he does not bite his tongue when discussing Cortés's love affairs, Gonzalo de Guerrero's wife's violent reaction when Jerónimo de Aguilar tries to take him away, or his comrades-in-arms' desperate need to obtain Indian women throughout the Conquest of Mexico. Instead, Bernal Díaz describes his heroine as the central mediator who helps Cortés obtain the desired object: Moctezuma's throne (Estrada, *La imaginación* 97). She appears not as a protagonist blinded by Cortés's love but as an astute woman of action who facilitates a productive dialogue between the Spanish conquistadors and the soon-to-be conquered *Mexicas*. When Malinche translates Cortés's speech for the Cempoalans, for instance, Bernal recalls her astuteness and good judgment and the fact that she even threatened them: "y aun les amenazaba" (LI, 88).

As if she were posing in front of a modern camera, however, in *Amor y conquista*, Malinche declares her love for Cortés whenever she has a chance to do so, for he is a good man, a hard-working soldier, and a good friend. Along these lines, she happily announces that their son, Martín Cortés, has brought them closer as a couple. She embellishes her sickly sweet discourse, arguing that: "En privado soy su amante y me transformo en una mujer que sólo anhela tomar y dar placer, pierdo la cabeza, el sentido del cuerpo y del lugar, busco erizar su piel, sacarlo de quicio, nada nos detiene, nos amamos violentos, insaciables, acabamos exhaustos" (In private I am his lover and I transform myself into a woman that only wishes to give and receive pleasure; I lose myself, my body, my sense of place; I try to drive him insane. Nothing stops us. We love each other violently, insatiably, and we finish exhausted) (376). Malinche's melodramatic speech is unbelievable. Or do we actually believe that "En esos encuentros no somos ni Malinalli ni el capitán Cortés, somos un hombre y una mujer que se atraen y se sacian, no tenemos dioses, reglas, convenciones, sólo hambre de nuestros cuerpos" (During those encounters we are neither Malinalli nor Captain Cortés; we are a man and a woman attracted to each other and that satiate each other; we have no gods, rules, conventions; just the hunger for our bodies)? (376).

If we read the novel with enthusiasm, we might be tempted to conclude it is crafted from a gendered perspective that seeks to portray Malinche as liberated by her own love. That might be true. Ultimately, the novel that we read presumably has been written with the words of an Indian woman, Ozlaxiuchitl, who tells her daughter the story of Malinalli, and it touches briefly on such issues as maternity, female inferiority, awareness, and consciousness (Aracil 27–28). Missing from this fiction, however, is the genuine attempt to rewrite history from a contestatory point of view and not simply from a supposedly "feminine perspective" that portrays "female identity" as a fixed essence (Richard, "Sexo" 130). Absent from the novel, in other words, is the articulation of a feminist discourse that successfully confronts dominant portrayals of women and femininity, or the construction of a dissident identity that fights against masculinist worldviews, guided by a spirit of transgression, subversion, and rebellion.

Esquivel's *Malinche* is just as problematic in this sense. Written as the colonial sequel to her romantic novels, *Como agua para chocolate* (*Like Water for Chocolate*) (1989), *La ley del amor* (*The Law of Love*) (1995), and *Tan veloz como el deseo* (*Swift as Desire*) (2001), *Malinche* attracts global audiences with a modern fairy tale but sacrifices her protagonist's agency. Hers is the story, as Irma Cantú points out, of an Indian princess or modern "Cinderellatl" who is unjustly sold into slavery by her mother until Cortés, acting as Prince Charming, saves her from a fatal destiny and elevates her above other women of her time as the mediator between the Spanish conquistadors and the Aztec emperor (153–54). After having a child with Cortés, she marries Juan Jaramillo and lives happily ever after, until her mythical transformation at the end of the novel, when she becomes a stream of water.

The conquest in Esquivel's novel takes place in a romantic and hypersexualized scenario, long before the Spaniards enter Tenochtitlan. This time, Cortés and Malinche (known as Malinalli in this work) make passionate love in a river and, thanks to the residual wonders of magical realism, affect their surroundings:

> Cortés y Malinalli, dentro del agua, uno frente al otro, se miraron a los ojos y descubrieron su destino y su unión inevitable. Cortés comprendió que Malinalli era su verdadera conquista, que ahí, en medio del abismo de los ojos negros de esa mujer, se encontraban las joyas que tanto buscaba. Malinalli, por su lado, sintió que en los labios de Cortés y en su saliva había un trozo líquido de dios, un pedazo de eternidad y que a ella le urgía saborearlo y conservarlo entre sus labios. Las nubes en el cielo se comenzaron a mover con una velocidad extraordinaria. El ambiente se cargó de humedad y lubricó tanto las plumas de las aves, las hojas de los árboles como la vagina de Malinalli. Las grises nubes, al igual que el pene de Cortés, hacían un gran esfuerzo por contener el agua, por retenerla, por no dejarla caer, por no soltar su preciado líquido.
>
> (In the water, facing each other, Cortés and Malinalli looked into each other's eyes and found their destiny and their inevitable union. Cortés understood that Malinalli was his true conquest, that there, in the depths of her black eyes, were the gems he had been searching for all this time. Malinalli, for her part, felt that on Cortés's lips, in his saliva, there was a taste of the divine, a piece of eternity, and she wanted to savor it and guard it with her lips. The clouds in the sky

> began to move with extraordinary swiftness. The air became laden with humidity, moistening the feathers of birds and the leaves of trees, as well as Malinalli's vagina. The gray clouds, like Cortés's member, made a great effort to contain their waters, to hold back, not to let them fall, so that their precious liquid would not be released). (74–75/77)

The scene continues with more graphic details that present Cortés and Malinalli as an overly sexualized couple destined to be together and incapable of controlling their animal instincts. Cortés, the alpha male of this erotic drama, lifts her up from the water, takes her to the side of the river, and penetrates her with violence. Unsure of whether she belongs here or in a pornographic scene, Malinalli also plays her part well: she acts like a fragile and helpless young woman who secretly thanks Cortés for hurting her, for pleasuring her beyond her wildest dreams, and for making her feel like a real woman who does not have to translate for others. Suddenly, thanks to Esquivel, Malinalli is just that: "Una mujer que, lejos de lo que podía esperarse, sintió alivio de recuperar su condición de sometimiento, pues le resultaba mucho más familiar la sensación de ser un objeto al servicio de los hombres que ser la creadora de su destino" (A woman who, contrary to what would be expected, felt relief in reclaiming her condition of submission, for it was a much more familiar sensation to be an object at the service of men than to be a creator of destiny) (76/79).

This sort of reverse female empowerment is further emphasized in other scenes of the novel, where Malinalli spends endless moments admiring Cortés's body, his strength and courage, his audacity in the battlefields, his natural gifts as a leader and negotiator. She thinks he is the reincarnation of her lost father, that their separate lives were predestined to be one, even if that makes her a weak person. Soon after the Spaniards are received by Moctezuma, Cortés rapes her again and, once more, Malinalli interprets the always available role of La Chingada:

> mandó llamar a Malinalli y fornicó desenfrenadamente con ella, como una manera de celebrar su triunfo y al mismo tiempo negarlo. . . . Besó su boca, sus senos, su vientre, sus muslos, su centro, para satisfacer una voluntad tan furiosamente ambiciosa que casi la partió en dos, la lastimó, la rasgó.

> ([he] sent for Malinalli, with whom he engaged in unbridled fornication as a way of both celebrating his victory and at the same time denying it. . . . He kissed her mouth, her belly, her thighs, her center, to assuage a longing so feverishly ambitious that he almost broke her in two, wounded her, ripped her apart). (121/123)

Against her lascivious inclinations, however, this time Malinalli feels that she has sinned and seeks forgiveness from Huitzilopochtli.

Is this portrayal of Malinche convincing? Not only does her twisted syncretism make little sense but the entire fiction embraces patriarchy and confines the protagonist to a domestic space without any room for contestatory tales.[6] When she becomes pregnant with her first child, Malinalli feels complete, knowing that in her womb she carries the blood of the Spanish and the Indians. A few pages later, however, when she realizes that Cortés will never be her husband or an ordinary family man, Malinalli delivers a sad discourse, completely incongruent with the portrait of a strong woman who supposedly played a major role in the conquest:

> Soy la bestia de carga de tus deseos, de tus caprichos, de tus locuras. . . . Lo que quiero es que despiertes y que aceptes la oportunidad que te ofrezco de ser felices, de ser una familia, de ser un solo ser. Te ofrezco el beso de los astros, el abrazo del sol y de la luna. Olvídate de esta idea absurda de ir a conquistar las Hibueras, por favor, Hernán, destierra de tu mente esa locura. Detén el delirio interminable de tu corazón y bebe de la paz para que cese tu ambición y tu delirio. Eso es lo que quiero y está en tus manos entregármelo.
>
> (I am the beast of burden of your desires, your whims, your madness. . . . What I want is for you to awake and accept the opportunity I am offering you to be happy, to be a family, to be one being. I offer you the kisses of the stars, the embrace of the sun and the moon. Forget this absurd idea of going to conquer Hibueras, please, Hernán, banish such madness from your mind. Stop the interminable insanity in your heart and drink peace to quench your ambition and your delirium. That is what I want, and it is in your hands to give it to me). (152–53/154)

Malinalli's words draw attention to her exoticism and otherness, her marginal place as a colonized subject, and her exclusion from all spheres of power. In this distant and imaginary world that Esquivel creates for Malinche, the interpreter of the conquest relegates herself to a secondary role and cancels herself out as an exotic indigenous subject who has little to do with the civilized Spanish conquistadors. The problem with Malinalli is that she thinks with her heart and interprets her world exclusively in terms of love, feelings, and emotions. Consequently, Esquivel's fiction of passive otherness does not resolve unanswered questions regarding Mexico's identity, inferiority complex, and coloniality.[7]

Malinalli's discourse is further weakened in the novel when Cortés marries her off to Jaramillo, and she interprets this action as an act of genuine love: "Tuvo que reconocer entonces que Cortés la amaba, no como hubiera querido, pero la amaba" (She had to face the fact then that Cortés loved her, not as she would have wanted it, but that he loved her) (160/161). Unconvincingly, Malinalli's heart quickly adapts to her new lover, and she thanks Cortés for choosing her new partner. Embracing her role as a romantic heroine, almost immediately Malinche melts for her new lover, and the narrator registers her metaphoric transformation into milk and tears, saliva and sweat. Still thankful to Cortés, she fully immerses herself in a new sexual relationship with Jaramillo, as if her ultimate mission in life was to have sex:

> A los dos les deleitaba el agua. Gustaban de acariciarse mientras uno bañaba el cuerpo del otro con agua que Malinalli previamente había perfumado con nardos del jardín. A veces, tenían que interrumpir el baño para besarse, para lamerse hasta el agotamiento, hasta que terminaban mojados de sudor y semen y de nuevo tenían que bañarse.
>
> (Both were delighted by water. They liked to caress each other while one washed the body of the other with water that Malinalli had perfumed with spikenard from the garden. Sometimes, they had to interrupt the bath to kiss, to lick each other till they were exhausted, till they ended up dripping in sweat and semen and had to wash again). (169–70/172)

Some critics might see in this erotic display of love, sex, and sexual practices between Malinche and the Spanish conquistadors a liberating narrative that pulls her away from mythical and ideological interpretations (Aracil 37). But Malinche's mythical and absurd conversion at the end of the novel, when she magically becomes water—"Su espíritu se fundió con el del agua. Se desparramó sobre el aire" (Her spirit became one with the water. It scattered in the air) (182/185)—cancels out the possibility of a positive interpretation. Not only is Malinalli in love—or "in heat," if we take into account the numerous passages in which her vagina literally cannot resist the conquistadors' penises—she is ultimately liberated in a sort of mythical and unreal afterlife: "Su piel se expandió al máximo, permitiéndole cambiar de forma e integrarse a todo lo que la rodeaba. Fue nardo, fue árbol de naranjo, fue piedra, fue aroma de copal, fue maíz, fue pez, fue ave, fue sol, fue luna. Abandonó este mundo" (Her skin expanded to the limit, allowing her to change shape and become one with everything that surrounded her. She was spikenard, she was orange tree, she was stone, she was aroma of copal, she was corn, she was fish, she was bird, she was sun, she was moon. She abandoned this world) (182–83/185).

In 1950, coincidentally the same year Octavio Paz published *El laberinto de la soledad*, Fernando Benítez, in *La ruta de Hernán Cortés* (*Hernán Cortés's Route*), cautiously wrote about the danger of misinterpreting Malinche's feelings for the Spanish conquistador from a contemporary perspective:

> ¿Amó Marina a Cortés? Le tuvo la fidelidad de la esclava, la adoración de la sierva al amo omnipotente, mezclada a la conciencia muy clara en ella del honor que suponía para una india ser la amante de un hombre blanco en el que se daban las circunstancias que hicieron célebre a Cortés. *De cualquier manera, su sentimiento por él debió de haber sido en todo diferente al que hoy damos el confuso y terrible nombre de amor.*
>
> (Did Marina love Cortés? She was loyal to him like a slave, she adored him as a servant does an omnipotent lord, well aware that it was an honor for an Indian woman to be a white man's lover within the circumstances that made Cortés famous. *In any case, her feelings for him must have been very different from that which today we give the terrible name love*). (124, emphasis added)

Regrettably, the habit of fictionalizing Malinche's love and unequaled passion for the Spanish conquistador still persists. Written three years after Esquivel's novel, Fanny del Río's *La verdadera historia de Malinche* illustrates this pattern of representation. In close connection to other fictional Malinches of the twenty-first century, this one openly admits that she would travel to the end of the world for Cortés, claims to be able to read her lover's mind, and wishes to die in his arms.

Perhaps because of her excessive religiosity, this Malinche is not as sensual as Esquivel's, but she is hopelessly devoted to him and not afraid to say it. In the novel she confesses to her son that she was nobody before Cortés found her, that he shaped her life, that his words were sacred to her, and that she worked hard to be a model partner. In Cortés's arms, she forgets her life as a slave, dismisses her doubts regarding her participation in the conquest, and thinks of living in a just world, embellished by their love. "Y Fernando fue mío y yo de mi señor" (And Fernando was mine, and I was his), she recalls, "y los dos sabíamos que unidos éramos inquebrantables, porque 'fuerte es, como la muerte, el amor' " (and we both knew that together we were unbreakable, "for love is as strong as death") (127). Quoting from the Bible in this fashion, specifically Song of Songs, Malinche claims that she lives for Cortés and does not shy away from revealing her complete submission to him; "era tan parte de mí, y yo tan parte suya" (he was such a part of me, and I was such a part of him), she tells her son, "que parecía, no mi esposo y señor, sino más: mi padre, mi carne" (that he was not just my husband and lord but more like my father, my flesh) (132).

Del Río's Malinche is not as explicit in her sexuality as Martín del Campo's or Esquivel's protagonists. But the language of love and female subordination that we find in the novel, closely related to the one that William Prescott attributes to Malinche in his *History of the Conquest of Mexico* (1843), debilitate any subtle hints of gender empowerment or political agency. This time, against all odds and verisimilitude, Malinche marries Cortés in secret on May 27, 1521, in Cempoala. Although they are never able to live together as husband and wife, her love for Cortés is so strong that Malinche continues loving him with a true sense of devotion and self-sacrifice even after she marries Jaramillo. Not only does she consider Cortés to be her greatest hero, she sees him as her protector, best friend, and true family. This Malinche has little to do with the image of resistance against female slavery to patriarchy that Chicanas have created for her in contemporary discourses associated with "a woman's freedom to use her mind, her tongue, and her body in the way that she chooses to cultivate her intellectual skills for her own survival and empowerment" (Gaspar de Alba 78). This one awkwardly accepts her secondary role and relegated destiny. As a matter of fact, when she recalls her last night as the conquistador's concubine, Malinche tells her son:

> Acepté, Martín, a Cortés sin ningún reparo: tal era la naturaleza de mi apego. Si conmigo cometió fallas, antes de hacerlo ya estaban perdonadas, y cada lugar que ocupé en su vida fue para mí un privilegio inesperado . . . esa última noche que pasé con mi señor, y el recuerdo de su abrazo enamorado, todavía hoy me consuela y me hiere al mismo tiempo.
>
> (Martín, I accepted Cortés without any reservations: such was the nature of my attachment to him. If he ever did wrong toward me, before making them he was already pardoned, and every place in his life that I occupied was, for me, an unexpected privilege . . . the last night that I spent with my lord, and the memory of his loving arms, both comfort and hurt me even now). (152)

One of the major setbacks of these novels is not that Malinche depicts herself in love with the conquistador(s), but the fact that her sexuality prevents her from rebelling against calcified misconceptions regarding her negative portrayal as La Chingada who never has the chance to become a Chingona, an empowered woman of political resistance in a male-dominated world.[8]

Traduttore, Traditore

Set in neoliberal Mexico's Cámara de Diputados, Víctor Hugo Rascón Banda's play *La Malinche* provides the eponymous protagonist with an empowered rewriting of her life and forced surrender to the will of Cortés and his soldiers (Day 126). Although several cultural critics and scholars have criticized Rascón Banda for featuring the protagonist's *malinchismo*, Malinche's interventions as interpreter are remarkable, at least from a gender perspective. I say this because her words reflect the determination of a woman who manipulates the course of history as she misinterprets information for the *Mexicas* and the Spaniards:

MENSAJERO: (A *Malinche*) Pregúntales que de dónde llegaron en sus barcos que parecen templos sobre las olas.

MALINCHE: (A *Jerónimo*) Qué de dónde han venido ustedes.

JERÓNIMO: (A *Cortés*) Preguntan que de dónde somos.

CORTÉS: (A *Jerónimo*) Diles que yo vengo de parte de un gran emperador, Señor de la mayor parte del mundo.

JERÓNIMO: (A *Malinche*) Diles que él viene de parte del Señor del Mundo.

MALINCHE: (A *mensajeros*) Díganle a Moctezuma que él es el gran Señor del Mundo.

(MESSENGER: (*To Malinche*) Ask them about where they came from in those ships that look like floating temples on the water.

MALINCHE: (*To Jerónimo*) Where do you come from?

JERÓNIMO: (*To Cortés*) They want to know where we are from.

CORTÉS: (*To Jerónimo*) Tell them that I am here on behalf of a great Emperor, a Lord that owns most of the world.

JERÓNIMO: (*To Malinche*) Tell them that he is here on behalf of the Lord of the World.

MALINCHE: (*To messengers*) Tell Moctezuma that he is the great Lord of the World). (36)

Acting as a true ambassador on behalf of the Spaniards, of her own initiative Malinche tells Moctezuma's messengers not to anger Cortés and his men, distorts meaning, supplements the discourse of the conqueror with knowledge of her own, trusts her intuition, summarizes sentences, creates a third language, falsifies speech, and invents words. Inevitably attached to a set of derogatory names and adjectives that highlight her archetypical role as "La rajada" (the ripped), "La violada" (the raped), "Barragana" (concubine), "Traidora" (traitor), and "Amante" (lover) (89–90), in this play Malinche is nonetheless "La lengua" (the tongue), "Una intermediaria" (an intermediary), "Un Puente" (a bridge), "Embajadora" (ambassador) (89–90). In a powerful monologue, Malinche explains this privileged and simultaneously unfortunate situation:

> Eran dos lenguas. Eran dos mundos. No. Dos universos. Tan lejanos, tan opuestos, imposibles de unir y hacer uno solo. Y entonces lo decidí. Yo era la lengua, yo era la intérprete. Ser traductora era mi oficio. Me di cuenta de que los que llegaban no se podían entender con los que acá vivían. Los vencedores jamás se entendían con los vencidos. Tan diferentes eran. Y me di valor. Me atreví. Mentí a unos y a otros. Cambié las palabras. Me propuse convertir en verdad la gran mentira del entendimiento . . . Yo inventaba una verdad hecha de mentiras cada vez que traducía de ida y vuelta entre los dos mundos. Una verdad que sólo podía ser verdad para otro mundo, para otro ser que estaba todavía por llegar. Lo intenté. No me arrepiento . . . Yo estaba sola entre los dos. Al lado, a la sombra, sin más poder que mi lengua. Despreciada de unos y de otros. Usada.
>
> (There were two tongues. Two worlds. No. Two universes. So distant and opposed to each other, impossible to unite and to become one. And then I made the decision. I was the tongue; I was the interpreter. It was my job to be the translator. I realized that the newcomers could not understand those who already lived here. The victors could never understand the defeated. That's how different they were. And I was courageous. I dared to do it. I lied to them. I changed words. I wanted to make true the great lie of understanding . . . I invented a truth made up of lies every time I translated back and forth between the two worlds. It was a truth that could only be true for another world, for another being that had not yet

> arrived. I tried. I don't regret it . . . I was alone in the middle of them. On the side, in the shadows, without any other power than my tongue. I was despised by both. Used). (95)

The previous monologue rejects any simplistic characterizations of Malinche as either virgin or whore, aggressor or victim, patriot or traitor. It also validates the idea that the act of translation inevitably alters meaning (Chandler 8, 12). Furthermore, the passage invites us to consider that Malinche took advantage of the precious opportunity to become an invaluable agent in the Conquest of Mexico. Although her actual words are lost to us, "buried within the artifice of interpretation as reported in Spanish and Nahua accounts of the Conquest, hidden within the speech glyphs that emanate from her mouth in illustrations of the *Florentine Codex*" (Restall 85), Rascón Banda creates for her a coherent discourse within a possible, sensible, and well-rounded world, thanks to an inward narrative turn that captures her personal and historical contradictions. And we believe her, even though she remains in an ambivalent position at the end of the play, when she asserts: "Sigo viva. Humillada, insultada. Viva mientras sigan odiándome. Soy el río de todas las culpas" (I am still alive. Humiliated, insulted, alive as long as they continue to hate me. I am the river of all sins) (143).

Apparently in sync with this picture of Malinche as a wise interpreter in the hands of the Spaniards, Martín del Campo's protagonist falls in love with their language, learns it faster than does any other Indian slave, and soon begins working with Jerónimo de Aguilar as Cortés's interpreter. When Aguilar is no longer needed to complete the translation process with his knowledge of the Maya language once Malinche, a native speaker of Nahuatl, becomes fluent in Spanish, she depicts herself in absolute control of the word that changes the course of the conquest. "Si yo quisiera" (If I wanted), she realizes, "con sólo traducir al revés, con agregar palabras o dar malos consejos, el capitán y los suyos estarían en seis soles ante el gran Motecuhzoma, listos para subir los peldaños del teocalli y ser sacrificados" (just by translating backward, adding words or giving bad advice, in no time the captain and his men would be in front of Moctezuma, ready to go up the *teocalli* to be sacrificed) (113).

At first glance, her words convey the transgressive potential of the interpreter, who appears to be armed with the female spirituality and self-determination that several feminist artists, writers, and scholars—particularly Chicanas—see in Malinche toward the end of the twentieth century (Romo 149). Her words allow us to picture her as a true *faraute*, or herald, capable of interpreting two different cultures not just by translating words but, more important, by modifying the plot or by altering the links, the hidden messages, the content and form of the speeches produced by the conquered and the conquerors (Glantz, "La Malinche" 98–99). Initially, then, this portrayal of Malinche revives Bernal Díaz's chronicle, where she is depicted as an articulated meddler—"entremetida y desenvuelta" (XXXVI, 59), he calls her—who walks on the communicative bridge between the Spaniards and the Indians and manages to insert herself into the narrative she attempts to interpret, altering its final meaning.

Unfortunately, though, in *Amor y conquista*, Malinche's love for Puertocarrero prevents her from acting as a genuine "entremetida," as an interpreter whose main job is to talk, to communicate what others say but also, more important, to intervene in the development of the plot (Glantz, "La Malinche" 99). To her disadvantage, Malinche keeps her ephemeral transgressive dreams to herself and translates with such accuracy and conviction that she even memorizes and internalizes the discourse of the conquistadors: "Traduje muchas cosas de tu religión" (I translated many things about your religion), she tells Puertocarrero, "ya me las estoy aprendiendo de memoria" (I am already memorizing them) (124). Only through the words of other characters in the novel can we intuit that Malinche is, indeed, a transgressive interpreter. Ozlaxiuchitl, for instance, tells her daughter, the metafictional writer who crafts this story, that she hates Malinalli for being Cortés's lover, "pero, sobre todo, por enseñarle nuestra manera de sentir, nuestras debilidades . . . *decía sus palabras falsas de manera tan natural* que si no me ponía en guardia correría el riesgo de ser engañada" (but, above all, for teaching him our way of feeling, our weaknesses . . . *she would say her false words in such a natural way that*, if I wasn't cautious, I was at risk of being deceived) (203, emphasis added). But Malinche's supposedly "false words" never make it to the surface of the narrative.

We notice a similar problem when Cuauhtémoc wants to capture Malinalli because he realizes that she is not just any kind of interpreter but the woman who reveals the secrets of the Tenochca heart to Cortés. How exactly she does this remains unclear. The novel is more invested in portraying her as a faithful lover, in recording the two pregnancies that bring her incomparable happiness, or in showing that she stands against violence. In this novel she is primarily a slave who interprets—she is repeatedly called a slave by the narrator and some of the characters, like Cuauhtémoc. Toward the end of the novel, she even admits to herself: "Sé que soy una esclava" (I know that I am a slave) (396), and when Cortés marries her off to Jaramillo, she does not use any words to protect herself. Instead, she passively accepts her destiny: "Permanecí en silencio. Tragándome las lágrimas, no quise que me viera llorar" (I remained silent. I swallowed my tears. I didn't want anyone to see me crying) (396).

The fact that Malinche simply interprets back and forth, from Spanish to Nahuatl and vice versa without any sort of political intervention, reminds us that historically interpreters have been treated as enslaved bodies, as ventriloquists whose voices are not their own (Glantz, "La Malinche" 105). But the fact that Malinche appears in this fashion in a novel published at the dawn of the twenty-first century seems incongruent with previous works that, precisely in reaction to her lack of voice—in the sense that her discourse is always that of others—empower her with transgressive attitudes, dissident behaviors, or revolutionary words. In Fuentes's "Las dos orillas," for example, Doña Marina resolves internal conflicts between Cortés and Moctezuma out of her own initiative and uses the word as a weapon to fight for the construction of a new world. No less ambitious is Ignacio Solares's novel *Nen, la inútil,* whose main character, constructed with Malinche's DNA, uses her mythical visions, her otherness, and even her masturbatory practices to manipulate people around her and create a liberated space of her own.

These narrative twists, developed in tune with a number of "new" historical novels that in the 1980s and 1990s established their domain explicitly contradicting the course of history, often empowering marginal voices, playing with anachronism, parody, intertextuality, and the Bakhtinian carnival (Menton 22), seem to be completely absent from the Mexican literary scenario of the twenty-first century. In Esquivel's novel, for instance, Malinche considers her job as an interpreter a heavy burden, a spiritual endeavor for which she feels unprepared. "Ser 'la lengua' implicaba un gran conocimiento espiritual" (Being "The Tongue" was a great spiritual duty), the narrator explains, "era poner todo su ser al servicio de los dioses para que su lengua fuera parte del aparato sonoro de la divinidad, para que su voz esparciera por el cosmos el sentido mismo de la existencia, *pero Malinalli no se sentía preparada para ello*" (for it meant putting all her being at the service of the gods so that her tongue was part of the resounding system of the divinity, so that her voice would spread through the cosmos the very meaning of existence. *But Malinalli did not feel up to the task*) (62–63/64–65, emphasis added).

Esquivel's Malinche is often afraid to use her words: "al hablar, se dejaba guiar por sus deseos y entonces la voz que salía de su boca no era otra que la del miedo. Miedo a no ser fiel a sus dioses, miedo a fallar, miedo a no poder con la responsabilidad y—¿por qué no?—miedo al poder" (when translating, she let herself be guided by her feelings and then the voice that came out of her mouth was no other than the voice of fear, fear of being unfaithful to the gods, of failure, fear of not being able to bear responsibility. And truthfully, also fear of power) (63/65). Apparently, she understands the power of the interpreter who controls meaning and information, the transmission of a specific discourse, the development of a particular situation. As an interpreter, however, she is conflicted because of a number of moral obstacles that make her feel like a traitor and keep her in a permanent state of misery:

> o trataba de servir a los dioses y ser fiel al significado que ellos le habían dado al mundo o seguía sus propios instintos, los más terrenales y primarios, y se aseguraba que cada palabra y cada acto adquiriera el significado que a ella le convenía. Lo segundo obviamente era un golpe de Estado a los dioses y el temor a su reacción la llenaba de miedos y culpas.
>
> (Either she remained faithful to the gods and to the meaning that they had given to the world, or she followed her instincts, her most earthly and primary instincts, and made sure that each world and each action acquired the meaning that most suited her. The second choice was clearly a rebellion against the gods, and their eventual reaction filled her with fear and guilt). (65/67)

When reflecting on the historical Malinche, Bolívar Echeverría considered her intervention as an interpreter to be admirable because she combines wisdom and audacity. Malinche, he reasons, successfully alters communication: she lies to both parties involved in the dialogue of the conquest and creates a utopian discourse of mutual understanding. To carry out this task, the translator acts as a mediator between two languages that can only meet in the midst of a utopian "third language," a bridge language that is neither one of the two in question and yet produces an invented reality that connects a set of symbolic and cultural values, in a convoluted space governed by misunderstanding (Echeverría 174).

Esquivel's *Malinche* could not be more removed from Echeverría's positive portrayal of the interpreter. In this novel, Malinche is always afraid of her words and feels guilty every time she interprets for the Spaniards and the Nahuas. She spends most of her energy not necessarily interpreting but trying not to disappoint Quetzalcoatl and wanting to please Cortés. In the end, torn between opposing languages, cultures, and beliefs, Malinche just wants to be left alone, in silence: "¡Imploró silencio a todos sus dioses! Lo que más la atormentaba, aparte del ruido exterior, era el ruido interno, las voces en su cerebro que le decían que callara, que no hablara" (She implored the gods for silence. What most tormented her, aside from the external noises, were the noises within, the voices in her mind that told her not to say anything) (67/69). In tune with Esquivel's romantic fictions, Malinche is not proud to have served as an interpreter; she is just thankful to have learned a new language of love:

> Inspirada por esa verdad que ilumina todas las cosas, le habló a su hijo en Español y fue en ese momento que descubrió la belleza del idioma de Cortés y agradeció que dios le hubiera regalado esa nueva forma de expresarse, en un lenguaje que abría nuevos lugares en su mente y gracias al cual su hijo podría comprender su amor de madre.
>
> (Inspired by that truth that illuminates all things, she spoke to her son in Spanish. It was at that moment that she discovered the beauty of Cortés's language and appreciated that god had given her that new method with which to express herself, in a language which opened new spaces in her mind. Thanks to it, her son could understand his mother's love). (165/167)

Malinche appears no less thankful to God in Fanny del Río's novel for having learned Maya and Spanish to better serve Jesus Christ, Spanish emperor Charles V, and Cortés. When she realizes that Jerónimo de Aguilar is not a great language teacher, she asks other soldiers to teach her Spanish because she wants to become an authentic Christian. Soon after, with her knowledge of Spanish, Malinche becomes the only interpreter of the conquest and translates Cortés with vehemence and passion, from the heart, as if she were genuinely transformed by his imperial arguments and religious beliefs.

As readers of these novels, we might be puzzled by the fact that Malinche's role as cultural intermediary and her alleged skills as a persuasive interpreter are either diminished or completely vanished. The three romantic heroines who translate from Spanish to Nahuatl and vice versa do so as an act of love, following their hearts, in confirmation of their passions. Conceived like soap opera characters of the twenty-first century, these women seem to cater to contemporary middle-class audiences interested in the portrayal of intimacy, or in melodramatic plots that "sell," often with spectacular undertones, a set of cultural values (García Canclini 28). Unlike Rascón Banda's theatrical rendering of Malinche as a cunning interpreter and shrewd manipulator who confirms "the myth of (mis)communication" between Cortés and Moctezuma—namely, that "Spaniards understood what they needed to, and natives understood what that meant" (Restall 99)—these recent novels relegate her to a private sphere of feelings and emotions, moral dilemmas, religious contradictions, and carnal addictions that practically erase her fundamental agency in the Spanish conquest.

Some critics might argue that these depictions of an enamored Malinche who is less interested in the art and power of translation than in her own intimate desires as a woman, lover, mother, and sexual companion, represent a feminist attempt to reclaim her interiority. But a mere fictionalization of the realm that has been traditionally marginalized for its "feminine" markers does not necessarily constitute a feminist work. A contestatory feminist fiction should not only privilege the fictionalization of so-called feminine spheres. Ideally it would also question the confinement of women to various domestic environments that keep them away from the production of knowledge and change. As Nelly Richard argues, a feminist fictionalization of the "private" must also challenge the validity of a set of cultural values that stereotype "privacy" and reduce it to the feminine realm ("Sexo" 137). What some of us would like to see in these novels by Esquivel, Martín del Campo, and Del Río is precisely that: a clear confrontation of all stereotypes associated with the "feminine" and the "private," or, simply put, a transgressive articulation of various "intimate" scenarios traditionally linked to women or the female experience, as if they had nothing to do with the world of men and masculinity.

Malinche's Religion

In a recent comparative study on Malinche, Pocahontas, and Sacagawea, historian Rebecca K. Jager writes that Malinche was a "strategic diplomat and passionate evangelist," and that she served not only as a cultural negotiator and consultant but as a "spiritual adviser" and "persuasive orator" who "convinced thousands of apprehensive Natives to believe in Spanish promises of liberation and salvation" (97–99). Surprisingly, her main source to back up this claim is Bernal Díaz's *Historia verdadera*, a historical manuscript nonetheless known for its literary undertones, which transport readers to a hybrid world of fact and fiction, unparalleled storytelling and effective writing strategies, medieval tales, popular sayings, and affected modesty. If we believe Bernal Díaz, then Malinche would be the best example of an indigenous woman embracing Catholicism in no time, almost immediately after her baptism. According to this colonial account, written by a Spanish conquistador who needs to justify the effectiveness of evangelization in a world that creates profit for the *encomenderos* and the Spanish Crown, Doña Marina tells her mother "que Dios la había hecho mucha merced en quitarla de adorar ídolos y ser cristiana" (that God had been very gracious to her in freeing her from the worship of idols and making her a Christian) (XXXVII, 62/86). Hence, in Díaz's chronicle, she translates Cortés's Christian speeches for the Indians very well, even the Franciscan prayers when Cuauhtémoc is sentenced to death.

How likely is it that Malinche would convert to Christianity in a moment, with the strong Christian conviction that Bernal Díaz attributed to her? Of course, we will never know the answer to this question, although her key participation in transmitting Christian values to the Indians is undeniable, as can be observed in several indigenous accounts of the conquest. In the *Lienzo de Tlaxcala*, Malinche is standing right next to Fray Bartolomé de Olmedo as a cross is erected in Tlaxcala; she is also present in the baptism of the lords of Tlaxcala. Yet even if we consider other Spanish chronicles that highlight Malinche's belief in God, such as Francisco Cervantes de Salazar's *Crónica de la Nueva España* (*Chronicle of New Spain*),[9] we can never know for certain her level of religious conversion. As anthropologist Cristina González Hernández writes, it is impossible to know whether her religious zeal was genuine or a political strategy, if she considered herself indigenous or Spanish or both after the conquest, and yet one set of possibilities does not exclude the other ones. What matters in the end is that Malinche inaugurated a new discourse of transculturation and cultural hybridity.[10]

Clearly, Malinche's religion speaks volumes about her elusive identity, and contemporary literature finds no middle ground for her religious beliefs: she is either a full-blown Christian or she remains faithful to her indigenous deities. Torn between these extremes, Malinche continues perpetuating Mexico's historical archetypes, those that portray women as either good or bad. Esquivel's *Malinche* and Del Río's *La verdadera historia de Malinche* exemplify this situation. In Esquivel's novel, Malinche welcomes her Christian baptism, convinced that Christ can be no other than Quetzalcoatl and that the Spaniards are his emissaries in charge of eradicating human sacrifice. Although externally she is a good Christian, deep down she believes in her indigenous deities. This internal conflict becomes more evident when she feels that her true God is mad at her:

> ¿Estaría enojado el señor Quetzalcóatl con ella? ¿Por qué? Ella no lo había traicionado, todo lo contrario. Había participado en la ceremonia del bautizo con la mente impregnada de su recuerdo. Es más, ¡desde antes de la ceremonia! Pues recordó que al entrar al templo donde se ofreció la misa, su corazón brincó de emoción al ver en el centro del altar una cruz, que para ella era la del señor Quetzalcóatl, pero que los españoles consideraban como propia y no pudo evitar conmoverse. En ningún momento había traicionado sus creencias.
>
> (Was Quetzalcoatl mad at her? Why? She hadn't betrayed him, quite the opposite. She had participated in her baptism with her mind impregnated by her memories of him. Even before the ceremony. She remembered that before entering the temple where mass was celebrated, her heart pounded with excitement when she saw a cross at the center of the altar that for her belonged to Quetzalcoatl, although the Spaniards called it their own, and she could not help but feel moved. Not once did she betray her own beliefs). (49–50)

Even though this passage tries to express the syncretism with which many Indians must have embraced Catholicism in the early stages of the conquest, throughout the novel Malinche continues to be true to Quetzalcoatl, adores Tonantzin, and talks to the goddess Tlazolteotl in the temple of Huitzilopochtli.

One could argue in defense of Esquivel that these associations make sense, considering that the first missionaries who arrived in New Spain shortly after the conquest taught Christian values and beliefs using what was already familiar to the indigenous population; after all, it is well known that the friars correlated indigenous deities, symbols, and rituals with their European counterparts (Curcio-Nagy 157). But Malinche, in Esquivel's novel, is unable to make that religious transfer. In fact, she blames Quetzalcoatl for not defending himself when the Spaniards destroy his temples and blames him for leaving her helpless in the middle of a religious battle. Furthermore, since she does not quite grasp the Spaniards' teachings regarding an invisible God and the kingdom of Heaven, she continues believing in the spiritual world of her ancestors, or more explicitly, in the power of the moon and the sun, whose light is capable of unifying time and space. Loyal to this mentality, then, in secret Malinche visits Tlazolteotl, the goddess of purification and patron of adulterers, to seek forgiveness for her sexual sins and transgressions.

As in Bernal Díaz's account, when Esquivel's Malinche finds her mother, she expresses her new religious beliefs, asserting that she is "la nueva ciudad, la nueva creencia, la nueva cultura" (the new city, the new beliefs, the new culture) (150/151). But her purported "new" beliefs are very similar to her "old" ones. At the end of the novel, for instance, Malinalli seeks spiritual refuge in Tonantzin's arms. Desperate to find her goddess, Malinche asks quietly: "'¿Dónde estás, alma de las cosas, esencia de lo visible, eternidad de las estrellas? ¿Dónde puedo buscarte para encontrarte, si estás prohibida, si te han desaparecido, si te han arrancado de nuestra fe, si han intentado borrarte de nuestra memoria?'" ("Where are you, soul of things, essence of the visible, eternity of the stars? Where can I search in order to find you, if you are forbidden, if they have made you disappear, if they have ripped you from our faith, if they have tried to erase you from our memory?") (178/180). Thanks to the wonders of this romantic, magical-realist novel, Malinche finds Tonantzin in the hill of Tepeyac, communicates with her in a dream-like moment that affects nature and even foresees her syncretic reappearance as the Virgin of Guadalupe: "Aparecería arropada por los rayos del sol, sostenida por la luna, en medio del aire, temblando en el viento, con una forma nueva" (She would come dressed in the rays of the sun, sustained by the moon, in midair. Trembling in the wind, in a new shape) (178/181).

To complete the magical and anachronistic apparition,[11] Guadalupe/Tonantzin tells Malinche without any hints of verisimilitude: "'Cambiarán de forma nuestros ritos, será otro nuestro lenguaje, otras nuestras oraciones, distinta nuestra comunicación . . . pero los dioses antiguos, los inamovibles, los de cerca y del junto, los que no tienen principio ni fin, no cambiarán más que de forma'" ("Our rituals would change in form, our language would become another, our prayers others, our communication different . . . but the ancient gods, the immovable ones, the gods of all things, those that have no beginning and no end, will only change in form") (178/181). As further proof that Malinche remains loyal to her indigenous beliefs, in her final hour she blends herself with Tonantzin and other female deities, in the presence of Quetzalcoatl, as she magically disappears in her patio's water fountain:

> El silencio era total. Aspiró el aroma de los nardos, metió sus pies al agua, caminó por en medio de los canales y llegó al centro del patio. Ahí, en el centro de la Cruz de Quetzalcóatl, en el centro de la encrucijada de caminos, donde se aparecían las Cihuateteo, las mujeres muertas en el parto que formaban la comitiva que acompañaba a Tlazolteotl, a Coatlicue, a Tonantzin—diferentes manifestaciones de una misma deidad femenina—ahí, en el centro del universo, se volvió líquida.
>
> (The silence was complete. She breathed in the aroma of the spikenard, put her feet in the water, walked through the middle of the canal, and reached the center of the patio. There, she entered into the center of the Cross of Quetzalcoatl, the center of all crossroads, where the Cihuateteo, the woman who had died during childbirth, who made up the entourage of the women who follow Tlazolteotl, Coatlicue, and Tonantzin, the different manifestations of the same feminine deity, appeared; and there, in the center of the universe, Malinalli became liquid). (182/184–85)

On the opposite side of the spectrum, Del Río transforms Malinche into a devoted Catholic woman who has fully internalized the conqueror's religion. Although at the beginning of the novel she admits that the Lord of the Christians is an enigmatic figure to her, Malinche undergoes a dramatic transformation as soon as she hears the Apostle's Creed: "entonces, deslumbrada por la hermosura de aquellas palabras, comencé a abrazar la fe de mis nuevos amos" (then, overwhelmed by the beauty of those words, I began to embrace my new masters' faith), she admits (43). Like Esquivel's Malinche, initially this one also finds analogies between her indigenous beliefs and her newly acquired religion but almost immediately adopts Christianity with true conviction. As she reflects on her instant reaction to the creed, Malinche tells her son:

> Sentía como si esas palabras fueran sucesivas llaves que abrían cerrojos a las pesadas cadenas de mi alma, liberándome de mentiras y falsedades, y entonces posé la mirada en la venerada imagen de la Virgen, que abrazaba a ese Hijo que el Espíritu Santo había protegido del recelo de José antes incluso de que naciera, y te juro, Martín, que al punto me despojé de todas mis creencias anteriores y fui cristiana en mi corazón a partir de aquel instante, mientras fray Bartolomé daba la primera misa de la Nueva España.
>
> (I felt as if those words were keys that unlocked the heavy chains of my soul, liberating me from lies and falsities, and then I looked upon the venerated image of the Virgin who holds in her arms the Son that the Holy Spirit had protected from Joseph's doubts even before he was born, and I swear, Martín, that at once I let go of my previous beliefs and I became a true Christian in my heart from that moment, while fray Bartolomé was giving the first mass of New Spain). (44)

For sure, the Spanish conquistadors would have wanted this type of automatic and miraculous conversion as the early priests baptized thousands of Indians at once, even if their understanding of Christian doctrine was obviously very limited (Cursio-Nagy 156). But what we see in Del Río's novel is an unbelievable extreme. Malinche learns Spanish mostly to become an authentic Christian, and she professes her new faith even better than the Spaniards. *Más papista que el Papa* (more Papist than the Pope), Malinche speaks in the novel like a New World mystic, discussing Jesus's Holy Calvary and the Virgin Mary's incomparable love and compassion:

> Me inspiraba Cristo la mayor admiración que sentirse podía, pero encontré la fe verdadera, si fe es esperanza y consuelo, en la

> virgen María, cuya imagen tan hondamente caló en mi corazón que no podía mirarla sin que al instante se humedecieran mis ojos; *había sido herida, sí, pero dulcemente de su amor.*
>
> (Christ inspired me a great deal, but I found the true faith, if faith is hope and comfort, in the Virgin Mary, whose image touched my heart so deeply that I couldn't look at her without crying; *I had been wounded, yes, but sweetly by her love*). (47, emphasis added)

Surprisingly, Malinche appears more like a close relative of Santa Teresa de Jesús or San Juan de la Cruz—the Spanish mystics—than as an Indian woman who might have had some internal conflicts with her newly imposed religion. Regardless of how native conversion was depicted in the early Spanish chronicles, in reality the Indians adopted Catholicism out of fear. Their alleged "conversion," as Monsiváis reminds us, was only possible by violent means; the Indians were enslaved, punished, and forced to learn and practice Catholicism as they witnessed the destruction of their world, including their gods and sacred books (*Imágenes* 17). Despite these facts, Del Río's Malinche defines herself as an authentic Christian, abominates idolatry, speaks against the practice of sodomy, and abhors human sacrifice. Unlike any of her indigenous fellows, she is a full-blown convert: "era una cristiana auténtica, y a cuantos me han acusado de equivocarme les he dicho que de buen grado volvería a hacerlo, pues con ello obedecí las escrituras sagradas, y mi fe todavía no ha conocido límites" (I was an authentic Christian, and I tell those who think that I made a mistake that I would gladly do it again, because I obeyed the Scriptures, and my faith knows no limits) (118).

Can we trust her words? Exceeding all plausible limits, in this particular novel Malinche prays like a faithful woman, constantly thanks the Virgin Mary for guiding her life in the midst of a turbulent world, puts herself in the hands of Christ, and blindly believes in the power of divine forgiveness. Although this type of conversion may have taken place in real life, at least in some cases, we as contemporary readers have a hard time believing that such a wise indigenous woman as Malinche would convert to Catholicism without any resistance. Catholicism was not necessarily understood by the recently converted Indians, oppressed by slavery, terror, and lack of knowledge. The smooth Christian conversion that Del Río depicts has very little to do with the cruelty of the

Spanish evangelization, a process that immersed Indians in the destruction of their world and the simultaneous creation of a new one, aided by prayers and punishment, in a new horizon of candles, saints, and virgins (Monsiváis, *Imágenes* 17).

In *La verdadera historia de Malinche*, the eponymous protagonist is too exceptional and therefore unreal. At the end of the novel, Malinche enters the Hospital de la Sagrada Concepción to dedicate her life to the salvation of those who are in desperate need of help. Like an exceptional woman, she convinces her spiritual mentor, a Franciscan friar, that she wants to spend the rest of her life among the poor. She leaves her family because she feels God's calling to abandon worldly matters in the middle of a portentous night:

> En el año del 20 y el siete apareció en el cielo una luz a manera de espada que no se mudó en toda la noche, y fue cuando azotó a la ciudad una pestilencia de sarampión y otra como de lepra que desfiguraba el rostro a quienes la padecían, infectándolos de tan nauseabundo hedor que no se podía sufrir su compañía: comprendí que Dios me estaba llamando, y no tardó en iluminarme con un plan.
>
> (In 1527, a light in the shape of a sword appeared in the sky and stayed there all night, and that's when the city was struck by a plague of measles and by something like leprosy that disfigured the faces of those who suffered from it and infected them with an unbearable stench: I understood that God was calling me, and he soon illuminated me with a plan). (165)

Her entrance into this famous hospital of the early colonial era (founded in 1524 as the Hospital de la Purísima Concepción) reminds us that many indigenous noblewomen were indeed targeted by the first missionaries as ideal individuals to accept and propagate Catholicism in the conquered territories. But Fray Juan de Zumárraga's request to establish a place to teach Christianity to indigenous women was rejected precisely because of their recent indoctrination and because of their overall inability to live in a cloistered environment. Although women of the Indian nobility received formal religious education in several "houses" or "schools" between 1529 and the following decade, their evangelization did not take place in a cloister (Díaz, *Indigenous* 6). In spite of this, in

Del Río's novel, after faking her death, Malinche secludes herself in the Hospital de la Sagrada Congregación, pays for her own dowry, and behaves like an exemplary nun, separated from the world and attached to her new spiritual life: "Recluida y desembarazada, al fin, de la odiada mundanidad que me aprisionaba, me aboqué a servir a los demás; ningún trabajo, por expuesto o repugnante, bastaba para colmar mi sed de sacrificio y humildad; suplicaba a los demás que no me lo encomiaran, pues había sido por procurar alivio a mi alma que huí de halagos y de vanidad" (Secluded and away, finally, from the worldly matters that trapped me, I turned to the service of others; no job, no matter how dangerous or repugnant, was enough to fulfill my thirst for sacrifice and humility; I asked others not to praise me as it was in search of peace that I had fled flattery and vanity) (166).

It is worth noting that when Zumárraga wrote his *Doctrina breve cristiana* (*A Brief Christian Doctrine*) (ca. 1545; a manuscript "para los adultos que se han de bautizar; y para los nuevos baptizados necesario y saludable documento" [for those adults who will be baptized; and a necessary and healthy document for the newly baptized]), the bishop of New Spain considered that successful catechization would lead the Indians not necessarily to understand Christian doctrine but to simply "stutter" the articles of faith (Rabasa 70). Unlike other Indians who presumably limited themselves to memorizing the doctrine, Del Río's Malinche is genuinely transformed by her new faith: "Entregada a las manos del verdadero rey del Cielo, cuando sentía que las fuerzas me escapaban, recordaba el suplicio de Jesús, ¡mi verdadero esposo celestial!, y nada resultaba suficiente para obtener su divina gracia. El amor de Cristo era mi inspiración y mi fuente de alegría" (Devoted to the true king of Heaven, when I felt that I had no strength, I would remember Jesus's torture—my true heavenly husband!—and nothing was good enough to obtain his divine favor. The love of Christ was my inspiration and my source of happiness) (166). Unquestionably, this Malinche surpasses Bernal's enhanced model of a Christian woman and leaves us speechless. Like a good pious woman, she suffers for the lack of faith that surrounds her and believes that only the Virgin Mary, as the mother of Christ and the perfect manifestation of clemency and forgiveness, can lead the sinners of the world to salvation, liberty, and redemption.

Without doubt, the proliferation of novels that fictionalize Latin American history confirms that the past constitutes an indelible part of the continent's identity, and also that historical memories preserve individual and collective experiences that express ways of thinking, representations of the world, beliefs, and ideologies (Aínsa, *Los guardianes* 119–20). But the author who works with the past is, for better or worse, responsible for making it legible, in the sense that even the smallest narrative transgressions and "lies" should fit comfortably within the boundaries of a "possible" fictional world.[12] It is hard to accept a character's interiority, personal drives, or conflicts if they are inserted into an impossible scenario of weak and illogical narrative structures. Sadly, Del Río's re-creation of a pious Malinche is simply incompatible with her historical context and the limited possibilities for a woman of her ethnicity and social status. The more Malinche embraces her new religion in this novel, the less credible she is. Or do we actually believe, as readers of contemporary fiction, that Cortés's interpreter decides to seclude herself in a hospital, "para alcanzar la verdadera riqueza de la consagración a Cristo y a su divina madre" (to reach the true wealth of consecration to Christ and his divine mother)? (168). When did Malinche learn these words? How did she have time to fully comprehend these foreign discourses and internalize them with such vehemence? Much to her detriment, Malinche's over-the-top Christianity turns her into an artificial protagonist. Her Catholicism is far-fetched and makes it difficult to believe that she flagellates herself to cleanse her sins before she dies, "pues anhelo encontrarme con el Creador y ponerle fin a las penas de este mundo" (because I wish to be with the Creator to put an end to the sorrows of this world) (168).

At least Marisol Martín del Campo tries to re-create a sound picture of Malinche's conversion, allowing her to recall that the indigenous women who served the Spaniards were forced to become Christians. Dignified, this Malinche asserts the Indians' loyalty to their original beliefs and traditions: "ninguna creíamos en sus dioses y vírgenes, ni en sus historias ni en sus demonios, ninguna deseaba traicionar nuestra religión o cambiar nuestras creencias" (none of us believed in their gods and virgins, nor in their stories or their demons, none of us wanted to betray our religion or change our beliefs) (70). As the narrative progresses, Malinche realizes that the conquest has changed her, and she is torn between two ways of thinking, two different cultures and religions. "Ya no sé en quién creer" (I don't know in whom to believe), she mentally admits to her lost lover Puertocarrero, "porque también creo en tu dios y en tus santos y vírgenes; sin su ayuda, ustedes no hubiesen podido conquistar el imperio mexica" (because I also believe in your god and your saints and virgins; without their help, you wouldn't have been able to conquer the *Mexica* empire) (366). Her words construct a possible world of fiction that contains the seeds of ambiguity, indecision, and internal conflict. Malinche's intermediate position is kept throughout this novel, especially when she demonstrates that she does not fully understand the new religion or various concepts related to sin and corporality, legitimate sex, and illegitimate children. In the end, she sees herself as a hybrid product of the new system and claims: "creo en el dios de Malinche y me siento más apegada al blanco, aunque también amo lo nuestro, no en balde soy mexica y soy de estas tierras, *no sé cómo explicar*" (I believe in Malinche's god and I feel closer to the white man, although I love our own beliefs as well. Not for nothing I am a *Mexica* and from these lands. *I don't know how to explain it*) (393, emphasis added).

Why does Malinche have to explain her faith in any of these novels? Better yet, why does she have to justify what must have been a forced process of transculturation? Perhaps because religion is an integral part of contemporary Mexico and because it is attached (thanks to the spiritual conquest) to the birth of the Mexican nation. Indisputably, the Virgin of Guadalupe that appears in these novels, either as a new manifestation of Tonantzin (Esquivel) or as the mother of all Christians (Del Río), reminds us that her figure is considered not only a religious fact but, more important, a national project that facilitates the spread of Christianity and trespasses the colonial era, the War of Independence, the Mexican Revolution, and the long twentieth century of Church–state tensions, social activism, Marxism, economic development, human rights, and liberation theology. Coincidentally, these novels dealing with Malinche's religion were published when the Mexican government improved its relationship with the Catholic Church after a long period of anticlericalism to enhance the administration's image with foreign lenders and private investors whose support would be crucial in a neoliberal era (Coerver 431). We cannot overlook the fact that these novels were produced in a tense political environment as the Church and the state moved closer to each other, thanks to the establishment of new diplomatic relations between Mexico and the Vatican in 1992, the role of the Church as mediator after the Zapatista uprising in 1994, the fourth visit of Pope John Paul II to Mexico in 1999, and Juan Diego's canonization in 2003. Malinche's religion speaks of Mexico's identity, of the government's thorny relationships with the Church, and more important, of the national culture of a country that even in the twenty-first century sells Catholicism—and the Virgin of Guadalupe as a symbol of Mexicanness—as its true religion, largely discrediting any other cults and beliefs. The thriving TV series *La rosa de Guadalupe* (produced by Televisa since 2008), confirms my hypothesis, as it continues to sell over the course of more than 800 episodes the spectacular idea that Mexico's moral, sexual, ethnic, and social problems can be solved—as we see in the novels of Esquivel and Del Río—thanks to the divine interventions of the Virgin of Guadalupe.

A Story of Her Own

Whether or not we like these literary representations of Malinche that individually or collectively explore her true religion, her internal conflicts as a translator, or even her love for the Spanish conquistadors, each novel is conceived as a counterfactual story or as a dissident narrative that provides an alternative reading of the history of a stigmatized character. The literary intention to rewrite history against the grain is not new, of course. Numerous historical novels, particularly those that were published in the last two decades of the twentieth century, explicitly complement historiography with undocumented information, subvert the course of history, propose contradictory interpretations of historical realities, and consequently challenge historical accuracy (Lefere 80–88). What distinguishes this set of recent novels penned by Del Río, Esquivel, and Martín del Campo is the fact that they give Malinche the opportunity to write down her own counterfactual story, draw an alternative codex, or give her true story to someone who can preserve it in writing, respectively.

Del Río's *La verdadera historia de Malinche*, whose title is reminiscent of Bernal Díaz's *Historia verdadera de la conquista de la Nueva España*, is an epistolary novel made up of thirty letters written by Malinche. She writes these letters to her son, Martín Cortés, to rinse her tainted memory. "Voy a contarte todo como pasó" (I will tell you everything as it happened), she writes to him, "no como lo narró a la Corte don Fernando, sino como lo sufrí yo, Malinalli, la heredera traicionada, la esclava india que aceptó la hostia y, con ella, el nombre de Marina" (not the way that Don Fernando reported it to the court, but as I endured it all, I, Malinalli, the betrayed heir, the Indian slave who accepted the host and, with it, the name of Marina) (16). She writes these letters to seek forgiveness for her wrongdoings, especially from her son. Ultimately she wants to clarify that she did not sell her people into slavery, that she is not responsible for the ruin of the Mexican nation, and that she is not, as most people want to remember her, the mother of the new Mexicans who wonder around aimlessly, feeling lost and carrying on their shoulders the weight of abandonment.

These words in the novel openly confront Malinche's stigmatized portrayal as La Chingada. In the process of cleaning her reputation, the narrative does what other historical novels are able to do thanks to the wonders of literature: it inserts an individual consciousness into the body of a collective past to problematize the present and its inherited memory (Aínsa, *Los guardianes* 122–26). In her version of the story, Del Río's Malinche describes herself as a beautiful woman used and abused by her indigenous masters long before the arrival of the Spaniards. She explains that Cortés used her as his personal messenger and secretary and that she was constantly afraid of being sacrificed and eaten by the indigenous warriors that the Spaniards encountered during the Conquest of Mexico.

Much to our surprise, while Malinche depicts Cortés writing his *Cartas de relación* to the Spanish Crown, she also reveals herself mastering the written language and writing her own history: "emprendí la tarea, llevada a cabo con el mayor de los sigilos, de escribir mi propia relación de la conquista de México, inspirada en la admiración que a todos nos causaba la gran Tenochtitlan" (I began to write, with the utmost discretion, my own account of the conquest of Mexico, inspired by the admiration that we all felt for the great Tenochtitlan) (104). That Malinche would ever write her own chronicle surpasses all limits of verisimilitude. Interestingly, she gives her written account to Bernal Díaz. Although he promises to pursue its publication, the manuscript gets lost when he gives it to an Italian sailor on his way to the Iberian Peninsula. We are left to wonder if this man threw it into the sea or burned it to keep himself warm.

This passage may seem insignificant (or even absurd), but it actually opens a can of worms in regard to Bernal Díaz and the true origin of the *Historia verdadera*. In the same year Del Río published her novel (2012), French historian and anthropologist Christian Duverger published *Crónica de la eternidad* (*The Chronicle of Eternity*), a book that proposes that the *Historia verdadera* was written by Hernán Cortés. The book's hypothesis has been largely discredited by several academics, as there are, indeed, numerous episodes of the *Historia verdadera* that disqualify such an assertion.[13] Del Río's novel makes us think, at least within the framework of a fictional pact between the narrator and the reader, that Doña Marina could have been the true author of the most famous chronicle of the conquest, and that Bernal Díaz published it under his name. More important, though, this passage forces us to reflect on a woman's impossibility—even more so for an indigenous woman—to participate in writing history and disseminating historical knowledge.

In a metaphorical sense, Malinche's fictional letters and chronicle confront the writing of history and validate counterhegemonic expressions that were never included in any official records. Although it is pretty unbelievable that Malinche would learn how to read and write or that she would take the time to study an assortment of books, for the first time she is in charge of writing her own story. Because she controls the construction of her own discourse, in her will she tells her son to be proud of his lineage, clarifying that she allied with the Spaniards to liberate her people from idolatry and the practice of human sacrifice: "Tú, Martín Cortés, hijo de Malinche, tienes en la sangre al pueblo nuevo de Dios: sostén el orgullo de ser quien eres; lleva siempre en alto la frente; haz comprender a todos que no hay vergüenza alguna que pueda mancillar a quien sabe dar su vida por la libertad" (You, Martín Cortés, son of Malinche, carry in your blood God's new world: be proud of who you are; keep your head up high; let everyone know that there's no shame in giving up your life for freedom) (176). These words represent an alternative ending to her story, one that allows us to see that the past is malleable or that it can always inscribe itself in the context of the present, even if historical dominant discourses have mostly destroyed or silenced any form of dissidence produced by minorities (Aínsa, *Los guardianes* 137).

Esquivel's *Malinche* provides readers with an alternative story that is created through written text and a set of illustrations that make up a codex, which is folded up and used as the book cover. Taking into account that Malinche's agency is represented in several native sources that address her fundamental role as Cortés's interpreter, such as the *Florentine Codex*, the *Lienzo of Tlaxcala*, the *Texas Fragment*, or the *Codex Tizatlán*,[14] Esquivel includes a contemporary codex with Jordi Castells's illustrations to better portray her story. She explains in her opening note that she wanted to include in this novel the codex that Malinche would have painted—had she had the opportunity or the skills to do so—to show through a set of images what words express differently. In sync with the romantic story we find in the novel, the codex that Malinche paints here is very personal, full of intimate passages that include her birth and indigenous baptism, her relationship with her mother and grandmother, her sexual encounters with Cortés, her marriage to Jaramillo, her meeting with her mother and brother, the birth of her children, and her death.

Whereas indigenous sources portray Malinche as a political agent, as ambassador and interpreter, messenger and secretary, Esquivel's codex relegates Malinche to a domestic sphere. In most illustrations, for instance, Malinche is learning domestic chores, or she is knitting, praying, and crying over her grandmother's death, the destruction of her world, her Christian conversion, her children, and Cortés. Only once does she appear as an interpreter, perhaps because the author believes, as she states in her introductory note, that

> el códice simboliza un proceso de conciliación, unifica el esfuerzo mental de explicarse los hechos razonablemente con la experiencia artística y religiosa de expresar el mundo de las emociones, los sentimientos y la espiritualidad por medio de imágenes materiales, llenas de color y formas caprichosas.
>
> (the codex symbolizes a process of mediation, it unifies the mental effort to explain events rationally with the artistic and religious experience of expressing the world emotionally and spiritually through concrete images full of color and whimsical shapes). (viii/xii)

This romantic vision of what Malinche's fictional codex symbolizes does not automatically appeal to every reader. But as in Del Río's case, the attempt to rewrite history from a divergent perspective is quite evident. As readers, we may not like the story of a character who is closely related to Tita, the protagonist of Esquivel's *Como agua para chocolate*, in the sense that she is moved by love and emotions, sexual drive, carnal passion, and magical intuition. Yet the creation of an alternative pictographic story attempts to validate other types of knowledge, or the fact that indigenous "writing" did exist long before the *Mexicas* encountered an alphabetic writing system (Boone, "Writing" 3–5). I say this because Malinche is conceived as a romantic "tlamati" who has the ability to paint and interpret transcendental personal stories. In the novel, her grandmother teaches her how to paint her life to exercise her language skills and memory. Like a true mentor, the grandmother actually revises her granddaughter's sketches until she masters the art of codex writing, using a set of interconnected images to narrate particular events.

Knowledgeable readers familiar with the history of "writing without words" will be less bothered by the fact that the wise grandmother turns out to be blind—perhaps in imitation of an old Úrsula Iguarán, in *Cien años de soledad* (*One Hundred Years of Solitude*)—than by the intimate and private nature of the *tlamati*'s codex. As Kelly S. McDonough observes in *The Learned Ones*, the Mexicas' painted codices—on various sociopolitical, religious, and economic issues—were produced and interpreted by very specialized intellectuals, "the tlamatinimeh (sages and scholars) and tlahcuilohqueh (painters/writers)" (9). On one hand, it is somewhat transgressive to depict Malinche, an indigenous woman, as the painter of her own personal codex. On the other hand, what she depicts inevitably takes away the wisdom and complexity contained in the books that were painted and interpreted by learned historians and orators, poets and priests, diviners and physicians (Boone, "*In Tlamatinime*" 13–14). As I have discussed before, in Esquivel's *Malinche*, the protagonist lacks any of these intellectual qualities, and she uses her codices to show her own emotions and feelings or to win personal battles. When Malinche confronts her mother for selling her into slavery, for instance, she tells her: "Tú no existes en mis códices, hace mucho que te borré" (in my codices you don't exist, I erased you long ago) (150/151).

In Martín del Campo's *Amor y conquista*, Malinche does not write her own chronicle, as in Del Río's novel; nor does she paint any codices, as we see in Esquivel's bestseller. But her servant, Ozlaxiuchtl, tells her story to her daughter, so she preserves it in writing. At the beginning of the novel, this woman of indigenous and Spanish blood writes:

> Hace más de cincuenta años de la muerte de la señora Malinalli . . . no vi con los ojos de este cuerpo los hechos que he de narrar, los miré con el corazón a través de las palabras de mi madre Ozlaxiuchitl, testigo de la grandeza y del desamparo de la india Malinalli, tan semejante, ay, al de la raza colhúa: ganaron mucho, perdieron poco.
>
> (It has been more than fifty years since Señora Malinalli's death . . . I didn't see with my very own eyes the events that I shall narrate. I felt them in my heart through the words of my mother, Ozlaxiuchtl, witness to the greatness

> and hopelessness of the Indian Malinche, whose luck was, alas, so similar to that of the *colhúas*: they gained a lot and lost very little). (11)

Thanks to this story we find out that Malinche makes up a biblical narrative about her honorable lineage, the same one that Bernal Díaz, as her loyal friend and accomplice—a good *mentiroso* (liar) (25)—convincingly develops in his *Historia verdadera*. Later on, we find out that Malinche could not have come from a rich family, as Bernal Díaz wants us to believe, since only the poorest people, the *macehuales*, sold their children into slavery.

In the epilogue, the mestiza who writes the story confirms the dissident intention of her alternative account. She writes, in sum, to fulfill a promise to her mother and honor the elderly who knew Malinalli and showed her their secret codices where they kept their own account of the conquest. More important, she writes to reconcile and repair the memory of her people, one that has been ignored or misinterpreted in multiple ways. Understandably, then, throughout the novel Malinche is described as a good and cautious woman, as an individual of great intentions who has the opportunity to repair her reputation as a traitor. "Por primera vez sé quién soy" (For the first time I know who I am), she tells Puertocarrero, "me identifico más con los tuyos que con los míos, y es que, aunque mi origen sea mexica, no tengo recuerdos ni experiencias mexicas, no siento haberlos traicionado al estar del lado del capitán" (I identify myself more with your people than with my own; although I have *Mexica* roots, I don't have any *Mexica* memories or experiences. I don't regret having betrayed them by siding with my captain) (381).

In one way or another, the three novels that I have discussed here allow Malinche to tell a story of her own, relying on various types of "writing" as tools of empowerment. Interestingly, Rancón Banda's Malinche does not write her own story, but in her multiple visits to a psychoanalyst she confronts what has been written about her. When the psychoanalyst tells Malinche that she is, according to Paz's *El laberinto de la soledad*, Mexico's raped mother in opposition to the Virgin of Guadalupe, she protests: "Estará en la soledad de los laberintos o en las Sagradas Escrituras, pero no estoy de acuerdo" (That might be written in some solitary labyrinths or in the Sacred Scriptures, but I don't agree) (111). When the psychoanalyst reads directly from Paz's book that Malinche does not resist her physical abuse and passively accepts her destiny, she objects:

> ¿Eso dice? ¿Y él estuvo ahí? ¿Él vio todo cuando me agarró a la fuerza el soldado español, cuando me luchó? ¿Él no vio cuando me defendí como gato boca arriba y cómo fui sometida? ¿Él no escuchó mi llanto? ¿Él no vio mis uñas clavándose en su espalda y mis dientes mordiéndole los brazos? ¿El no vio cómo me abrieron las piernas por la fuerza y cómo me taparon la boca para que no gritara?
>
> (Is that what he says? Was he there? Did he see everything when the Spanish soldier violently grabbed me, when he forced himself on me? Did he not see that I fought tooth and nail to defend myself and how I was suppressed? Did he not hear me crying? Did he not see my nails clawing at his back and my teeth biting his arms? Did he not see how my legs were forcefully opened and how my mouth was covered so that I wouldn't scream?) (112)

Undoubtedly, Malinche's words "rewrite," although in a less literal manner within the play, her stigmatized story. This time she contests the fact that she has been considered a traitor by Mexicans and consequently tells them to leave her alone with an insult that originates with her own stained self: "O sea que soy traidora. O sea que no me perdonan. ¡Chinguen a su madre todos!" (So I'm a traitor. So they don't forgive me. They can all go fuck themselves) (113). Along these lines, in her closing statements Malinche admits that she is indeed "el río de todas las culpas" (the river that contains all sins) (143), but she immediately asks to be left alone and disowns her children: "Ya no los reconozco. Me los han cambiado. Yo no parí esos monstruos" (I don't recognize them. They have changed them. I didn't give birth to those monsters) (144).

Armed with these words, Malinche assures us today that she will continue reappearing in the twenty-first century to redeem herself or to remind Mexicans that they have an undesirable mother who rejects them as much as they reject her. For instance, in Álvaro Enrigue's *Muerte súbita* (*Sudden Death*), a novel that won the Herralde Prize in 2013, Malinche is not a protagonist per se, but she appears in several of the fictional fragments as Cortés's interpreter, political adviser, lover, and second wife. As we have seen in other novels that market intimacy in neoliberal times, Malinche appears in bed with Cortés, and the graphic descriptions of her sexual practices and fantasies attempt to portray her as a liberated woman, momentarily in charge of her destiny. In this novel, Malinche is Malinalli Tenépatl, the princess of Painala who becomes a slave until she ends up with Cortés and wisely decides her future as an interpreter: "prefería ser la mujer de un viejo casi amable y más bien distraído que volver al oficio de esclava sexual de un cacique y todos sus amigos" ([she] preferred to be the wife of an absentminded old man than to go back to being the sex slave of a cacique and all his friends) (175/178). This Malinche is astute and self-driven. She learns how to take advantage of her misfortunes, translates with a sense of freedom, becomes indispensable during the Conquest of Mexico, and behaves like a true ambassador. However, she disappears from the narrative when she is no longer needed, just as she suddenly evaporates from Bernal Díaz's chronicle without any warning. And we close the book thinking that she is condemned to remain alive but only in a mythical afterlife with other female icons and archetypes whose real-life transgressions and limited acts of empowerment are securely locked away.

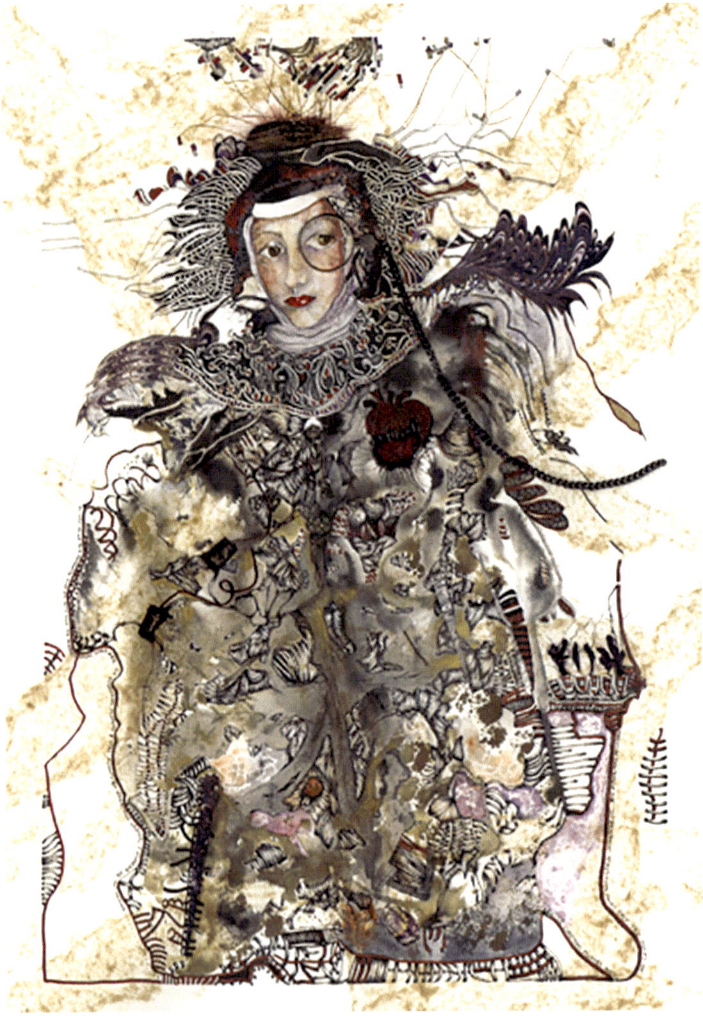

Sor Juana Inés de la Cruz. *Y diversa de mí misma entre vuestras plumas ando*, painting by Perla Estrada.

2

Impossible Nun

Sor Juana and the Traps of Representation

Vosotros me concebisteis
a vuestro modo . . .

(The conception you hold of me
is proportionate to yourselves . . .)

—Sor Juana Inés de la Cruz
(*Obras completas*, I 161/*Anthology* 106)

There is something mysterious about Sor Juana that continues to attract the attention of postcolonial Mexico. It is no coincidence that Carlos Monsiváis includes a famous oil portrait of the enigmatic Baroque poet-nun within a multifaceted quilt of visual images that represent his country's living tradition (*Imágenes* 491).[1] After all, how can we not be attracted to a cloistered woman who fights for her intellectual freedom in misogynist and restricted seventeenth-century New Spain? Following the verbal image Sor Juana crafts for the bishop of Puebla in her autobiographical *Respuesta a Sor Filotea de la Cruz* (*Answer to Sister Filotea de la Cruz*) (1691), writers, historians, painters, musicians, playwrights, and critics of all calibers for three centuries have propagated the story of a child who begs her mother to dress her like a boy to attend the all-male university. Hers is the life of a woman who surprises the most knowledgeable nobles of her society with logical arguments that supposedly could only be produced by men. And hers is the tale of a free thinker who enters the convent of San Jerónimo in 1669 not because of religious vocation but to read and write, without the hardships and obligations of a conventional marriage. Despite the numerous discrepancies regarding her pious conversion in her last years or her determination to continue writing until her premature death, Sor Juana enters this new century as a popular legend or, more accurately, an official habit of Mexican culture (Hind, "Official" 247).

In the past three decades, we have come to understand that Sor Juana Inés de la Cruz (1648–1695), known to her contemporaries as the Tenth Muse, used her writing to create a multifarious image of herself. Readers of today can distinguish in her work the historical individual, the writing subject, and the textual self that emerges from her ventriloquist reproductions of different literary discourses. Employing various methods of literary self-fashioning, the nun uses her poetic voice to construct controversial images of herself in her love and portrait poems, letters, essays, plays, and *villancicos* (carols) written for religious ceremonies. This artifice is particularly noticeable when she becomes Isis, the goddess of wisdom, in her *Neptuno alegórico* (*Allegorical Neptune*) (1680), when she speaks through Leonor in *Los empeños de una casa* (*The House of Trials*) (1692), and also when she uses Teseo's speech in *Amor es más laberinto* (*Love Is More Labyrinth*) (1725) to declare that human beings are either wise or foolish, regardless of their gender (Luciani 62). In short, the poet successfully invents several versions of herself—as a woman, man, or neutral individual—borrowing the language of others and using emblematic and metaphysical artillery, even when composing sacred lyrics (Glantz, "Letras" 173; Estrada "San Bernardo" 39 and "Exploraciones" 70).[2] This controversial literary persona is precisely what attracts contemporary audiences to Sor Juana's rejection of any feminine conventions of silence and traditional gender boundaries (Franco, *Las conspiradoras* 52).

Rendered masculine by a few, feminist by others, Sor Juana's complex figure is continually re-created through artistic production. The acclaimed Mexican actress Ofelia Medina, for instance, has traveled all over Mexico, Europe, and the United States with *Sor Juana Hoy* (*Sor Juana Today*), a theatrical production that incorporates Sor Juana's life, poetry, philosophical worries, and desire for a world where a woman can speak. Since the late 1990s, playwright Karen Zacarías has introduced the nun to numerous English-speaking audiences with the play *The Sins of*

Sor Juana. María Luisa Bemberg's film *Yo, la peor de todas* (*I, the Worst of All*) (1990) still seduces viewers with its suggestion of a lesbian relationship between the famous nun and the lady who protected her, Countess María Luisa de Paredes. Counterbalancing the antique portraits where Juana Inés is wearing her immense religious gown with an emblematic badge on her chest and a long rosary with an unfailing cross, Jorge Sánchez provocatively paints her with long hair, a sensual neck, and a busty torso.[3] Others, such as Southwest artist Marta Arat, sanctify her with a crown of roses over her black veil, making her look like a close relative of Santa Rosa de Lima.[4] Along these lines, musicians cannot resist the temptation to put music to her words.[5]

These sorts of dialogues with Sor Juana are also present in contemporary literature. Not only has she been repeatedly quoted by many Latin American writers, including Rosario Castellanos, Carlos Fuentes, and Rosario Ferré, she appears as the main protagonist in Electa Arenal's *This Life Within Me Won't Keep Still* (1986), Alicia Gaspar de Alba's *Sor Juana's Second Dream* (1999), Rafael Humberto Moreno-Durán's *Cuestión de hátitos* (*A Matter of Habits*) (2004), Gloria Durán's *Catalina, mi padre* (*Catalina, my Father*) (2004), and Paul Anderson's *Hunger's Brides* (2005).[6] Although the Sor Juana archetype is undoubtedly a constant in recent works by Mexican women writers such as Ángeles Mastretta and Laura Esquivel (Hind, "Archetype" 91), or Rosa Beltrán, Ana Clavel, and Cristina Rivera Garza (Estrada, "Gender Transgressions" 56), here I analyze four Mexican novels published between 2007 and 2010 that explicitly re-create Sor Juana's life: Mónica Zagal's *La venganza de Sor Juana* (*Sor Juana's Revenge*) (2007), José Luis Gómez's *El beso de la virreina* (*The Vicereine's Kiss*) (2008), Mónica Lavín's *Yo, la peor* (*I, the Worst*) (2009), and Kyra Galván's *Los indecibles pecados de Sor Juana* (*The Unspeakable Sins of Sor Juana*) (2010). In reaction to the orthodox Sor Juana, "a smart but sexually inactive woman who pursues knowledge and procreates only through art and not through a genetic legacy" (Hind, *Femmenism* 34), these novels pluralize our conceptions of Sor Juana as they demonstrate that historical truth is fragmented and dispersed, that memory elaborates and intertextualizes its own palimpsests, and that our relationship with the past is never neutral (Aínsa, "Guardianes" 15). The end product of these historical re-creations varies from one author to the next and does not always stand safely on its own as a "possible world." Nevertheless, the fact that each novel fictionalizes gender construction, sexual behaviors, identity, physicality, feminisms, marginalization, and domesticity, among other topics, speaks for the present need to adjust a historical role model to Mexico's social, political, and cultural dilemmas in a postnational age.

In this sense, Sor Juana shares Malinche's fate: regardless of her intellectuality, the nun is rearticulated in twenty-first-century literature from a voyeuristic perspective that exploits intimacy the same way current mass media markets privacy, hidden sexual practices, obsessions, and disorders. This confirms not only that neoliberalism has affected the production and commercialization of literature but the fact that novels produced now are crafted with new ethical principles and reveal other aesthetics, in agreement with multiple societal changes, the pervasive demands of bestsellers, and the massive consumption of so-called light literature (Voionmaa 118–19). If Malinche appears as the protagonist of a neoliberal melodrama in the novels discussed in the previous chapter, Sor Juana reveals her interiority in several contemporary works where she behaves like the main actress of her own *telenovela*.

The Phoenix Portrait

Conceived as a detective novel of the Baroque and published under the pseudonym of Mónica Zagal, apparently to demonstrate that men can also write feminist novels,[7] Héctor Zagal's *La venganza de Sor Juana* unfolds when the nun's first biographer, Father Diego Calleja, approaches Don Antonio Sebastián de Toledo Molina y Salazar, the marquis of Mancera and former viceroy of New Spain, to resolve certain mysteries surrounding Sor Juana's life:

> Quería saber cómo era la madre Juana Inés. Cuáles eran sus aficiones y sus defectos. Por qué no contrajo matrimonio. Por qué ingresó al convento. ¿En verdad era tan inteligente como decían? ¿Y su relación con los confesores? ¿Por qué murieron tan de repente? ¿Era cierto lo que se contaba? ¿Por qué había vendido su biblioteca? ¿Qué pecado horrible había cometido la monja para verse obligada a dejar de escribir? ¿Alguien le había impuesto esa penitencia?
>
> (He wanted to know about Mother Juana Inés. About her predilections and faults. Why she didn't get married. Why

> she entered the convent. Was she really as smart as they said she was? What about her relationship with her confessors? Why did they die so suddenly? Was it true what they said? Why did she sell her library? What horrible sin did she commit that forced her to stop writing? Did anyone impose that punishment on her?) (13)

The priest's questions are illuminating not necessarily for their originality but for their accurate reflection of the recurring tendency to anchor almost every contemporary rewriting of Sor Juana to the nun's biography, physique, sexual transgressions, exceptional intelligence, lack of religious vocation, political connections, secret trial, and final conversion.[8]

Not surprisingly, Zagal's novel gives much attention to what Sor Juana looked like. Perhaps taking into account Miguel Cabrera's painting of Sor Juana and Juan de Miranda's famous portrait *Sor Juana Inés de la Cruz*, painted in the late seventeenth century,[9] Zagal writes that the nun: "No era fea. Delgada, no precisamente alta. Su rostro oval no carecía de encanto. Tenía la piel tersa, aunque ligeramente ajada por el sol. Sus delgadas manos eran expresivas; sus ojos chispeantes . . . Su voz era tenue y firme . . . Sus palabras se oían con nitidez" (She wasn't ugly. Thin, not particularly tall. Her round face was charming. Her skin was terse, although slightly withered by the sun. Her delicate hands were expressive; her eyes, sparkling . . . Her voice was tenuous and firm . . . Her words were heard with clarity) (14). Almost immediately, Zagal's Calleja retouches this verbal portrait with information that adds another layer of mystery and austerity to the profile of a poor woman whose fortune is about to change. After numerous interviews with the aging viceroy, the Jesuit father and narrator imagines that Juana dressed with modesty because she did not have any money. Among other things, he points out that she never wore fashionable dresses and, except for a pearl necklace, she did not own any jewelry.

This perfect set-up for a Mexican Cinderella story, evincing colonial accents and contemporary resonances, prepares readers for Juana's opportune entrance into the viceregal court, where she serves as one of the vicereine's companions. Quite different, however, is the description presented by Gómez in *El beso de la virreina*, where a young Juana Inés appears as a fragile and nervous child, stripped of any hints of beauty and deprived of intellectual curiosity. In Gómez's novel we learn that the future prodigy of New Spain "Es tan fea como un lirio. Usa sandalias rústicas. Su vestido atemoriza a los sabios . . . Come muy poco, no duerme la siesta, moja el colchón . . . no se peina como una dama" (She is as ugly as an iris. She wears rustic sandals. Her dress scares the wise men . . . She eats very little, doesn't take naps, wets her mattress . . . she doesn't comb her hair like a lady) (7–9). In the same manner that Zagal finds it necessary to begin his novel with a physical description of Sor Juana, Gómez pays close attention to her body, as if her unattractive looks had something to do with her future development as a writing woman:

> Lo peor en Juana . . . no eran ni sus pies dormidos ni su humedad inoportuna, sino su cuerpo. Económica de carnes y generosa de huesos. Nada de grasa, nada de panza. Sus piernas eran apenas tan gruesas como los brazos de una cortesana. Estatura mediana, pantorrillas redondas, pies pequeños. Su cintura es casi tan torneada como la de una guitarra. A sus caderas les faltan muchos kilos para despertar deseo. Quizás es belleza quizá no, hermosura de otro tipo. Pero apostura no es.
>
> (The worst thing about Juana . . . was neither her dead feet nor her unfortunate dampness, but her body. No meat and lots of bones. No fat, no belly. Her legs were as thick as the arms of a courtesan. Medium height, rounded calves, small feet. Her waist is shaped like a guitar. Her hips are too thin to awaken desire. She might be beautiful or not, beautiful in a different sense. But she does not impress.) (10)

Why does it matter so much whether Sor Juana was beautiful? Surely, we can attribute much of this contemporary fascination with the nun's physical attributes to her first biographer, who propagated the hyperbolic image of a rare, discreet, and beautiful woman, "que nació al mundo para lograr a la naturaleza las vanidades de prodigiosa" (who came into this world as a natural prodigy) (13). We wonder, however, if this voyeuristic attraction to Sor Juana's body is only present because she is a woman, because she is conceived in a neoliberal era that highly values physical appearance and commercializes beauty (Elias et al. 5), or because she is once again in the hands of men. As Rosa Perelmuter unpacks a large library of criticism that describes Sor Juana's alleged rarity, the critic confirms that since the sixteenth century the nun-writer has been cataloged by numerous men of letters as a mythical phoenix and rare beauty, a prodigal monster of manly attributes trapped in the body of a woman, and as a singular and/or exemplary woman (104–6). One of the main problems with these labels also attached to Sor Juana in the twentieth and twenty-first centuries is, of course, that they portray her as an anomaly, in the midst of two extreme representations that only accentuate her exceptionality (Grossi, *Sigilosos* 19; Perelmuter 109). In these two novels, she is too feminine or too masculine, either ugly or beautiful, never just an average human being. She is either extremely confident or a nervous wreck, unable to control her incontinence in the company of men. To their own detriment, these contemporary depictions reproduce the historic male habit of using women as raw material for their own writing (Franco, *Las conspiradoras* 29). The composite Manichean model that we gather from reading Zagal's and Gómez's individual but inevitably dialogic novels unfortunately exhibits the well-known tendency to reduce and homogenize a woman's life to make it fit within a polarized scheme of male domination and female subordination (Moraña, "Pensar" 330).

Unlike Zagal and Gómez, Lavín spends more than half of her novel situating Sor Juana within a community of women whose feminine point of view controls the entire narrative (Guillén 97). Contrary to our expectations, the novel primarily fictionalizes the lives of Sor Juana's mother and grandmother, older sister, and aunt, as well as the mentor who teaches her how to read and write and the vicereine who becomes her life-long protector, friend, and literary accomplice. When we finally discover Sor Juana's body, it is through the intimate gaze of her slave, Juana de San José, whose serene eyes are able to see the woman behind the religious habit as the nun is about to take a bath:

> Ajena a la desnudez de su cuerpo, como si no le perteneciera porque sin pudor alguno la monja siguió despojándose de las prendas, entregó a la esclava el escapulario negro, el hábito blanco que le pesó en sus brazos y por último deslizó por sus piernas delgadas esas bragas deshiladas que Juana lavaba con cuidado como el resto de las prendas de la monja . . . Apenas cuatro años mayor que ella no podía evitar hacer comparaciones con su propio cuerpo. Le asombraba el contraste de su pubis oscuro con su piel blanca olivo y los pezones púrpura de sus pechos. Pensaba que ningún hombre los vería jamás. No era un cuerpo desbordado como el suyo, porque las caderas eran

> menudas, casi varoniles, pero era armónico . . . Juana Inés cerró los ojos ajena al esparadrapo que Juana frotaba por su cuerpo. Se dejó alzar los brazos como una muñeca y limpiar las axilas velludas, los senos bajo el doblez con el que reposaban sobre el tórax.
>
> (Unaware of her naked body, as if it didn't belong to her, without any reservations the nun continued to get rid of her clothes, gave to her slave the black scapular, the white habit that weighed on her arms, and took off the worn undergarments that Juana washed carefully like the rest of the nun's clothes . . . Just four years older than her, she couldn't help comparing her own body to hers. She was amazed by the contrast of her black pubis, her white olive skin and her purple nipples. She thought that no man would ever see them. It wasn't an abundant body such as hers, for her hips were small, almost masculine, yet harmonious . . . Juana Inés closed her eyes, unaware of the washcloth that Juana used to rub her body. She let her lift her arms like a doll in order to wash her hairy armpits, her breasts under the fold on her thorax.) (241–42)

In this act of literary striptease, the long passage presents Sor Juana as an average-looking woman. In the silence of this intimate encounter, her slave realizes that the nun's body is simply the soul's shell in need of cleanliness. Diverging from Zagal's and Gómez's portrayals, Lavín uses her description of Sor Juana's naked body to cast doubt on earlier depictions. Lavín's naked Sor Juana represents the fullness of what for other male writers is a transcendental beauty or ugliness, and thus constitutes an example of what Roger Shattuck calls forbidden knowledge.[10] Even though Sor Juana is described in other passages of the novel as a *rara avis* for being simultaneously intelligent, eloquent, beautiful, and elegant, Lavín's work openly reveals its feminist agenda. In *Yo, la peor* a woman writes another woman's life to contest women's historical silence and misrepresentation, to recuperate the lost voices of a female individual or group, and to situate their life stories within a safe place that is different from the one that has been consistently assigned to an entire female population over centuries of male domination (Lorenzano, "Mujer y narrativa" 351). The novel would be stronger, though, if Sor Juana did not write herself as "un animal acorralado, un animal acusado de su naturaleza" (a cornered animal, an animal accused of its natural impulses) (15). The contemporary melodramatic touch weakens the portrayal of a courageous and determined intellectual.

As readers of these novels, we may not like their aesthetic quality, explicit agendas, or bipolar descriptions of the writer-nun that often lack verisimilitude. Is it credible to portray (as Gómez does) a filthy Juana Inés, "encargada de barrer, trapear, limpiar los corrales, asear el gallinero, tirar las basinicas y darle de comer a los cerdos" (in charge of sweeping, mopping, cleaning the barn, emptying the bedpans, and feeding the pigs) (22)? The unfortunate and ill-fated story that Gómez offers is that of a servant who is routinely mistreated, abused, and beaten up; it is an incredible story of failed dialogues, impossible situations between the nun and her confessors, enormous anachronisms that ridicule historical facts, and numerous contradictions that distort the venerated figure of a renowned colonial writer. Not surprisingly, the novel whose sensationalist plot resembles the traumatic stories developed in a TV series such as Silvia Pinal's *Mujer, casos de la vida real* (*Woman: Real-Life Stories*) has received little critical attention since its publication in 2008. As Alberto Ortiz points out, the novel, supposedly based on a historical character, lacks any sense of historicism, and the intertextual references to recognizable names, places, and times do not correspond to Sor Juana's historical reality but to an unconvincing fantastical framework (161). Yet it is possible to perceive in *El beso de la virreina* and other Mexican novels that re-create Sor Juana's life in the twenty-first century an overt authorial intention to show the nun as a sexual or sexualized woman radically different from the iconic, saintly, unreachable, and exclusively intellectual figure that permeates Mexico's collective memory. In Galván's *Los indecibles pecados de Sor Juana*, for example, the nun's niece, Sor Isabel María de San José, describes her aunt as a tall, beautiful, and distinguished woman, whose seductive full lips—and perhaps crooked teeth—attract her own uncle, the viceroy, a famous painter, and the vicereine. In a way, then, Sor Juana frees herself from the Tenth Muse trap that emphasizes her singularity as an eccentric writing phenomenon of colonial Mexico (Merrim, *Early Modern* xiii) and instead invites us to imagine her in unprecedented and fictional processes of self-fashioning that today respond to a wide range of political, sexual, and intellectual hopes. The price that we have to pay for these renewed literary portraits, however, seems a bit high, especially when some of the fictional works at stake sacrifice their verisimilitude and authenticity with impossible details and awkward situations.

Sex and the Convent

In his seminal work *Sor Juana Inés de la Cruz o las trampas de la fe* (*Sor Juana Inés de la Cruz or the Traps of Faith*), Octavio Paz carefully suggests the likely possibility that the young writer actively participates in the so-called *galanteos de palacio*, the erotic or sexual encounters between the vicereine's single ladies-in-waiting and the married courtiers, as part of an institution that stimulated erotic freedom at the same time as limiting its execution (134–35). Intriguingly, when considering Sor Juana's participation in the palace *tertulias*, José Pascual Buxó follows up, however briefly, on Paz's suggestion that these erotic retreats in some way become a hospitable background for the nun's development as a writer (*Sor Juana* 236). If we take into account that such *galanteos* or wooing of women became a common courtly practice that did not stop at the doors of convents, it is not difficult to see why this erotic code of conduct would be taken as an optimal place of departure to imagine a sexual Sor Juana today (Lavrin, *Brides* 209).

The seven-episode TV series *Juana Inés*, produced by Canal Once in 2016 and currently streaming on Netflix, in many ways exemplifies a neoliberal trend I observe in the novels of the early twenty-first century that revolve around Sor Juana: the explicit exploration of the nun's sexual orientation, illicit sex in the convent, secret pregnancies, and other scandalous stories that are consumed by audiences interested in alternative or forbidden sexual practices, hidden desires, and transgressive behaviors. This current tendency to exhibit an individual who wants to confess his or her most intimate sins in front of a camera for a massive audience willing to play the role of a psychoanalist (Monsiváis, *Aires* 237), is also found in the literature that rearticulates the life of a famous and enigmatic colonial figure.

In confirmation of the worn-out hypothesis that Juana Inés entered the convent after an amorous disenchantment, Zagal re-creates her engagement with Captain Sandoval, the gentleman willing to accept her in spite of an illegitimate origin and a modest dowry. The arrangement, according to the narrator, is convenient not only because it finds an acceptable social place for Juana Inés but because such a marriage would silence "esos estúpidos rumores que circulaban sobre doña Leonor y su dama" (those stupid rumors that circulated about doña Leonor and her lady-in-waiting) (37). If this first hint of Sor Juana's lesbianism is nothing more than a mere rumor, her sexual persona is overtly exposed when her drunken suitor attempts to rape her before the wedding, and even more so when her confessor, Antonio Nuñez de Miranda, implicitly blames her for causing this sexual aggression. Aware of her beauty and disturbing intelligence, the priest questions her with morbid fascination:

> ¿Lanzó usted alguna mirada lasciva? ¿Vestía atrevidamente? ¿Intercambio complaciente de sonrisas? ¿Por qué le abrió la puerta? ¿No sabía que no deben recibirse visitas durante la noche? Por un momento, aunque fuese por un instante, ¿consintió usted en la propuesta indecorosa? ¿No consideró que sus versos podían enardecer las pasiones?
>
> (Did you give him a lascivious look? Were you dressed provocatively? Did you exchange smiles? Why did you open the door? Didn't you know that visitors are not allowed at night? For a moment, even if it was just an instant, did you accept his indecent proposal? Didn't you consider that your poems might trigger his passion?) (45)

As the fictional Calleja tries to solve the puzzle of Sor Juana's life, he also succumbs to the powerful image of the nun's sexual self and justifies his Jesuit brother's inquiries: he worries about her ability to fascinate men.

This story of Sor Juana's sensual powers, which reproduces the idea that women are the devils behind the cross, the body's weakness, or an inevitable savage temptation that should be controlled by men, is developed to an unbelievable extreme (Castellanos, *Sobre cultura* 58, 81). In *El beso de la virreina* Sor Juana has rough sex with Duke Fernando Manríquez, and she is often referred to as "Marimacho" (tomboy) (97), "machorra" (butch) (229), and "soneto de carne" (sonnet of meat) (103). She seduces her worst enemy, the misogynist archbishop Francisco de Aguiar y Seijas, who is infatuated with her breasts; she engages in amorous relationships with several women around her, in and outside of the convent. The narrative fails, I argue, from the moment it sacrifices the authenticity of a possible world and becomes the unbelievable staged production of an unreal scenario (Doležel 31). The fact that the imaginary alternative reconstructs Sor Juana's world as a constellation of impossibilities (the nun hypnotizes insects, speaks four languages at the same time, and magically cures the leprous with lustful kisses) does not, however, remove from the page the explicit urge to demystify her iconic figure. Evidently, the novelist seeks to weaken our solidified notions of the historic nun, who is now trapped in the midst of countless sexual scenes, erotic postures, and rather compromising sensual acts.

Lavín does not explicitly portray Juana Inés as a lesbian in *Yo, la peor*, but she cannot help showing her virginal body tainted by a man. In one of the novel's many acts of confession, the narrator recalls that before entering the convent "una parte de Juana Inés había sido descubierta entre las manos y los besos, las caricias y los apretujones, y la forzada entrada de quien le hacía prometer silencio" (one part of Juana Inés had been discovered by the hands and kisses, the strokes and embraces, and the forced entry of someone who asked her to promise silence) (170). Aware that nuns have been consistently praised as the ultimate forbidden fruit because of the physical and moral barriers around their female communities (Lavrin, *Brides* 210), Lavín reveals Sor Juana with an aura of mystery. During the day she displays an immaculate face, protected by the wimple, and at night she appears stripped from her habit with her hair tied up. If Fernando Benítez, in *Los demonios en el convento* (*Demons in the Convent*), vividly imagines that a naked nun stopped being a nun and became a sexual woman of beautiful breasts, an avid vagina, and round thighs covered with very fine hair (48), Lavín's narrator visualizes Sor Juana's aura catching the attention of the vicereine María Luisa de Paredes:

> Mientras la virreina escuchaba, sus ojos miraban constantemente a la monja atrapada en un hábito intentando comprender por qué una mujer que le hablaba de Platón lo mismo que de Virgilio, y que luego citaba a Góngora y a Lope, tan novedosos, podía estar dedicada a la oración y al encierro. En tanto hablaba Juana Inés y soltaba algún giro gracioso, María Luisa *le hurgaba los pedazos de piel visible*. El atavío la confrontaba porque no podía pensarse encerrada en esas ropas sin colores, lisas y poco ceñidas al cuerpo, porque no imaginaba esconder el escote que paseaba en las recepciones de las cortes.

> (While the vicereine listened, her eyes constantly observed the nun trapped in a habit, trying to understand why a woman who spoke of Plato and Virgil, and who quoted Góngora and Lope, both so fashionable, could be dedicated to prayer and reclusion. As Juana Inés spoke and made graceful comments, María Luisa *analyzed the visible pieces of her skin*. The attire gave her pause because she couldn't imagine herself trapped in those colorless clothes, so plain and loose, because she couldn't imagine hiding the cleavage that she showed off in the receptions of the court). (264, emphasis added)

On one hand, Benítez's voyeuristic narrative confirms the fascination that nuns and their convent space have inspired throughout history (Kirk, "Power" 50), on the other, Lavín's subtle suggestions about the woman under the habit create suspense around the possible start of a love relationship between Sor Juana and the vicereine. Although the novel does not portray these women engaged in any sexual acts, the narrator describes the passion that a sexual Sor Juana awakens in the vicereine's body and psyche. As the nun and the pregnant María Luisa de Paredes become closer, in spite of the walls that separate them:

> La virreina leía por enésima vez las líneas de Juana Inés mientras acariciaba su vientre fuerte, restirado por aquella vida que palpitaba próxima a aflorar. Y al hacerlo rozaba sus pechos frondosos, sus pezones reventando de vida. Estar próxima a parir la exaltaba y aquellas bondades del cuerpo no las podía expresar más que a la vera de Juana Inés, más mujer que monja, más cercana que su propio marido tan preocupado por ella . . . necesitaba los versos de la monja, su amistad, su amor y la generosidad de sus palabras . . . la vida le había dado la oportunidad de estar ante una inteligencia poco usual, una mujer como no había conocido alguna. Y aquello la regocijaba; la sapiencia la entusiasmaba, pero la sensibilidad de su persona transmutada en Lysi en los versos de la monja la extasiaban.

> (The vicereine read Juana Inés's lines for the umpteenth time while she caressed her robust belly, stretched out by the beating

> life soon to be born. And doing so she also touched her large breasts, her nipples full of life. Being so close to giving birth excited her, and she could only express the greatness of her body through Juana Inés, more a woman than a nun, closer than her own husband who was so worried about her . . . she needed the nun's poems, her friendship, her love, her generous words . . . life had given her the opportunity to come before an unusual intelligence, a woman like no other. And that pleased her; wisdom excited her, but her own sensibility transformed into the Lysi of the nun's poems made her ecstatic). (273)

The fragments that allude to the love and friendship between Sor Juana and the vicereine reenact not only the historical fact that the nun composed numerous "romances de amiga" (friendship poems) for her friend María Luisa (Poot Herrera, *Guardaditos* 290–91) but also, more problematically, the bad habit of reading her poetry as the mirror of an amorous narrative or as the diary of her impossible love stories and truncated passions (Grossi, "Revisión" 37). In reading these passages, we can only agree with Georgina Sabat de Rivers, whose academic expertise on Sor Juana did not prevent her from writing in the late 1990s that we were still far away from thoroughly understanding the nun's personality (*En busca* 11). Still, it is impossible not to see that these and other passages of Lavín's novel seek to present Sor Juana and the women around her with the internal insecurities, tribulations, and fears of any human being (Vargas).

In many ways, the graphic exposure of Sor Juana's unverifiable sexual orientation and behavior, potential lesbianism, *galanteos*, and possible love affairs comes across as daring, irreverent, and anachronistic. But it is expected within a neoliberal environment whose sexual politics promote individual transgressions and actively reward explorations of the inner self. Evidently, the authors who expose Sor Juana's sexuality today intentionally want to disturb her respected figure to humanize her, drawing from her own historical context. As challenging as it might be for some readers to imagine Sor Juana engaged in various erotic and sexual activities, in colonial Spanish America premarital sexual relations, homosexual acts, polygamy, out-of-wedlock births, and clandestine affairs between religious and lay persons were common occurrences (Lavrin, "Scenario" 2). Well aware of these facts and their continuity within the convent, in *Apariciones* (*Apparitions*) (1995) Margo Glantz fictionalizes the fragmented stories of Sor Lugarda de la Encarnación and Teresa Juana de Cristo, whose lives become one as they feed off of each other's erotic mysticism, perverse whippings, and bloody torments, hoping to physically feel, embrace, and enjoy Christ, his "cuerpo amante . . . la sangrante presencia de su cuerpo enjuto" (loving body . . . the bleeding presence of his gaunt body) (83). Kyra Galván does not re-create these mystic explorations and brutal flagellations through which men and women of the Church presumably experienced various types of sexual pleasure.[11] But she situates Sor Juana in the heart of several sexual experiences that indicate why her confessor would want to redeem her as the most perfect bride of Christ.

In *Los indecibles pecados de Sor Juana*, the nun engages in consensual sexual relations with her uncle, Juan de Mata, after he rapes her and she feels "una combinación de horror, rechazo, placer, atracción y latidos que no sabía que podían existir, culpa, agradecimiento, todo mezclado en un caldo que hervía a borbotones en su pecho" (a combination of horror, rejection, pleasure, attraction, and heartbeats that she wasn't aware of, guilt, gratitude, all mixed in a broth that boiled in her chest) (64). Years later at the viceregal palace, Juana Inés falls in love with Don Carlos de Olmos y Villegas and arranges to sleep with him in disguise. Following the typical style of a *comedia de enredos* (comedy of errors), the sexual meeting with Don Carlos never takes place. Instead, that night she ends up sleeping with the viceroy, Don Antonio Sebastián de Toledo, becomes his mistress thereafter, and a few months later gives birth to a daughter in the convent of the Discalced Carmelites. In the fictional search for Juana Inés's fate after her daughter dies and she takes her religious vows in San Jerónimo, we discover in her niece's diary that the nun falls in love with the painter Cristóbal de Villalpando and sustains an affair with him for eight years until the day she gives birth to their son, in the secrecy of the convent. With a sense of complicity, Sor María Isabel de San José writes:

> Yo no puedo describir los momentos de amor que vivieron Juana y Cristóbal, porque fueron privados, les pertenecieron a ellos y a nadie más. Lo que sí sé es que fueron momentos robados a la muerte, al encierro, a las reglas. Y debieron haber sido celestiales. Únicos. Maravillosos. Algunos de los poemas que según le escribió a la virreina, en realidad eran

para Cristóbal, por eso se reía María Luisa cuando la gente, horrorizada, decía que eran indecentes. Ella sabía a quién iban dirigidos y lo ocultó para darle un gusto a su amiga.

Juana tenía cuarenta años cuando se descubrió preñada, y lejos de recurrir a las curanderas nos lo confesó a todas con una sonrisa en el rostro, como si se hubiera tratado de una concepción virginal. Como si no hubiera habido nada que ocultar y hubiera sido un hecho natural y mágico. Fue nuestro secreto por muchos meses . . . Al enterarse de que el resultado de su amor era un varoncito, pidió que buscáramos al padre para que pudiera llevárselo lo más pronto posible . . . Le costó mucho trabajo separarse de él. Pero todas le ayudamos. La mimamos, la acariciamos, rezamos por ella y por el niño. Y sobre todo, guardamos fielmente el secreto. Su amiga la virreina, que tenía dos años de haber dejado estas tierras, nunca se enteró del final de la historia.

(I can't describe the moments of love shared by Juana and Cristóbal, because they were private and belonged to them and no one else. What I do know is that those moments evaded death, reclusion, and the norms. And they must have been celestial. Unique. Wonderful. Some of the poems that she apparently wrote to the viceireine were really for Cristóbal, that's why María Luisa laughed when people, horrified, said they were indecent. She knew who they were meant for and kept the secret to make her friend happy.

Juana was forty years old when she found herself pregnant and, instead of going to the healers, she told us with a big smile on her face, as if it had been a virginal conception. As if she didn't have to hide it, as if it were a natural and magic happening. It was our secret for many months . . . When she found out that the fruit of her love was a boy, she asked us to look for the father so that he could take him as soon as possible . . . It was hard for her to let go of him. But we all helped her. We took care of her, and prayed for her and the boy. And, above all, we kept the secret. Her friend, the vicereine, who had been gone from these lands for two years, never learned of the end to the story.) (199–200)

Is this portrayal of Sor Juana believable? It is hard to recognize the prodigy of New Spain in the description of a nun who practically lives for sex, arranging her multiple sexual encounters, and having children with two different men. Considering this fictional layout, Alfredo Cerda Muños enthusiastically points out that Sor Juana's demystification in Galván's novel creates an intimate and humane protagonist who loves and suffers, questions maternity, and fights for her cultural independence, in sync with a contemporary world (55). But the full-blown picture of Sor Juana's sexual self, taken to a farfetched extreme, seems bizarre, even if these sorts of sexual affairs were fairly common in Spanish America between nuns and their confessors (Lavrin, *Brides* 225–32).

It is true that in Sor Juana's time a single woman could be nine months' pregnant, in private, and maintain her public reputation as a virgin and woman of honor. Her relatives, certain members of her social circle, or some outsiders could be aware of her condition, but they would all conspire to maintain her virtuous reputation. The Church would also protect her honor by not writing the mother's name on the child's birth certificate (Twinam 125). That these pregnancies also took place within the convent is no mystery, although we only have limited official records of such "sinful" matters (Lavrin, *Brides* 235). But these facts make little sense when they are applied to a renowned historical figure whose private and public life is part of a national culture that has already solidified her image as a true intellectual devoted to her poetry, her philosophical endeavors, her argumentative nature. What may work for large viewing audiences of a TV series such as *Juana Inés*, in need of juicy stories of sexual transgression, does not always find a comfortable fit within the framework of a novel.

The practice of transforming sexual actions and intentions into narrative—originally devised in ascetic and monastic settings—is not new, of course (Foucault 21). What I find unique about these novels—putting aside their literary competence—is the fact that their telling of sexual behaviors does not convey spiritual reconversion, turning back to God, reorientation or modification of desire itself. If the past is not only necessary but inevitable in any process of identity construction (Aínsa, "Guardianes" 13), these contemporary rearticulations of Sor Juana as a sexual being strive to humanize her for middle-class audiences less interested in her literary production than in the woman under the habit. This sexualized Sor Juana desperately wants to empower herself from a liminal space, seeks to contest female and colonial marginality, and pretends to defy regulatory sexual practices dictating that women should be either "in" sexual control, or "out of" such control, but not "in between" (Twinan 120). A novel's literary quality, however, is not judged based on the author's efforts and good intentions. The sexualization of Sor Juana in these novels is destined to fail from the instant it crosses the boundaries of what seems logical and plausible within a fictional framework that rearticulates a previous work of art—her letters and philosophical essays, her love poems and plays.

In his introduction to a recent volume on modern representations of Sor Juana, Mario A. Ortiz points out that the diverse and "imagined" portrayals of the writer-nun that we find in contemporary literature cater to various social groups in Latin America, Europe and the United States that see her as an adjustable symbol of gay and lesbian identity, female liberation, human rights, and social justice ("Introducción" 15). This is true, as evidenced in the slogans, comic books, posters, T-shirts, bookmarks, pamphlets, and web pages that reduce or extinguish her intellectual passions and commercialize her as another Frida Kahlo (Grossi, "*Sueño*" 114–15; Bergmann 178). And the fictional works that portray her as a woman of carnal passions, failed relationships, love adventures, and maternal instinct defy the past. We may not like the final product, as I have pointed out before, but these works, influenced by the spirit of neoliberalism, undoubtedly want to portray her as a subject capable of ruling her life. Because of this process, Sor Juana is not fictionalized as a *perfecta religiosa* (model nun), whose narrative is manipulated by the Catholic Church to stay in tune with other saintly *vidas* (life stories) (Myers 113), but as an imperfect transgressor who makes the best of her marginal situation. Consequently, the past in these novels becomes an ambivalent and disturbing scenario, a shattered mirror where contemporary Mexico can no longer look for its identity.[12]

When Laura—the metafictional researcher who comes across Sor María Isabel de San José's diary—figures out Sor Juana's sins, she immediately worries about the consequences of demystifying such an iconic woman: "La figura de Juana Inés de la Cruz era casi mítica en México, y aunque nadie se atrevería a decir que había sido una santa ni nada por el estilo, de hacerse público algo así quizá sería capaz de destruirla, como figura ejemplar, intocable, a pesar del tiempo transcurrido" (The figure of Juana Inés de la Cruz was almost mythical in Mexico and, although nobody would say that she was a saint or anything like that, if this became known, it could destroy her exemplary, untouchable, figure, even after all this time) (65). If we take into account what these novels reveal, not only do they distort Sor Juana's respected figure but that of the past itself, its monolithic structure, and the archaic practice of kneeling before history as if it were the sacred graveyard of the future, or the place that provides answers to an uncertain present. The literary fabrication of the past in these recent novels aims to transform certain human experiences naturally connected to historical realities; it also explores a larger and transcendental human condition that only in the best aesthetic scenarios becomes significant, plausible, and persuasive (Buxó, "Historia" 19).

Feminist Avenues

Many studies have been written on Sor Juana's feminism, her status as the "first feminist of the New World," and the multiple ways she uses her literary works to empower herself as a woman writer and a woman writing in the cloistered society of seventeenth-century New Spain (Merrim, *Feminist* 7). These feminist perspectives are well justified, more so if we place Sor Juana's brilliant intellectuality alongside other women writers of the early modern period (Arenal, "Sor Juana" 39). In response to the legendary dichotomy that identifies men as rational and capable of universally valid thought and women as emotional and tethered to the particularity of their body and situation (Jehlen 264), the writer-nun creates around her a powerful female community ruled by Saint Paula, Saint Teresa of Ávila, Saint Gertrude, Mary of Jesus of Ágreda, the Queen of Sheba, the Virgin Mary, and Saint Catherine of Alexandria. This creation of a virtual and exemplary female society is present throughout her literary production.

In her first *villancicos* to the Assumption of the Virgin (1676), Sor Juana portrays Mary as "Soberana Doctora / de las Escuelas divinas" (Sovereign Doctor / of divine Schools) (Cruz, *Obras completas* [OC], II 6) and "Valiente de aventuras, / Deshacedora de tuertos" (adventurous Brave, / problem Solver) (OC, II 10–11). Speaking the mother tongue (Arenal, "Speaking" 93), in her *villancicos* to the Immaculate Conception of 1689, the nun goes above and beyond any traditional expressions of Marian devotion to state that "Dios en Ella restituye / al Orbe sus perfecciones" (God restores in Her / the perfections of the World) (OC,

II 100). True to her beliefs, in 1691 Sor Juana continued to use the poetic space as a "metaphorical classroom" (Estrada, "Ejercicio" 91–92 and "Venid" 90), this time to defend Saint Catherine's right to study, arguing that the prodigy of Alexandria "Estudia, arguye y enseña, / y es de la Iglesia servicio, / que no la quiere ignorante / El que racional la hizo" (Studies, disputes, and teaches, / and thus she serves her Faith; / for how could God, who gave her reason, / want her ignorant?) (OC, II, 171; *Answer* 179–81).

This voice that transgresses gender assignments, produced by a religious woman who insists on the primacy of reason and the equality of sexes (Arenal and Martínez-San Miguel 188), is most noticeable in Sor Juana's *Autodefensa espiritual* (*Spiritual Self-Defense*) when she asks her confessor, "¿no tienen [las mujeres] alma racional como los hombres?" (don't women have rational souls like men?) (*Poesía* 1414). To contest any calcified differences between male and female, good or bad, superior or inferior, passive or active, Sor Juana argues, "sólo sé que mi cuerpo, / sin que a uno u otro se incline, / es neutro, o abstracto, cuanto / sólo el alma deposite" (I know only that my body, / not to either state inclined, / is neuter, abstract, guardian / of only what my soul consigns) (*Poems* 140–41). Sor Juana employs a similar voice of transgression in the lines "Ser mujer, ni estar ausente, / no es de amarte impedimento, / pues sabes tú que *las almas / distancia ignoran y sexo*" (That you're a woman far away, / is no hindrance to my love: / for the soul, as you well know, / *distance and sex don't count*) (*Anthology* 38–39, emphasis added), and also when she asserts that "el sexo / no es esencia en lo entendido" (sex is not / the essence of intelligence) (*The Answer* 178–79).

Along these lines, in *Los empeños de una casa*, Castaño, dressed as Doña Leonor, seems to understand that gender is a performance and men may fall in love with him because he is perceived as a woman: "que a bulto se amartelan, / no de la belleza que es, / sino de la que ellos piensan" (they fall in love en masse, not with real beauty but with what they have imagined) (OC, IV 138). If we take this and other literary instances that justify a feminist reading, it is undeniable that the nun uses her own writing not only to speak the way a woman speaks but to pull away from any gender norms or social habits that relegate women to the outskirts of power and knowledge, where language and experience tend to reproduce similar stories of marginalization (Olivares 60). Simply put, "while highly and in many instances encoded, her poems, plays, and prose texts refer consistently to the female condition, to the colonial context in which knowledge was produced, and the emergence of a creole perspective that challenged the existing notion of a knowing subject" (Arenal and Martínez-San Miguel 189).

I reflect on Sor Juana's granted early feminist spirit because it is persistently rearticulated in a contemporary fictional arena where feminism and neoliberalism coincide, as they both set forth a critique of traditional authority (Fraser 115). Unfortunately, though, the fictionalization of Sor Juana's feminism does not always work, particularly not when it is taken to an impossible extreme, or when it appears separated from its true intellectual roots. In *El beso de la virreina*, for instance, Juana Inés teaches other women how to modify the law, behaves like a lawyer in court, and forms an unbelievable Women's League to prove that women are as talented as men. This hyperbolic and anachronistic feminism is further exposed when the young writer is examined at the viceregal palace by 400 lawyers, professors, and several men of the Church. Instead of reproducing the now familiar picture that her first biographer gives us, "que a la manera que un galeón real . . . se defendería de pocas chalupas, que le embistieran, así se desembarazaba Juana Inés de las preguntas, argumentos y replicas, que tantos, cada uno en su clase, la propusieron" (like a royal galleon . . . that defends itself from a few small canoes, Juana Inés answered the questions, arguments and replies proposed by each one of them) (17), Gómez transforms the event into a massive feminist demonstration that affects the entire society of New Spain. While the future nun answers all kinds of questions with admirable knowledge, displayed in Spanish, Nahuatl, Latin, and Greek, among other languages:

> Afuera, más de tres mil mujeres se han abierto camino entre los callejones y han invadido las calles aledañas al palacio y la están cantando. Son mujeres de la ciudad. Pero también son mujeres venidas de pueblos y rancherías, de aldeas y villorrios, de feudos y caseríos, de montañas y desiertos. Desdichadas que caminaron durante semanas con la única finalidad de estar cerca del debate. Mujeres que surcaron distancias colosales con tal de arribar al sitio de la polémica.
>
> Están ahí para apoyar a Juana, su única esperanza.
>
> Hay amas de casa, obreras, campesinas, esclavas, limosneras, damas, prostitutas, pueblerinas, aristócratas, vendedoras, cargadoras, barrenderas, recolectoras, afanadoras, peonas,

> pescadoras, arrieras, pastoras y puerqueras. Josefa de Asbaje y María de Asbaje dirigen el enorme coro.
>
> Es trova femenina. Balada de cargar en la espalda doscientos años de tristeza. Canción incomprendida, himno de fugitivas.
>
> (Outside, more than three thousand women have invaded the streets around the palace, and they're singing to her. They're city women. But they're also women from towns and farms, villages and one-horse towns, from the country and farmhouses, the mountains and the deserts. Unfortunate women who walked for weeks just to be close to the debate. Women who traveled colossal distances just to arrive to the site of the polemic.
>
> They are there to support Juana, their only hope.
>
> There are housewives, workers, peasants, slaves, beggars, ladies, prostitutes, town women, aristocrats, vendors, carriers, sweepers, collectors, cleaning girls, laborers, fisherwomen, mule drivers, shepherdesses and pig raisers. Josefa de Asbaje and María de Asbaje are the leaders of the enormous choir.
>
> It's a female song. A sad song carried on their shoulders for two hundred years. A misunderstood song, an anthem for fugitives.) (134–35)

The allegedly historical moment becomes a fantastic feminist carnival—a suspension of established order, hierarchical rank, and acceptable codes of conduct (Bakhtin 10)—in this scene, which comes to a climax when Juana Inés passes the exam with flying colors and the multitude of women commanded by her sisters celebrate her with hugs and kisses, words of praise and songs of encouragement.

Like most passages in Gómez's *El beso de la virreina*, this one comes across as an implausible and false setting that does not correspond to the historical framework of colonial Mexico. The genuine problem here is not that the novel fails some absolute documentary fidelity to reality but that it presents false tales without the authenticity and persuasiveness of a good story (Eco 17–19). The nun's feminism is reduced to a magical realist illness that originates in the convent of San Jerónimo and affects wives, concubines, mothers, grandmothers, daughters, sisters, nieces, and brides. Unlike the historical Sor Juana, who stays in San Jerónimo for more than two decades to live alone and avoid obligations that could distract her from the silence of her books, Gómez's protagonist enters and leaves the convent at will, uses her leadership to organize other women, fights for women's rights, hardly ever reads or writes, and manages to incite an entire women's community to change their subordinated condition. Thanks to her:

> [Las mujeres] quieren independizarse. Trabajar por su cuenta. Poner su propio negocio. Salir a divertirse. Tener amantes. Beber licor. Acurrucarse con pelados. Meterles mano . . . Que se las padroteen. Pagar el revolcón.
>
> Del marido sólo requieren los servicios sexuales. Y eso, siempre y cuando anden de verdad necesitadas.
>
> Es padecimiento audaz, incontrolable. Se filtra por abajo de las puertas y sale por las ranuras de las ventanas.
>
> Inicia en los ovarios. Sube por la matriz y se apodera de todas las glándulas. Afecta tanto a damas como a doncellas. A vírgenes y a hembras paridoras.
>
> Se propaga con una palabra, con una explicación.
>
> ([Women] want to be independent. Work on their own. Have their own business. Go out and have fun. Have lovers. Drink alcohol. Cuddle with nobodies. Make out with them . . . Be pimped. Pay for sex.
>
> From their husbands they just want sexual services. And only when they are in desperate need.
>
> It's bold and uncontrollable suffering. It seeps under the door and goes out the window.
>
> It begins in the ovaries. It goes up through the womb and seizes onto the glands. It affects ladies and maidens. Virgins and birthing women.
>
> It is propagated with one word, with one explanation.) (181)

As legitimate as some of these claims might be in contemporary societies, insofar as they reproduce a conscious and organized female battle against a phallocentric and oppressive, sexist system of power (Gargallo 32), they make little sense within the context of New Spain, precisely because women's historical existence and personal stories were largely marginalized and assigned a subaltern position within the matrix of colonial hegemony. Certainly, under the rubric of Latin America's "new" historical novel, numerous writers of the twentieth century have explicitly distorted the course of history through omissions, exaggerations, and anachronisms (Menton 23). But only the most accomplished, from the canonical Alejo Carpentier, Reinaldo Arenas, Juan José Saer, Carlos Fuentes, and Mario Vargas Llosa to the more innovative Carmen Boullosa, Rosa Beltrán, Enrique Serna, William Ospina, and Mayra Santos-Febres, among others, have carried out their individual projects without sacrificing the aesthetic coherence of their fictional (re)creations. Convincing (and therefore good) fiction cannot simply overlook that the discursive and vital space of colonial women was systematically controlled by a number of strategies designed to confirm and fortify a monolithic power structure (Moraña, "Mujer" 7). By the same standards, a credible and compelling novel about Sor Juana should not ignore that women were forbidden to go out of their convents unless they had first obtained proper episcopal permission (Kirk, *Convent Life* 5).

The other three novels that revisit Sor Juana's feminism are much more successful: their fictions rearticulate the aesthetics of a primary work of art, such as Sor Juana's *Respuesta a Sor Filotea de la Cruz*, in a way that allows us to identify the original pieces of the first articulation within a second artistic arrangement that expands in our imagination, without trespassing the limits of credibility (Lévi-Strauss 7). In an attempt to internalize Sor Juana's "total negación . . . al matrimonio" (absolute unwillingness to enter into marriage) (*Respuesta* 50, 51) and her ultimate desire "de querer vivir sola; de no querer tener ocupación obligatoria que embarazase la libertad de mi estudio" (of wanting to live alone and not wanting to have either obligations that would disturb my freedom to study) (*Respuesta* 50–51), Zagal gives us the ambivalent picture of a young woman placed by her own confessor between a rock and a hard place:

> ¿Qué esperaba del matrimonio? Viviría uncida al capricho de un hombre, sin derechos, sin horas para el estudio. Su marido la embarazaría en la noche de bodas y desde entonces su principal obligación sería parir y criar hijos. ¿No entendía que era preferible caer en las manos de Dios? . . .
>
> Núñez la animó a pensar en el convento. Ahí también seguiría sola, pero al menos contaría con una celda donde

> estudiar. No estaría obligada a compartir su lecho con otra persona; no estaría obligada a compartirse con otra persona. Podría leer cuanto se le antojase, sin levantarse a medianoche para amamantar hijos, sin tener que limpiar una casa, sin verse en la necesidad de satisfacer a su marido.
>
> (What did she expect of marriage? She would live under the control of a man, without any rights, without any time to study. Her husband would get her pregnant on their wedding night and from then on her principal duty would be to give birth and raise children. Didn't she understand that it was better to end up in God's hands? . . .
>
> Núñez encouraged her to think about the convent. She would still be alone there, but at least she would have a room in which to study. She wouldn't have to share her bed with another person; she wouldn't have to share herself with any other person. She could read as much as she pleased, without having to wake up in the middle of the night to breastfeed her children, without having to clean a house, without having to satisfy her husband.) (46–47)

As Zagal problematizes the dilemmas of a woman intellectual who combines talent and beauty, we envision the major problem that Sor Juana faces for contesting, as a feminine Aristotle or as a renewed Catherine of Alexandria, the expectation that women had to be sweet, beautiful, and submissive. Hence, with a couple of delicate brushstrokes, Zagal retouches Sor Juana's feminism, her theological battles, love poems, polemical plays, and argumentative letters, so as to highlight the disturbing presence of a well-versed, intelligent, and most eloquent woman who writes with so much wisdom as to leave everyone speechless. The major paradox behind this feminist representation, as I argue next, is that Sor Juana's intellectual battles are quickly confined to the kitchen, as if a woman's intellectual hunger could only be satisfied in a domestic setting.

In the works of Lavín and Galván, the intention to rewrite Sor Juana's story as a postcolonial and feminist historical fiction becomes clearer, as each author crafts an "alternative" or "apocryphal" account that situates women on the axis of a collective memory that has been routinely forgotten by national discourses (Seydel 169). Unlike Gómez, Lavín traces Sor Juana's feminism on numerous occasions closely related to her intellectual development, from the time she attends the *Amiga* school as a very young girl,[13] or the day her *loa* to the Blessed Sacrament wins an award at the age of seven, to the memorable encounter with the men who test her knowledge. Acknowledging the dangerous profile of an intellectual woman whose art of *contra/diction*, sharp wit, and self-directed classical humanistic education defies women's status as the passive, peripheral, private and domestic other (Arenal and Martínez-San Miguel 187), Lavín's narrator presents Juana Inés as an individual unfit for marriage and with no option but the convent. As the vicereine reflects on Sor Juana's victory in front of the most knowledgeable, she concludes that perhaps she was not made for married life.

In tune with the late Hispanic feminine boom that subverts traditional content and form, as it simultaneously establishes female genealogies (Madrid Moctezuma 95–98), in *Yo, la peor* Sor Juana's first teacher, Refugio Salazar, strongly supports her decision to enter the convent: "Juana Inés haces bien, muchacha; perseguirás tu sueño, el estudio sin que la sociedad te infame y te reclame cordura y virtud de mujer y esposa . . . Escribe, muchacha, escribe. Si has negado la vida del matrimonio para casarte con el altísimo, que sea en provecho de tu notable talento" (Juana Inés, you're doing the right thing; you'll follow your dream, your studies, without being condemned by a society that asks you to be a virtuous woman and wife . . . Write, girl, write. If you have rejected a married life in order to marry God, take advantage of your notable talent) (198–99). Accordingly, throughout the novel readers are told that Sor Juana devises the *Neptuno alegórico* that highly impresses her colonial authorities; the narrator mentions on several occasions that she writes the ambitious poem *El sueño*, the play *Los empeños de una casa*, her argumentative *Crisis de un sermón*, and *Los enigmas de La Casa del Placer* (*Enigmas of the House of Pleasure*), all of which prove that she never renounced the word or the desire for knowledge.

The seamless introduction of these works in the body of Lavín's novel is illuminating because each reference completes the picture of an intellectual woman who lived to reason and by reason, challenging the cultural and historical paradigm that has gendered knowledge as male and trespassing a forbidden zone to which women were denied access (Merrim, "Feminist Reading" 17; Kirk, "Women's Literacy" 141). The intertextual allusion to the enigmas, in particular, greatly fuels the novel's feminism. First, it supports the idea that Sor Juana continued writing near the end of her life, when she composed for a group of Portuguese nuns twenty *redondillas* (quatrains) on the nature of love. Second, the fact that her poetry successfully entered the Casa del Placer, an autonomous female textual space or academy, invites us to picture her as part of an ideal literary community that promoted the circulation of texts between several convents, within a sisterhood of shelter and protection from the hostility of the outside world (Kirk, *Convent Life* 144; Poot Herrera, *Guardaditos* 314). The reference to this "house" is key to the feminist foundation of the novel, for it once offered its virtual inhabitants "the luxury of dreaming up an all-female universe where women write for other women, free from the disapproval that normally would accompany such activities" (Kirk, *Convent Life* 144).

In Galván's *Los indecibles pecados de Sor Juana*, Sor María Isabel de San José writes her suggestive confession not because a man of the Church has asked her to do so, but as an act of obedience to her dearest aunt, Juana Inés. Her writing distances itself from the written testimonies and notes produced by other nuns whose biographies were manipulated by their confessors to produce acceptable hagiographies, crafted as exemplary models of poverty, chastity, and obedience that always ended with the climatic episode of a "good death" (Franco, *Las conspiradoras* 42). Sor María's testimony is born in the secrecy of female complicity, as an act of transgression that gets around male authorities, and it is addressed to another woman:

> La madre Juana Inés me encomendó escribir el recuento de estos hechos porque deseaba que quedaran asentados en algún lado y porque no debían ser escritos por su propia mano, sino por un tercero, un testigo de confianza como yo . . . Me instruyó para que cuando estuviera terminado, se lo enviara a la condesa—de Paredes—su amiga, que ella lo guardaría bien . . . Mi tía y yo nos reuníamos en su celda por las noches en absoluta privacidad, con el pretexto de que me ayudaba en mis lecciones de latín, y se iba confesando conmigo para que yo recordara y escribiera las cosas tal y como fueron, porque ella no podía contarlas al mundo. Pero quería que constara en actas.
>
> (Mother Juana Inés asked me to record these incidents because she wished to leave documentation of them, somewhere, and because she couldn't write them herself as they

> had to be written by a third party, a trustworthy witness like me . . . She told me that once I finished it, I should send it to the Countess—de Paredes—her friend, because she would guard it well . . . My aunt and I privately met in her cell at night, with the excuse that she was helping me with my Latin lessons, and she would confess to me so that I would remember and write things just as they happened, because she couldn't tell them to the world. But she wanted them to be recorded in writing.) (58–59)

This confession invites us to picture that Sor Juana managed to have if not a well-rounded life at least a well-experienced one as a lady-in-waiting, avid reader, passionate lover, controversial nun, mother, daughter, teacher, friend, muse, and woman of letters. Her feminism is present in all of her actions and determines the final outcome of her life. She wants to become a painter, for instance, not just to support herself before entering the convent but also to prove that men and women have the same capacity to produce a work of art:

> según ella, nada impedía ni en nada influía el sexo de una persona sobre el resultado pintado sobre un lienzo. Quería demostrar que si las manos de una mujer se aplicaban lo suficiente a la pintura, podían lograr un resultado igual o hasta superior al de las manos de un varón, y que el observador no sería capaz de distinguir la diferencia.
>
> (according to her, the sex of a person did not influence the final outcome of a painting. She wanted to demonstrate that if the hands of a woman took painting seriously, they could produce an equal or even superior result to the one generated by the hands of a man, and the observer would not be able to tell the difference.) (118)

Like Lavín's Sor Juana, however, in the end this one realizes that things would not change just because she said so. She decides to become a nun not because of religious vocation but because she is four months' pregnant.

As Laura, the metafictional researcher who deciphers Sor María Isabel's confession in the twenty-first century, compares her own life to Sor Juana's and wonders about her future as a single mother, she comes to the conclusion that men did not seem too worried about being responsible for their actions and that nothing had really changed since the seventeenth century. In a subsequent reflection of female recognition and drawing another set of parallel genealogies, Laura thinks of Rosario Castellanos and her denunciation of women's passive role while men go through life "libres como el viento" (as free as a breeze) (130). The quick but fortunate allusion to Castellanos's feminism immediately reactivates her words, particularly those that the author employs in *Mujer que sabe latín . . .* (*Woman Who Knows Latin . . .*) to emphasize that women have been historically denied the same certificate of citizenship as men, on the basis of their inferior status, fragility, mental deficiency, monotonous existence, and mythical portrayal (*Mujer* 9–16). As a way to fictionalize this historical marginalization of women in the context of New Spain, toward the end of the novel Galván's narrator finds a letter that Sor Juana writes to the son that she conceives with Cristóbal de Villalpando. As fictional as it is, this alternative memory attaches Sor Juana's feminism to her intellectual passion and female condition. She laments:

> En el siglo me condenaron por ser mujer y nada más por ser mujer. Lo que hice, que fue intentar aprender, escribir, indagar sobre el universo y la razón, enseñar a las que no tenían oportunidad de aprender, nunca fue una fechoría, a mi modo de ver. A cualquier varón se le hubiera perdonado y hasta celebrado.
>
> (In this century I was condemned for being a woman and only for being a woman. What I did, trying to learn, write, and explore the universe and reason, teaching those who didn't have the opportunity to learn, was never a misdeed, the way I saw it. Any man would have been forgiven and even celebrated for it.) (232)

This is how the novel ends: with a clear feminist message that presents the female act of writing—in the hands of Sor Juana, Sor María Isabel de San José, and Laura—as a strategy to conquer a new place or to baptize the infinite possibilities of a woman's desire, far away from any traps of historical determinism and any gendered catalogs of acceptable female conduct (Lorenzano, "Mujer y narrativa" 351). Together, this and other passages in Galván's work rearticulate an artistic, revolutionary, and by all means fictional version of Sor Juana's feminism and revisit the multiple ways the woman, poet, and nun of colonial Mexico experienced the personal as a political act (Arenal, "Where Woman" 130). What sets apart this Sor Juana from the others re-created elsewhere is that Galván cleverly fictionalizes the process that Yolanda Martínez-San Miguel observes in the writings of the historical individual: the well-crafted articulation of an intellectual subject who seeks access to various hegemonic spaces of intellectuality (51).

Had Sor Juana Cooked . . .

One of these intellectual spaces where Sor Juana establishes fruitful equivalences between writing and cooking is the kitchen, the domestic place suddenly empowered in her *Respuesta a Sor Filotea de la Cruz* as a privileged room to study "los secretos naturales" (the secrets of nature) and to test and practice "filosofías de cocina" (philosophies of the kitchen) (*Answer* 74–75). Rather than presenting herself as a master of cooking, in her famous letter to the bishop of Puebla Sor Juana appears as a natural researcher and observer who uses the kitchen to confirm the physical and chemical properties of food (Perelmuter 48–58). In fact, only as part of her intellectual quest does the nun assert, "Si Aristóteles hubiera guisado, mucho más hubiera escrito" (Had Aristotle cooked, he would have written a great deal more) (*Answer* 74–75). Interestingly, though, what we observe in the majority of these recent narratives is quite different. The multiple Sor Juanas readers find in these works spend a tremendous amount of time in the kitchen, not necessarily philosophizing but simply cooking, tasting all kinds of elaborate dishes, composing a recipe book, and preparing poisonous substances that she uses to her advantage.

In *Los indecibles pecados de Sor Juana*, the prodigy of New Spain is responsible for introducing the viceroy and the vicereine to the culinary delights of her country, and we constantly see her in the kitchen, where she feels at home surrounded by other cooks. Apparently, to please her authorities, Sor Juana exposes them to a rich variety of dishes that should win her a few favors in court:

> Un día pavo y otro venado y otro más chiles cubiertos de almendras y pasas. Torrejas y pastelillos otro día, huevos con

> nata o con nopales, pan con tomate y butifarras para que no extrañara[n] la Madre Patria. Variedad de frutas frescas y caramelizadas, chilaquiles verdes, rojos o marmoleados. Pescados blancos con tamarindo, con epazote y con rajas, claras con rompope, guisos con cacahuate, en fin, la lista era larga y deliciosa.
>
> (One day turkey and another one deer, and chiles covered with almonds and raisins on another one. French toasts and cakes on another day, eggs with cream or *nopales*, bread with tomato and sausages so that they wouldn't miss their homeland. A variety of fresh and caramelized fruits, green, red, or marbled *chilaquiles*. White fish with tamarind sauce, *epazote* and sliced chiles, egg whites with eggnog, stews with peanuts, anyway, the list was long and delicious.) (88)

Nowhere in this list of dishes is there a single reference to Sor Juana's intellectuality. Her hunger for knowledge is simply not present when she happens to be around food, which openly contradicts what we observe in her writings: the portrayal of the kitchen as another place to study or as an empirical laboratory (Ochoa 230; Perelmuter 58). The allusion to the kitchen appears again in Galván's novel when Sor Juana and her niece prepare a pecan pie for the countess of Paredes. Only this time the allusion to food is not accompanied by a poetic composition that highlights the superiority of the nun's writing over the gift she sends to the vicereine (Glantz, *Sor Juana* 69); instead, the scene presents itself as a natural moment of female complicity, where Sor Juana tells her niece the secrets of her tainted origin.

Also divorced from any intellectual projects are the references to the kitchen that we find in Gómez's *El beso de la virreina*, where Juana Inés enters several cooking spaces like a witch to prepare magic potions. Contrary to our expectations, throughout the novel she distinguishes herself as a woman who uses potions and narcotics and makes spells. In fact, when her religious sisters become ill due to a deadly epidemic, Sor Juana prepares drinks following a secret recipe that should revive them:

> Treinta gramos de azufre compuesto, diez gramos de nuez vómica y treinta gramos de sal; todo diluido en cinco damajuanas de agua hervida. Se deja descansar una noche. Se les

> da de beber una cucharada cada seis horas durante el inicio del padecimiento. Si están muy enfermas entonces cada hora. Para las fiebres utilice baños de pies y té caliente de limón.
>
> (Thirty grams of composite sulfur, ten grams of nux vomica and thirty grams of salt; all diluted in five demijohns of boiled water. It should sit for one night. They should be given one teaspoon every six hours at the beginning of the illness. If they're very sick, then every hour. For the fevers, give them a foot bath and hot lemon tea). (354–55)

Clearly, the interrelation between cooking and writing prevalent in Sor Juana's life and poetry is once again absent. Even more problematic is Juana Inés's depiction as a madwoman who empowers herself through various acts associated with witchcraft that only devalue women's power within a male-dominated system (Behar 200). This paradox, as I explain shortly, is also present in Zagal's *La venganza de Sor Juana.*

Only in Lavín's *Yo la peor* Sor Juana makes allusions to the kitchen with the same intellectual passion that she portrays in her *Respuesta a Sor Filotea de la Cruz*. Displaying a well-defined scientific spirit that Lavín also acknowledges in a recent interview (Zapata), the nun protests: "Si nos es dado experimentar en la cocina y ver *que un huevo se fríe y une en la manteca y aceite y, por contrario, se despedaza en el almíbar*, ¿por qué no es posible indagar los terrenos de lo sagrado, donde [los hombres] por permiso de su anatomía sí lo pueden hacer? (If we can experiment in the kitchen and see *that an egg becomes solid and cooks in butter or oil, and on the contrary that it dissolves in sugar syrup*, why is it not possible to investigate the world of the sacred, where [men] have their anatomy's permission to do so?) (214, emphasis in original). Knowing that Sor Juana was an expert on "delicias gastronómico poéticas" (poetic gastronomic delights) (Lavín, *Sor Juana* 19), the author of *Yo, la peor* gives her intellectual protagonist the opportunity to make several references to food and the kitchen but only to create innovative metaphors of her ambivalent situation. When she feels trapped by her enemies, for instance, she writes to María Luisa de Paredes that she anticipates winning the final battle, "como el chocolate que tanto te gustaba beber en el convento" (like the chocolate that you liked to drink in the convent) (214). Later on, Lavín's Sor Juana offers sweets to her friend and protector and sends her "zapatos rellenos de dulces" (shoes filled with candy)

(267) to sweeten her difficult pregnancy. But the nun also highlights that the sweets and fritters were prepared by other women and not by her, the convent's accountant.

On the opposite end of this spectrum, Héctor (Mónica) Zagal's *La venganza de Sor Juana* revolves entirely around the kitchen and other equivalent spaces of domesticity. When Calleja approaches Mexico's former viceroy to get firsthand information about Sor Juana, during each interview the marquis's chef displays elaborate Mexican dishes that supposedly come from the nun's secret recipe book. That Sor Juana composed such a cookbook, at least partially or with the help of other nuns, is a historical fact. As Mónica Lavín explains in *Sor Juana en la cocina* (*Sor Juana in the Kitchen*), "En 1979 se publicó por primera vez un manuscrito que recoge 36 recetas del claustro de San Jerónimo; el soneto a manera de introducción y el autógrafo final son de Sor Juana Inés de la Cruz" (In 1979 a manuscript was published for the first time with 36 recipes from the convent of San Jerónimo; the sonnet that serves as an introduction and the final signature are by Sor Juana Inés de la Cruz) (7). Naturally, the existence of this book invites us to imagine the writer-nun in the kitchen cooking, although we may wonder with Lavín whether the writing or transcription of these recipes was simply another obligation among her many chores. Still, what could have been a mere circumstantial occurrence in Sor Juana's real life, or simply another way to win her benefactors, takes over the entire narrative in Zagal's novel and reconfigures her true intellectual endeavors.

The protagonist-chef that we find in *La venganza de Sor Juana* in many ways behaves like an amateur contestant on an episode of *MasterChef* but with an evil twist that markets Mexican culture as an exotic product, forever magical and primitive. I say this because in Zagal's novel Sor Juana cooks all kinds of delicious dishes for her friends and confessors, enjoys having a private space for her stews, and gladly shares the kitchen with her Indian servant Ignacia, who is an expert in the art of herbal remedies. As in Laura Esquivel's *Como agua para chocolate*, where Tita and her servant Nacha use the kitchen as a magical room of their own to create meals that affect the lives of everyone around them, Sor Juana and Ignacia prepare soups, salads and tamales, a variety of appetizers, and desserts that drastically affect people's moods. Aware of her confessor's gluttony, the nun deliberately feeds him a variety of spicy *moles*, *castañitas fingidas*, and *buñuelos* (sweet fritters) made out of figs, apples, milk curd, and sage. As if magical realism had not been completely exhausted by the ill-fated followers of Gabriel García Márquez in the late 1980s and early 1990s, Sor Juana uses egg yolks to cure melancholy, deciphers her confessor's health by examining the rigor of the penitence he imposes in the confessionary, and magically changes his temperament through different types of food. In agreement with this portrait, Sor Juana spends most of her time combining the art of medicine with cooking, trying to combat with food not just Núnez de Miranda but her next two confessors, all of whom end up mysteriously dead after being in close contact with her cooking.

What Zagal sacrifices in his representation of Sor Juana is the nun's love for experimenting with everything she saw and touched to formulate in-depth questions that expanded her interdisciplinary knowledge of the world (Paz, *Sor Juana* 546). Purposely or not, the author forgets that Sor Juana ends up in the kitchen because she has been forbidden to study her books and not by personal choice. She explains this in her *Respuesta*, as she recalls that a mother superior ordered her not to read:

> Yo la obedecí (unos tres meses que duró el poder ella mandar) en cuanto a no tomar libro, que en cuanto a no estudiar absolutamente, como no cae debajo de mi potestad, no lo pude hacer, porque aunque no estudiaba en los libros, estudiaba en todas las cosas que Dios crió, sirviéndome ellas de letras, y de libro toda esta máquina universal.
>
> (I obeyed her [for the three months or so that her authority over us lasted] in that I did not pick up a book. But in terms of absolutely avoiding study, as such a thing does not lie within my power, I could not do it. For although I did not study in books, I studied all the things that God created, using all the intricate structures of this world as letters and as a book.) (72–73)

In this context, Sor Juana makes acute scientific observations in the kitchen with the flour, the eggs, the oil and the sugar, as part of a natural research process she later describes to the bishop of Puebla "por daros entera noticia de mi natural" (to give you a full account of my nature) (74–75). In this sense, her kitchen inquiries expand her field of learning, and the kitchen becomes a space that generates wisdom and knowledge (Franco, *Las conspiradoras* 80; Perelmuter 61).

The numerous cooking passages we find in Zagal's novel have little to do with Sor Juana's intellectual traits and have nothing in common with Rosario Castellanos's "Lección de cocina," the subtle short story where a nameless protagonist ironically defines her stagnant and contradictory place in a white and immaculate kitchen that is supposed to define her.[14] If Sor Juana in her *Respuesta* resorts to various tricks of the weak to defend her intellectuality from the safe position of a marginal or subordinated female subject within the patriarchal matrix of New Spain (Ludmer 87), she acts quite differently in Zagal's novel, where most of her energy is spent trying to win her confessors with "la fineza de las semillas del anís, la escurridiza elegancia de las hojas del aguacate, la sensualidad de los mangos, la provocativa acidez de los tamarindos" (the gentleness of anise seeds, the slippery elegance of avocado leaves, the sensuality of mangos, the provocative bitterness of tamarind) (124). Although nuns in New Spain traditionally cooked sweets for their donors and used the convent kitchen to teach cloistered young girls how to cook as an essential part of their education (Gonzalbo Aizpuru 336), in *La venganza de Sor Juana* the nun's private kitchen is described as a war camp. Apparently, in this battlefield—perhaps more suited for the modern camera of a reality TV show than for the plausible rearticulation of a colonial intellectual—Sor Juana invests endless hours cooking meals with a servant known for her witchcraft activities to manipulate her superiors' health, temper, sleeping habits, and personal beliefs. On one hand, the preparation and astute delivery of these supposedly bewitched meals reflect a practice that was common in pre-Hispanic times and sixteenth- and seventeenth-century Spain and New Spain; on the other hand, the empowerment of a female subject through various witchcraft activities is unfortunately illusive, undeniably limited, short-lived, and ultimately insignificant (Behar 200–201).

The Lost Manuscript

Toward the end of Zagal's novel, Calleja attempts to save Sor Juana's secret recipe book from his Jesuit superiors, who want to avoid stirring up the nun's theological incursions, writing and cooking habits, and shady association with Ignacia. A storm surprises him, however, and the book falls in the mud. As Calleja tries to save the precious document, he discovers that another manuscript has been used as binding for the original recipes:

> Para matar el tiempo mientras la tormenta se disipaba, curioseó en las hojas que servían para empastar el recetario. Se sorprendió al identificar la letra de sor Juana. El agua había dañado bastante ese segundo manuscrito, pero se podían leer algunas frases. El título era perfectamente legible: "La muerte dulce. Doce recetas de la india Ignacia."
>
> (In order to kill time while the storm passed, he browsed through the pages that served as binding for the recipe book. He was surprised to identify Sor Juana's handwriting. The water had substantially damaged that second manuscript, but some phrases could still be read. The title was perfectly legible: "The sweet death. Twelve recipes by the Indian Ignacia.") (193)

The fictional recipes that Zagal includes after the novel's epilogue implicitly corroborate Sor Juana's direct involvement in the mysterious deaths of her confessors, particularly because each one is accompanied by suspicious subtitles, such as "Para engañar el alma en caso de engaños amorosos" (To trick the soul in case of love deceptions) (200); "Para ganarse la simpatía de un hombre hosco y frío" (To win the sympathy of a bad-tempered and cold man) (201); "Para alejar las obsesiones peligrosas" (To dispel dangerous obsessions) (202); and "Para apaciguar la cólera de un carácter violento" (To calm down the fury of a violent person) (206). Metaphorically speaking, both the recipe book and the hidden manuscript where Sor Juana transcribes Ignacia's recipes represent an alternative convent script, one that departs from the conventions of religious practice and literature without sacrificing its subversive presence within an intensely patriarchal world (Merrim, *Early Modern* 105–8).

Finding one of Sor Juana's lost manuscripts in the twenty-first century would certainly fascinate an entire community of *sorjuanistas*. Within the neoliberal context in which these novels have been produced, however, this added element corroborates the sensationalist content that is expected in works that promise untold secrets and private confessions. José Luis Gómez only hints at the possibility of a lost manuscript when Sor Juana asks her friend Marta Portes to burn her unpublished poems immediately after her death, at the very end of *El beso de la virreina*. However, both Lavín and Galván insert in their novels a series of fictional letters that could have been written by Sor Juana. In perfect agreement with the nun's practice of letter writing—as evidenced by her *Carta atenagórica* or

Crisis de un sermón (1690), the *Respuesta a Sor Filotea de la Cruz* (1700), and *Carta al Padre Núñez* (*Letter to Father Núñez*) (1981)—in *Yo, la peor*, we find four letters signed by Juana Inés on November 17, 1694; December 17, 1694; January 17, 1695; and February 17, 1695. Situated during the last six months of her life (she died in San Jerónimo on April 17, 1695), these fictional manuscripts addressed to the former vicereine María Luisa de Paredes present themselves as a composite symbolic and alternative testament that compresses Sor Juana's passions into a series of final sentences that recall her past, describe her present, and project her into a possible future (Lavrin, "*Lo femenino*" 169).[15] They contain the words we would like to have to understand Sor Juana from an intimate perspective, a possibility that the series *Juana Inés* also entertains unveiling an erotic and dangerous exchange of letters between the nun and the vicereine.

If, to a great extent, colonial women's testaments contained a woman's reaffirmation of her faith, the recounting of her life, the disposition of her belongings, and an overall view of a woman's life (Lavrin, "*Lo femenino*" 169), in *Yo, la peor* Sor Juana uses these last letters to reflect on her life-long accomplishments as a writer and on her current disadvantages as she is being cornered by ecclesiastical authorities. "Ahora me piden que sea otra de la que soy" (Now they ask me to be different than who I am), she protests. "Que me corte la lengua, que me nuble la vista, que me ampute los dedos, el corazón, que no piense, que no sienta más que lo que es menester y propio de una religiosa, de una esposa de Cristo" (They want me to cut off my tongue, to cover my eyes, to amputate my fingers, my heart, to stop thinking, to feel only what is necessary and proper for a religious woman, a bride of Christ) (17). Displaying the same determination that distinguishes her throughout her brilliant writing career, the nun assures her friend and secret interlocutor that she has pretended to be silent to save herself.

In the midst of her most difficult times, Sor Juana appears triumphant in anticipation of a final victory. She is happy, for instance, imagining how upset her confessor and the other ecclesiastical authorities of New Spain will be when they receive a printed copy of the enigmas of *La Casa del Placer* she sent to the Portuguese nuns. She laughs in private, knowing that she has tricked them, for she will never renounce writing. Lavín's Sor Juana confirms this positive attitude along with her true devotions in her last letter, with the words: "Renunciar a ser la que soy desde hace tanto me es imposible . . . Deben saber que si firmé *Yo, la peor de todas* con mi sangre fue por rubricar dramáticamente aquella representación" (It would be impossible to stop being who I am . . . They should know that I signed *I, the worst of all* with my blood to dramatically endorse that representation) (367–68). Thus the nun's final novelistic act of writing carries with it the seeds of female transgression, one that combats women's traditional simulacrum of silence (Porzecanski 53).

A parallel situation of explicit female empowerment that allows a woman to speak not with the words of others or with the residues of canonical and male-centered discourses (Porzecanski 54) is fictionalized in Galván's *Los indecibles pecados de Sor Juana*. In this novelistic scenario, Laura, the researcher, finds not only Sor María Isabel de San José's blunt confession concerning her famous aunt, but also the letters Sor Juana writes to her lover and to her illegitimate son. Although these letters are openly melodramatic and reveal themselves tainted with words typical of a lover's discourse, characterized by feelings of absence and anxiety, catastrophe, and the uncertainty of love (Barthes, *A Lover's* 13–15), Sor Juana simultaneously depicts herself as a woman in love and as a nun whose intellectuality is not an impediment to motherhood. Consequently, in the letter to her son, she writes:

> Quiero que me perdones por no poder ser una madre como cualquier otra para ti. Ya no podré quebrantar más los votos que tomé hace años y que deberé honrar en el futuro para morir con cierta dignidad. Nunca sabré cómo será tu carita, ni te veré corretear por ahí, ni podré limpiar tu naricita cuando estés enfermo. Tampoco me será posible enseñarte las primeras letras e inculcarte el amor por los libros y el conocimiento, ni podré contarte una fábula a la hora de dormir. Perdóname porque no estaré ahí, pero quiero que te lleves el regalo de mi amor por ti. Quiero que sepas que te amé desde el primer instante que supe de tu existencia y te amaré hasta la tumba.
>
> (I want you to forgive me for not being like the other mothers for you. I will no longer be able to break the vows that I made years ago and that I should honor in the future so as to die with dignity. I will never know what your little face will look like, nor will I see you running around, nor will I be able to clean your little nose when you get sick. I won't be able to teach you your first letters, the love for books and

> knowledge, nor will I be able to tell you a bedtime story. Forgive me for not being there, but I want you to take as a present my love for you. I want you to know that I loved you from the first instant that I knew of your existence, and I will love you until I die.) (232)

By situating herself like a multifaceted woman in this single act of writing, Galván's Sor Juana ends her own narrative by repositioning herself as a feminist artisan of her own identity. Symbolically, and in line with contemporary perspectives on gender, she humanizes her female individuality and concurrently validates her maternal feelings and intellectual passions, as a way of showing that a woman represents diversity, fluidity and multiplicity, and that her sexuality (á la Irigaray) cannot be captured under one rubric or masked by any fabricated femininities (Guerra 63–65). As a composite whole, then, these letters and the ones crafted by Lavín expand and renovate Sor Juana's real texts, those in which the nun assembles a complex semantic puzzle that situates the feminine within the privileged realm of official discourse (Martínez-San Miguel 53).

The fact that these novels have been written and published almost concurrently in the first decade of the twenty-first century undoubtedly speaks of Sor Juana's relevance as a cultural icon of Mexico today. Entangled in a series of contradictory representations, the fictionalized poet-nun speaks to us about gender marginalization, sexual discrimination, and the historical otherness that persists in contemporary societies. Against all odds and defying verisimilitude (at least in some cases), Sor Juana demolishes myth and history to appear triumphant, reconfigured, and renovated as a national symbol (Valero Juan 229, 241). As we have seen in this chapter, the contrasting fictionalizations of the Tenth Muse are inevitably influenced by our world, the books we read, and the theories that shape our imagination. We may like some of her contemporary representations more than others. And still, from the surface of a Mexican 200-peso bill or from the heart of one of her numerous paintings, portrait poems, or defensive letters, the nun challenges any definitive reading of her works and persona as she intuitively warns us: "La imagen de vuestra idea / es la que habéis alabado; / y siendo vuestra, es bien digna / de vuestros aplausos" (Your praises have been lavished / on an image of your idea / being yours, it surely deserves / the tribute of your applause) (OC, I 161/*Anthology* 109).

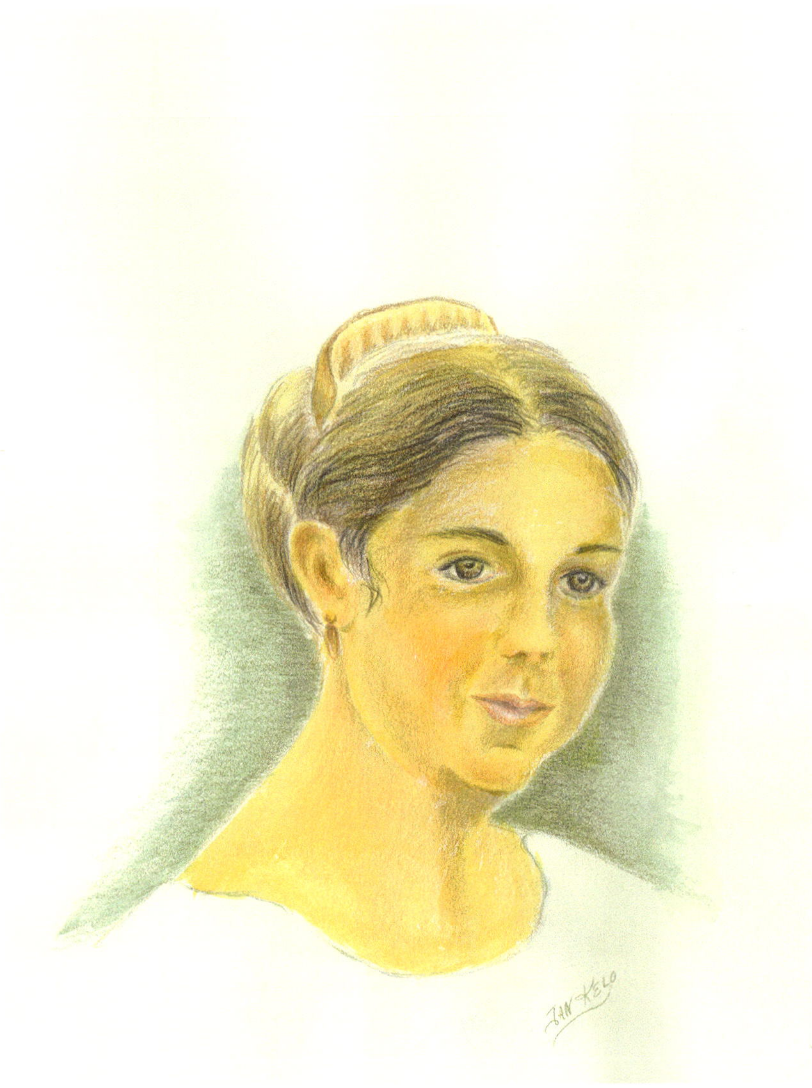

Leona Vicario. *Leona Vicario, Heroina insurgente*, colored pencil drawing with watercolor wash by Janet Kelo, 2017.

3

Leona Vicario

The Sweet Mother of the Nation

> Como, además de hermosa y elegante, Leona era, según dejamos dicho, naturalmente inteligente; de una virtud acendrada; de una perfecta religiosidad; hábil en el arte de la pintura; instruida en historia, política, ciencias naturales y literatura; conocía el idioma francés; descendía de padres honorables, y poseía un buen capital, debió sobresalir entre las demás señoritas de la alta sociedad de la Nueva España, por lo común extremadamente ignorantes . . .
>
> (Besides being beautiful and elegant, Leona was, as we have said, naturally intelligent, virtuous, religious, skilled in the art of painting, knowledgeable in history, politics, the natural sciences, and literature. She knew the French language, had honorable parents and was well off. Because of this, she must have stood out among the young ladies of New Spain's high class who were most likely extremely ignorant . . .)
>
> —Genaro García, *Leona Vicario* (46).

Genaro García's 1910 biography, *Leona Vicario: Heroína insurgente* (*Leona Vicario: Insurgent Heroine*), is a true gem of the early twentieth century. It stands out, as Amy Wright observes in a suggestive study, "as a progressive and anomalous revision of the 'Mexican woman' coming from within the highest ranks of the Porfirian intellectual world at a time of key debate regarding women's role in Mexican society" (147). In fact, given its exclusive focus on the life of a rebellious woman who actively participated in Mexico's War of Independence (1810–1821), precisely when Mexican women were encouraged to be submissive and domestic as perfect "angels of the house," the book has been recognized as a good example of early Mexican feminism, produced by a Mexican historian deeply committed to the study of women and their legal rights.[1] Other historians before García had written brief biographies of Leona Vicario, as he acknowledges in his preliminary note, but he solidifies the multifaceted and iconic portrait of a public Mexican woman whose actions change the course of history.[2]

According to García, María de la Soledad Leona Camila Vicario Fernández de San Salvador was born in the capital of New Spain on April 10, 1789. Her parents, Spaniard Gaspar Martín Vicario and criolla Camila Fernández de San Salvador y Montiel, provided Leona an exemplary education and made her a virtuous and compassionate Christian woman. Inevitably influenced by the nineteenth-century romanticism and its preference for nationalistic discourses,[3] García depicts Leona as a woman of unusual strength and exceptional kindness, a hybrid citizen of the emerging republic equally devoted to the Spanish Virgin of Los Remedios and the Mexican Virgin of Guadalupe. Enamored with his heroine, García imagines her as an avid reader whose hunger for knowledge has no limits: she cultivates the study of fine arts, science, and literature. She reads the history of her fatherland, books on politics and cosmography, and German, Spanish, English, and French literature. This representation of a new Mexican citizen committed to education is expected, of course, of a book still marked by nationalism and its not-so-subtle discourses on the power of education,[4] published 100 years after the start of the Mexican War of Independence.

Orphaned at the age of eighteen and holding a decent fortune (107,000 pesos), Leona Vicario, a self-sacrificing woman of exceptional morals and heroic spirit, is depicted as a treasure of the nascent nation. Looking at the painting with which Leona was later immortalized in Mexico's currency and stamps, García considers that she was good-looking: "de estatura regular, robusta y bien formada; movimientos graciosos; rostro lleno, afable y sonrosado; frente ancha, alta y vertical; cejas muy delgadas; ojos grandes, negros, de mirar luminoso, firme y enérgico; nariz fina y correcta, y boca pequeña y sonriente" (of average height, robust and well formed; gracious movements; with an affable face and rosy cheeks, a high forehead, thin eyebrows, big eyes of firm and luminous expression, a delicate nose, and a small mouth) (45). More important, García describes her as a transgressive and indomitable woman. Much to the dislike of her guardian uncle and tutor, lawyer Agustín Pomposo Fernández de San Salvador, Leona breaks off her engagement with the wealthy Octaviano Obregón; falls in love with the patriot Andrés Quintana Roo, a young lawyer from Yucatán; and uses her inheritance to fund insurgence activity, leaving behind a life of comfort and social prestige.

Thanks to these and other biographical details, Mexicans remember Leona Vicario as a secret insurgent messenger who suffered imprisonment and persecution since 1813. She is the brave woman who did not betray her liberal comrades, even under the threats of the Inquisition during her confinement in the Colegio de Belén. Leona Vicario is the courageous mother who gave birth to her first child in a cave in 1817, lacking food and proper medical care; she is the honorable wife of Quintana Roo; and last but not least, she is the mother of Mexican independence. When she died on August 21, 1842, at the age of fifty-three, "piadosamente, como había vivido" (piously, as she had lived) (García 144), Leona Vicario was shortly after named Benemérita y Dulcísima Madre de la Patria (Sweet Mother of the Fatherland) by President Antonio López de Santa Anna. After her state funeral, an honor that no other woman has ever received in Mexico, Leona was buried in the cemetery of Santa Paula until May 28, 1900, when her remains were taken to the Rotonda de las Personas Ilustres. In 1925, her remains were moved one more time to rest in the mausoleum of Mexico City's Columna de la Independencia, along with that of Quintana Roo and other male heroes of Mexico's independence, such as Miguel Hidalgo y Costilla, José María Morelos y Pavón, and Ignacio Allende.

In 1825, José Joaquín Fernández de Lizardi, the famous author of *El Periquillo Sarniento* (*The Itching Parrot*) (1816) and *La Quijotita y su prima* (*The Quijotita and Her Cousin*) (1818), published an essay on insurgent Mexican women, titled *Calendario para el año de 1825 dedicado a las señoritas, especialmente a las patriotas por el Pensador Mexicano* (*Calendar for the Year 1825 Dedicated to the Young Ladies, Especially to the Patriots by the Mexican Thinker*). In this work that honors María Josefa Huerta Escalante, Mariana Rodríguez de Lazarín, María Fermina Rivera, and Manuela Herrera, Lizardi considers that Leona Vicario was born in love with her country's freedom and notes that she became a true patriot after Miguel Hidalgo's *Grito de Dolores*. To fully express her heroic spirit, Lizardi compares the insurgent Mexican heroine to another Leona from ancient Greece: "Una dama ateniense llamada Leona sufrió constantemente los tormentos que la mandó dar el tirano Hippias, sin conseguir éste que aquella heroína descubriese a los codefensores de su patria" (An Athenian lady named Leona was constantly tormented by the tyrant Hippias, but she never revealed the names of those who defended her fatherland) (14).[5] Lizardi's writing reflects how nationalism—the ideological mechanism that attracted numerous intellectuals of the early nineteenth century—invents an ideal entity for a particular country such as Mexico; it is, after all, a legend that promotes devotion and pride, a sense of identity, or the idea that an entire community shares common beliefs (Monsiváis, *Esencias* 202–3).

Thanks to these hyperbolic discourses that praise female heroism, over the course of the nineteenth century the Mother of the Nation became an icon, along with other emblematic women of the Mexican War of Independence, such as Josefa Ortiz de Domínguez (1773–1829), popularly known as La Corregidora, and Gertrudis Bocanegra (1765–1817), even though their participation "did not bring about the social, legal, or constitutional reforms needed to improve the situation of women in society" (Pérez de Mendiola 17). In the company of other famous women, like Manuela Saenz (1793–1856), patriot of Quito and collaborator with Simón Bolívar, and Buenos Aires revolutionary Mariquita Sánchez (1786–1868), Leona Vicario is remembered because she had an unusual degree of independence from patriarchal authority. She adhered to the patriot cause, made impolitic public outbursts favoring Mexico's independence, defied the Spanish monarchy, used her house as a communication center for the patriots, and fought against the royalists of New Spain (Chasteen, *Americanos* 53, 102).

Like other Latin American icons, Leona Vicario draws her power from various signs of religious connotations, the world of commerce that massively reproduces an image, and the magic of the fetish, which privatizes and eroticizes what is repeated and propagated in a larger, public space (O'Connor and Niebylski, "Reflections" 1–3). She continues to evolve in her afterlife because she was an exceptional woman: her dissident actions against the royal authorities of New Spain allowed her to be known as the mother of a new nation, a title usually reserved for the Virgin of Guadalupe, the mother of all Mexicans.[6] Ultimately,

Leona Vicario became a mythical heroic figure not only because she is a transgressor but, more important, because her transgressions have an ethical motivation. She does what other mythical heroes have done throughout the course of history: she combats a fatal, deterministic life, becomes the architect of a better destiny, and presents us with an alternative story of empowerment that can be easily reactivated by our own hopes of self-improvement, fame, and immortality (Bauzá 162–63).

Rosario Castellanos is less fond of her figure in the late 1950s. In one of her reflections on Mexican women, written in 1959 but published posthumously under the title *Declaración de fe* (*Declaration of Faith*) (1996), Castellanos recognizes Leona Vicario's patriotism and the fact that she collaborated with the rebels during the War of Independence. She also notes, however, that Vicario most likely helped the rebels as a messenger because she was in love with Quintana Roo and calls her a romantic young lady who was excited to play a dangerous game for adults. After evoking the biographical snippets that make her famous, Castellanos points out that in the end, Leona and her husband gave up their ideals of freedom to save their own lives. What bothers her most about Leona's figure is not necessarily the fact that she gave up her altruistic ideals—perhaps out of fear and desperation—but her willingness to return home like a good wife and mother, accepting her confinement to the domestic sphere: "Al llegar la paz . . . Leona se reduce a su hogar. Una vida casi tranquila, de familia" (When the war ended . . . Leona stays at home living an almost serene, family life) (86). Upset about this state of women's passiveness, instead of including only those well-known details that transform Leona into a heroine, Castellanos writes:

> ¡Lástima que expresara sus descubrimientos tan mal! En una ocasión una de sus sirvientas sufrió un accidente al estar aplicando una sangría. Y al ver correr confundidas las dos sangres—la del amo y la del criado—sin encontrar diferencia, exclamó: "No hay más azul que el de los cielos a los que suben las buenas acciones, como las de mi madre cuando socorre a los pobres."
>
> (It's too bad that she expressed her findings so badly! On one occasion, one of her servants suffered an accident while she was in the process of bloodletting. And at the sight of the two sets of blood—of the master and the servant—running

> together, she exclaimed: "The only blue is that of the heavens where good actions end up, such as my mother's when she helps the poor.") (83)

This negative depiction of Leona Vicario is well justified. Castellanos, the great feminist of the twentieth century, considers that any heroic action is worthless if it does not overcome its ornamental quality and does not propitiate intellectual equality (Mejía 11). Understandably, in *Mujer que sabe latín . . .* (*Woman Who Knows Latin . . .*) (1973) when Castellanos denounces women's marginality in a world that keeps them away from the production of knowledge, she reminds us that Josefa Ortiz de Domínguez was illiterate and that Vicario was indeed an ignorant woman. She revisits the anecdote with which she had previously explained Vicario's intellectual limitations and incorporates additional details that distort her pristine portrait:

> otra de nuestras heroínas de la Independencia, doña Leona Vicario, es tan ignorante a pesar de sus lecturas de autodidacta que, en cierta ocasión en que se ocupaba de faenas de la cocina y se hirió con un cuchillo en un dedo, quedó maravillada de que la sangre que manaba de la herida no hubiera sido azul sino roja, roja como la de la servidumbre que la ayudaba, roja como la de las esclavas que la servían.
>
> (another one of our heroines of Independence, doña Leona Vicario, is so ignorant in spite of her self-taught readings that on one occasion, when she was working in the kitchen, she cut her finger with a knife and was amazed to see that the blood from the wound was not blue but red, red like the servants' who helped her, red like the slaves' who served her.) (23)

Several decades after Castellanos's denouncement of historical female ignorance and passiveness, we find a much more favorable portrait of Leona Vicario in three novels published in 2010 in celebration of Mexico's bicentennial anniversary of independence: Celia del Palacio's *Leona*, Carlos Pascual's *La insurgenta* (*The Insurgent*), and Eugenio Aguirre's *Leona Vicario: La insurgente* (*Leona Vicario: The Insurgent*). These literary rearticulations of "retrospective nature" confront individual and collective memories; or the survival of historical memory and nostalgia, on one hand, and the persistence, on the other, of historical amnesia, silence, and selective memory (Aínsa, *Los guardianes* 117–22). Together these works confirm the poetic and religious nature of patriotism, that there exists something called "la religión de la patria" (the religion of the fatherland), and that even today, this clear and simultaneously blurry concept expresses collective hope, the ideals of a community, and the remote possibility of liberation (Monsiváis, *Esencias* 36). As expected of historical works that fashion the name of a recognizable woman in their titles, the novels I discuss here fictionalize Leona Vicario as a wife, lover, mother, and rebel. In this sense, they promote a matriarchal discourse of melodramatic undertones that place women and their love conflicts in the center of the action (Pizarro Cortés 415).[7] Some of these works, however, sacrifice her political participation and emphasize her domestic existence and unfailing love for Quintana Roo.

In some ways, this fictional display of Leona's romantic portrayal speaks for the impossibility of alternative histories of women's empowerment. Often the individualistic and intimate narratives that revolve around a national icon sacrifice a woman's intellect, her potential to subvert an established order, and her abilities to resignify a marginal space. Like Malinche and Sor Juana, the Leona we find in fictional works of the twenty-first century is trapped in a neoliberal labyrinth that markets affect, personal emotions, the feeling subject, and the specificity of individual experience. Extending far beyond the particularities of economic and political policy, neoliberalism has influenced the creation of new subjectivities that can be acquired and managed (Smith 3–7). This commercial value, transferred to the realm of literature, has promoted the publication of numerous novels that can be consumed with minimal intellectual energy; their added bonus is a sensational content that promises to entertain as much as a soap opera, a talk show, a romantic comedy, or a sitcom. Only a few of them are able to craft sensible worlds for wholesome and genuine historical subjects.

A Female Patriot

In his reading of recent historical novels that revolve around the Mexican War of Independence, César Antonio Sotelo observes an attempt to revive historical characters that to some extent had been kept in the secret dungeons of history's official discourses (19). This is not, by any means, a new literary trend but a persistent one, as I discussed in previous chapters. Precisely to counterbalance the participation of the well-known Josefa Ortiz de Domínguez (La Corregidora) or María Ignacia Rodríguez de Velasco (La Güera Rodríguez), between February and April 2010 three different editorial houses—Planeta, Grijalbo, and Suma de Letras—published novels that revived the almost forgotten Leona Vicario. Using different fictional strategies, these works openly construct or deconstruct, reconfigure or summarize the convoluted figure of a female patriot in neoliberal times, or a feminine role model of nation-building that seems to contradict postnational literary trends.

Conceived and marketed as a bestseller, Eugenio Aguirre's *Leona Vicario* sells the story of a young woman of patriotic spirit and altruistic ideals associated with national liberation. In the sensationalist introduction, in fact, Aguirre asserts that Vicario merits a literary tribute given her firm personality, optimism, and limitless generosity. Prolific in the use of hyperbole, a priori Aguirre tells his readers that Leona Vicario fought next to the poor and oppressed during the War of Independence, that she never sought forgiveness from the Spanish Crown, and that her unparalleled intelligence and heart "supieron encontrar, en el caos, la esperanza y el amor" (knew how to find, in the midst of chaos, hope and love) (10). The Leona that Aguirre wants us to find in his novel is an exceptional woman destined to become Mexico's Benemérita y Dulcísima Madre, as we can infer from her initial conversations with other young men who discuss politics and the future of New Spain as an independent republic.

As the young Vicario realizes that rebellion is the only path to freedom—"¿qué le queda a la gente de estas tierras, que no sea el tratar de sacudirse el yugo al que la tienen sometida?" (what else can the people of these lands do other than trying to get rid of the chains that oppress them?) (21)—she becomes involved in the insurgent movement, knowing that she is giving up her position as a privileged young woman. As if she were posing in front of a camera, Vicario wonders out loud if she can do something for her country's independence; she asks the Virgin of Guadalupe to show her how to become involved in the liberation of her nation and subsequently determines to help the rebels, putting her own money and knowledge at their service. Within a few pages, Leona's house is described as a beehive where discreet and astute bees work for Mexico's independence, and we are repeatedly told that she is a woman of courage, prepared for the worst punishments and ready to face death.

Given Aguirre's lack of experimentation with the content and form—in the sense that he does not distort any historical facts or legends, and he sets forth a linear plot in chronological fashion—his novel has been cataloged as a light text of flat narrative structures that lacks creativity and critical reflection (García Argüelles, "Leona Vicario" 121), or as a poor fictional piece that risks very little and could only be useful to elementary school children (Sotelo 16). Although some of these judgments may be a bit harsh, the novel contains few surprises in the (re)construction of Leona Vicario as a female patriot. She does what she is supposed to do according to history, and only occasionally does she speak like an empowered woman. To her detriment, Leona's patriotism is explicitly stated by the narrator of the novel; we are "told" that she is an activist, capable of convincing many Mexicans to support the insurgent movement. In lieu of genuine actions, the narrator provides detailed descriptions that desperately seek to highlight her patriotism, unthinkable without a romantic touch. For instance, after a brief moment in which she expresses her excitement about the possibility of living in a free country—with no more slaves branded with a hot iron and no more masters—the narrator takes the lead and silences her potential transgressions with a ready-made synopsis that is there to be easily digested by a passive reader:

> A partir de entonces, la actitud de Leona frente al movimiento de Independencia se convirtió en firme dedicación, sin vacilación ninguna, con todo el entusiasmo de su corazón ardiente, con toda la clarividencia de su gran talento, con todo el placer de su extraordinario carácter, plenamente convencida de que al fin triunfaría aquella causa, que por ser la de los débiles y oprimidos, ni la justicia divina ni la humana podían contener.
>
> (Since then, Leona dedicated herself to the independence movement without any hesitation, with enthusiasm, with astute awareness of her great talent, with her extraordinary nature, fully convinced that the cause of the weak and oppressed would succeed, for it could not be contained by divine and human justice.) (57)

One of the main problems with these prepackaged descriptions is that they leave no room for the reader's imagination to wonder about the protagonist's internal dilemmas in the midst of historical turbulence. The more the discourse becomes hyperbolic, the less convinced we are of Leona's true actions as a female hero. Like Superwoman, in Aguirre's novel Leona is capable of doing too much. Or so we feel when we read that Leona helps the imprisoned rebels, that she pays for the weapons and for the young soldiers she sends to the battlefields, and that she financially supports the families of the soldiers she enrolls. Is she really capable of doing all of this? Instead of strengthening the protagonist's heroic profile, the hyperbole in regard to her patriotism gives us the impression, at least momentarily, that there is no there there. We feel just as disillusioned when she is imprisoned and speaks not like a heroic woman but like an actress reciting her lines in front of an audience that already knows what to expect: "Así es, que estoy presa—se dijo—prisionera por querer la libertad y felicidad de mi pueblo, de esta pobre patria pisoteada por déspotas que no ven en ella otra cosa que el medio de hacerse ricos. No me daré por vencida, ¡lucharé con toda mi inteligencia, con toda mi voluntad!" (So I am imprisoned—she said to herself—imprisoned for wanting the freedom and happiness of my country, this poor fatherland that has been stepped on by those tyrants who are simply looking for ways to become rich. I won't give up. I will fight with all my intelligence, with all my will!) (101).

In the end, Leona is recognized by the government for her numerous sacrifices to the nation. She is, according to the narrator, an exemplary woman among many others whose hands were at the service of the wounded rebels and whose words were like music to their ears. Aware of her transcendental role in the War of Independence, Leona admits to her husband: "somos los seres más libres del mundo . . . Porque hemos logrado una victoria personal. A estas alturas, después de los años de lucha, creo que nuestras personas, nuestros espíritus, ya no nos pertenecen. Nos hemos convertido en una parte vital para nuestra patria" (we are the freest people of the world . . . Because we have achieved a personal victory. Now, after all these years of struggle, I believe that we no longer own our selves, our spirits. We have become an essential part of our fatherland) (135). Unsurprisingly, the novel ends with a list of known historical facts about Vicario's last years, after she recovered part of her fortune and returned home to take care of her daughters. She dies in this book as she did in real life, on August 21, 1842, and the narrator summarizes her state funeral, her temporary stay in the Rotonda de los Hombres Ilustres, and her final transfer to the Columna de la Independencia.

Aguirre's novel exemplifies how bestsellers are tailored to attract large audiences interested in "easy" and "light" works that entertain and concurrently assure readers that they are being educated with very little intellectual effort (Vargas Llosa, *La civilización* 37). It also reminds us that a great number of individuals in contemporary, neoliberal societies buy books not necessarily thinking of their content but likely because the topic is in fashion (the bicentennial of independence, for example); because they have attractive book covers with seductive advertisement (the image of an "exceptional" woman always sells); and because their authors receive a great deal of attention in newspapers, public interviews, book presentations, TV shows, and so on. On one hand, if Aguirre's book confirms that contemporary societies are not organized to read but to buy books that are kept like trophies on a shelf, on the other hand, it allows us to speculate about the nature and readership of bestsellers. Like Gabriel Zaid, we wonder, for instance, if bestsellers of this sort are actually read by anybody and if they will ever be read a second time like the classics that permit return readings and are always willing to offer surprising experiences (57–66, 91).

At a safe distance from this and other bestsellers, Celia del Palacio's *Leona* articulates the intimate and complex narrative of a woman who is not afraid to express her feminist ideals over the course of almost 400 pages, without sacrificing her love and passion for Quintana Roo. Thanks to this feminist point of view, the protagonist speaks her mind in this novel, and her patriotism seems more convincing than that of Aguirre's heroine. As Elsa Leticia García Argüelles argues, one of the major accomplishments of Del Palacio's novel is its revival of Leona as a multifaceted woman—as a wife, mother, lover, and insurgent—without depicting her as a representative of the "bello sexo" (beautiful sex), as a "mujer de bronce" (iron woman), or as an "ángel del hogar" (angel of the house) ("La heroicidad" 37). We perceive this throughout the novel when Leona expresses her patriotic ideals, intimate beliefs, and unfailing heroism.

In the opening chapter, Leona reasons like a patriot of the early nineteenth century, displaying a sense of genuine political engagement and intellectual transgression. In a heated discussion with her uncle, Don Agustín Pomposo, Leona reminds him:

> Usted sabe muy bien que a los nacidos en este reino jamás les permitirán ocupar los puestos más altos y que lejos de ser considerados iguales, siempre seremos inferiores en todo.

> Nosotros tendremos que pagar con nuestro oro, nuestro trabajo o nuestra sangre los privilegios de los gachupines, quienes nos dirán qué podemos comerciar, qué podemos sembrar, cómo debemos vivir . . .
>
> (You know very well that those who were born in this kingdom will never be allowed to occupy the higher posts and that, far from being considered equal, we will always be inferior in every way. We will have to buy with our gold, our work or our blood the privileges reserved for the Spaniards, who will tell us what to sell, what to plant, how to live . . .) (20)

Her words are credible inasmuch as they revive and recharge the words of other criollo patriots, whose letters, essays, and speeches changed the destiny of colonial Spanish America. Just as Simón Bolívar, in his famous *Carta de Jamaica* (*Letter from Jamaica*) (1815), denounced that Americans were treated as second-class citizens within the Spanish system—"no ocupan otro lugar en la sociedad que el de siervos propios para el trabajo, y cuando más el de simples consumidores" (occupy a position in society no better than that of serfs destined for labor, or at best they have no more status than that of mere consumers) (18)—Leona protests: "¿Dónde está el honor de ser esclavo?" (Is there any honor in being a slave?) (20). Addicted to the insurgent movement, in this novel Leona wants to fight like a man but because General Rayón will not accept working with a woman under his command, she asks her lover to fight for both of them: "No seré tuya hasta que con tus palabras hayas construido una patria libre. Nos casaremos cuando nuestra causa haya triunfado . . . ¡A luchar, amor mío! ¡Hazme sentir orgullosa de amarte!" (I won't be yours until you create a free country with your words. We will get married after we win . . . Fight, my love! Make me proud of loving you!) (63).

Perhaps because Leona the patriot combines in a single discourse her passion for Quintana Roo and her undisputable love for Mexico as a free country, some critics have described her heroism as "tacky" and "pretentious" (Sotelo 18). Leaving aside the fact that these comments speak of the distress caused by a complex woman who is concurrently a free thinker, a rebel, and a passionate human being unafraid to hide her supposedly "feminine" emotions, throughout Del Palacio's novel Leona stays true to her patriotic ideals and demonstrates that "love" and "femininity" are not impediments to grow as a revolutionary. This becomes more evident when she educates other women on the importance of the insurgent movement, who live in a bubble of ignorance and claim to know nothing about politics. She asks them to question why there are so many different types of citizens, and why some are considered less than others, even though they were created equal. In view of their indifference, Leona further insists:

> ¿Se han puesto a pensar en quién nos gobierna? ¿Por qué ha de venir a gobernarnos un español desde tan lejos? ¿ . . . alguien que no entiende nada de nosotros, que no nació aquí y que procura no "mancharse" las divinas calzas con nuestro polvo? ¿Por qué la Nueva España es la hija menor? ¡Y peor que eso, la sirvienta, la esclava! Tenemos todo lo necesario para ser independientes.
>
> (Have you thought about who's governing us? Why are we governed by a Spaniard who comes from far away? . . . someone who doesn't understand anything about us, who wasn't born here and who tries not to stain his divine stockings with our dust? Why is New Spain the youngest daughter? And, even worse, the servant, the slave! We have everything we need to be independent.) (116)

Indomitable, Leona fights with words, arguing that it is easier to ignore the problems of New Spain than to try to solve them:

> Sí, es más fácil ignorar lo que ocurre allá afuera. La miseria de las calles y la injusticia constante en el campo y en la ciudad. Es más fácil ignorar que hace casi tres años se levantó un movimiento de mucha gente valiente que estuvo dispuesta a morir para cambiar las cosas y que los españoles de América fuéramos iguales a los de Europa, que no hubiera esclavos y que pudiéramos comerciar con quien nos diera la gana. ¡Tener libertad para escribir, para trabajar, para respirar!
>
> (Yes, it is easier to ignore what happens out there. The misery of the streets and the constant injustice of the country and the city. It is easier to ignore that almost three years ago many courageous people, willing to die, began a movement

> to change things so that the Spaniards from America could be equal to those from Europe, so that there wouldn't be slaves and so that we could trade on our own. To have the freedom to write, to work, to breathe!) (116)

As a dedicated historian, Del Palacio builds her fiction on a solid historical foundation that comes from an in-depth scholarly research,[8] allowing us to recognize Leona Vicario as a woman who used her personal fortune to support the insurgents; suffered imprisonment, poverty, and hunger; and so on. More important, though, Del Palacio does this from a subjective point of view that invites readers to internalize Leona's fears and motivations, her altruistic nature, and her dissident principles (García Argüelles, "Leona Vicario" 119). When Leona gets a copy of the Congreso de Chilpancingo's founding charter from General Morelos, she runs to the public plaza, reads it out loud, and convinces many people of the greatness of the insurgent movement with her tears and courageous spirit. Likewise, in Apatzingán Leona tells her friends, the deputies in charge of crafting a provisional constitution of independence: "Los principios tienen que ser claros para que los entienda todo el mundo. Por favor recuerden, de verdad, quién es el pueblo: no son sólo los americanos hijos de españoles y mestizos . . . el pueblo es el indio y el mulato; el campesino y la mujer" (The values must be clear so that everybody understands them. Please remember who makes up the fatherland: not just the American descendants of Spanish and mestizos but the Indian and the mulatto, the peasant and the woman) (208).

We will never know whether Leona pronounced these words with such vehemence. But they make sense within the world the author has created for the reader, who in turn accepts if not Leona's destiny as a national hero certainly her willingness to fight for an independent country.[9] After seeing Leona in action over the course of many episodes where she appears desolate and hungry, disinclined to betray her fellow insurgents, and wanting to change the future of children, peasants, and former slaves, we empathize with her indignation when she feels that Mexicans have traded one monarchy for another. Along these lines, we share her anger when she realizes that her husband has turned in his former comrades and when she slaps him with all her might, "no con la fuerza de una mujer furiosa, sino la de una verdadera leona enjaulada, de una guerrera desesperada" (not with the strength of a furious woman but that of a caged lioness, a desperate warrior) (298). With the same passion that Leona kisses him or cries for him throughout the novel, she now rejects him: "No quiero volver a verte nunca. Me das vergüenza y asco" (I don't want to see you ever again. You embarrass me. You disgust me) (298).

These twists and turns in the characterization of Leona present her as a rounded character who increases in complexity throughout the novel. By the time we close the book, we are convinced that Leona was a true patriot, committed to obtaining her country's liberty. She comes across as the heroine who would not hesitate to become involved in the insurgent movement if she had to do it again, as she claims in one of her final speeches. Aware of her importance in the War of Independence, a fictional Leona dies in peace, feeling that her mission was accomplished at least in part: "Con sus palabras, con sus sacrificios había contribuido a crear un país independiente, aunque no podía decir que la tarea hubiese concluido. Había ayudado, a golpes de miseria y hambre, a golpes de sangre y frío, a fraguar la libertad . . . aunque la libertad no fuera perfecta" (With her words, with her sacrifices, she had contributed to the creation of an independent country, although she couldn't say that her work had concluded. She had helped, in the midst of misery and hunger, bloody episodes and inclement weather, to forge freedom . . . even if that freedom wasn't perfect) (375).

Conceived as a theatrical farce, Carlos Pascual's novel, *La insurgenta*, questions precisely whether Leona Vicario should be considered the Mother of the Nation given the legends that promote a female profile of self-sacrifice, abnegation, and unquestionable patriotism. In a note titled "Habeas Corpus," at the end of the novel—a trend that we see in many historical novels of the twenty-first century—Pascual explains that he wrote a fictional piece on Vicario to find out more about Mexico's national mother, arguing: "Algo raro nos pasa a los mexicanos con nuestras madres. A la Malinche, nuestra madre primigenia, la odiamos o, por lo menos, nos avergonzamos de ella. Y a la Madre de la Patria, Leona Vicario, la olvidamos" (Something strange happens to us Mexicans with our mothers. We hate Malinche, our first mother, or at least we are embarrassed of her. And we forget the Mother of the Fatherland, Leona Vicario) (239). To save her from the dungeons of history, Pascual reconstructs her profile in a nontraditional narrative: through a series of testimonies gathered right after her passing by the Ayuntamiento de la Ciudad de México. Over the course of three days, during which Leona's corpse begins to rot, the Audiencia commissioned by Antonio López de

Santa Anna gathers in the city's town hall to hear contradictory opinions in regard to Vicario's type of funeral and her posthumous designation as Benemérita y Dulcísima Madre de la Patria.

Pascual's polyphonic narrative has been praised by several critics insofar as the novel gives a wholesome view of Leona Vicario, surrounded by numerous secondary characters who knew her personally and speak either in favor of or against her. As Gabriela Barroso observes, in the voice of each character readers recognize episodes, names, places, and dates associated with Mexico's independence. Instead of crafting a tedious historiographical account, with the typical heroic undertones we find in a number of history textbooks, Pascual composes a set of episodes full of irony and antiheroism, irreverent passages, sarcasm, and humor (Barroso 180). This enthusiastic reading is well founded. Although we do not hear Leona's voice, except when the Audiencia reads a letter published by her in the newspaper *El Federalista Mexicano* (*The Mexican Federalist*), we, as readers and members of the fictional jury, are asked to restructure her historical figure with subjective comments, conflicting opinions, and entertaining personal judgments.

Father Monte Agudo, for instance, one of Leona's former inquisitors, votes in her favor. Although he considers that she disturbed everyone with her rebellious acts, particularly the Catholic Church, the priest deeply admires her: "¡Porque era valiente! ¡Porque tenía cojones! . . . Sostuvo sus dichos, se negó a confesar, se negó a sí misma el miedo . . . ¡se negó la propia flaqueza!" (Because she was brave! Because she had balls! . . . She stuck to her beliefs and refused to confess. She didn't allow herself to be afraid . . . She didn't allow herself any weakness!) (21). María de Sotomayor, Leona's servant, argues with domestic metaphors that Leona deserves to be named Madre de la Patria because she educated many people around her and revolutionized the nation. Apparently, Leona taught her, an Indian woman, that the fatherland was a house that had to be swept and mopped, painted, repaired, and maintained as livable. Benito Juárez does not use any metaphors to defend Leona in the letter he sends to the Audiencia, but he claims that "Doña Leona Vicario de Quintana Roo es la representación máxima del sacrificio y la pasión femenina en la defensa de la Patria" (Doña Leona Vicario de Quintana Roo is the best representation of sacrifice and feminine passion in defense of the Fatherland) (108).

Those who vote against her also present convincing arguments that nonetheless add humor to the narrative. The alleged painter of one of her anonymous portraits, Don Domingo Ortiz, for example, says that he cannot vote in favor of a pretentious woman who told him that his painting was "una soberana porquería y que ella, además, no tenía semejante papada" (a royal piece of shit and that she didn't have such a jowl) (39). Doña María Ignacia Rodríguez de Velasco y Osorio, the famous Güera Rodríguez, argues that the nation does not need a Sweet Mother but could always benefit from having a great lover such as herself: "¡La Dulcísima Amante de la Patria!" (The Sweetest Lover of the Fatherland) (116). Always ironic, Rodríguez does not waste the opportunity to highlight her contributions to the nation as an exemplary patriot and the lover of Agustín de Iturbide. Her arguments become more belligerent as she says that although Leona Vicario fought for her country's independence, she did not do anything for the liberation of women. Instead, she continues, Vicario taught them to stay at home as virtuous and respectable wives and mothers.

The explicit confrontation of these comments in the novel requires readers to reflect on Leona's attributed patriotism, based on numerous bits and pieces that indeed question official and unofficial history, as well as popular myths and legends around the formation of a female hero (García Argüelles, "Leona Vicario" 123). After winning Random House's Premio Bicentenario de Novela Histórica, in an interview for *La Jornada* Pascual expressed that he wrote this novel to highlight the role of women in the revolutionary movement for independence, precisely during the creation of the country's heroes and most illustrious figures (Montaño Garfias). This is true. The novel itself is dedicated to a great number of revolutionary women who have not received as much attention as the men who fought for Mexican independence, such as "Carmen Camacho, fusilada" (shot), "Gertudris Bocanegra, fusilada" (shot), "Juana Bautista Márquez, ahorcada" (hanged), "Ana Villegas, muerta en prisión" (killed in prison), "Mariana Rodríguez de Lazarín, condenada a prisión" (sentenced to prison), or "Antonia Nava, 'La Generala,' que ofreció a sus hijos como soldados" (who offered her children as soldiers) (7–8).

At the same time, however, the novel denounces the political benefits of having national heroes in times of turmoil. We understand this better when President López de Santa Anna demands in a burst of anger that the Audiencia name Leona Vicario Benemérita Madre de la Patria as soon as possible. He wants the members of the Audiencia to grasp the idea that in difficult times unfortunate events like the death of an individual can be turned around for the well-being of the nation, thanks to the wisdom and astuteness of a wise politician such as himself. Just in case his message were not clear enough, he further argues:

> Refrescar la memoria a los ciudadanos de los actos valientes y honrosos de nuestros héroes es algo siempre útil que propicia un mayor afecto a nuestra patria y, en consecuencia, una mayor conciencia civil. Será bueno desempolvar un poco al señor Morelos, al señor López Rayón y a la misma señora Vicario. Hay que sacudir un poco el pantéon de la Patria y darle lustre a nuestros bronces, que bastante opacos los veo en estos días . . . El punto es que los ciudadanos necesitan fervientemente una distracción a tantas desgracias y apuros.
>
> (It is always useful to refresh the citizens' memory in regard to the brave and honorable acts of our heroes. This promotes stronger feelings for our nation and, consequently, a greater civil consciousness. It will be good to dust off Mr. Morelos, Mr. López Rayón and Mrs. Vicario. We must shake up a bit our nation's pantheon and shine our bronze statues that I see is rather lackluster these days . . . The point is that citizens earnestly need a distraction to forget about so many troubles and misfortunes.) (226–27)

In a country of recently acquired democratic rights, Licenciado Ortiz Vega, either confused or insulted by the president's speech, asks him: "¿Pan y circo, señor Presidente?" (Bread and circus, Mr. President?) (227), only to find out from a violent Santa Anna: "¡¡Pan y su tiznada madre si no se sienta en este momento a redactar el bando que quiero publicado mañana a primera hora en los periódicos nacionales!!" (Bread and your screwed mother if you don't sit down right now to write the proclamation that I want published first thing tomorrow morning in the national newspapers!!) (227).

No wonder Canal Once attracted large audiences in summer 2015 with *Réquiem por Leona Vicario* (*Requiem for Leona Vicario*), a TV mini-series produced by Patricia Arriaga with Carlos Pascual's screenplay, based on *La insurgenta*. The series was composed of four thirty-minute episodes addressing the formation of the nation and its main protagonists as well as its democratic flaws and failures. Not coincidentally, the series was filmed in November 2014, in the midst of numerous scandals associated with President Enrique Peña Nieto's corrupt government—his $7 million "White House" in Las Lomas de Chapultepec, the mass kidnapping and disappearance of forty-three male students from the Ayotzinapa Rural Teachers' College, and the growing number of unpunished femicides throughout the country. How can we not associate Santa Anna's despotism, authoritarianism, and hypocrisy—"¡Si no me han hecho Benemérita a la señora Vicario antes de una hora, los habré de considerar a todos ustedes como traidores de la patria y sabrán de la autoridad del señor Presidente!" (If you haven't named Mrs. Vicario Benemérita within an hour, I will consider you traitors to the nation and you will understand the president's authority) (227)—with Peña Nieto's empty speeches and aloof discourses that evade action and justice but assure Mexicans that they are "overcoming" their tragedies because "the best route to the future is the road of laws and institutions"? (Agren).

Female patriots like Leona Vicario are unfortunately recognized, as we read in her historical epitaph, included in Pascual's fiction, "por sus distinguidos servicios, superiores a su sexo" (for her distinguished services, superior to her sex) (230). She is an exception to the rule, and above all the virtuous wife of Quintana Roo. As Montserrat Galí Boadella states in her study *Historias del bello sexo* (*Histories of the Beautiful Sex*), Leona Vicario's situation shows that Mexican independence did not include the liberation of women (59). Ironically, her comment on a heroine of the early nineteenth century is still true today, in an age that promotes gender equality, equal rights, and social justice.

Interestingly, in 1994 US novelist Elizabeth Borton de Treviño, who lived in Mexico since 1935 until her death in 2001, published in English a novel titled *Leona: A Love Story*. "Based on a true story," the novel twists some of Vicario's scattered biographical facts and adds hyperbolic details in order to attract young readers. In this fictional version, Leona has a Spanish mother and a Mexican father who is related to the famous poet Netzahualcóyotl. When they pass away, she becomes "the richest heiress in the country" (5). She is first engaged to Don Conrado Obregón but soon meets the love of her life: Andrés, with whom she discusses literature, politics, and the future of the country. When she escapes with the rebels, this Leona dresses up as a boy; she does not have to give birth in a cave, as the legend goes; after the war, she is recognized with the "lovely title" of "Heroine of the Independence" (144). In the end, she confesses to her husband, in the last lines of the novel, "Ah, Andrés, no title could ever mean more to me than Señora de Quintana Roo" (144). Her patriotism does not represent a threat to the established patriarchal order.

Love in the Time of Independence

As has been noted in the analysis of these contemporary novels, Mexican intellectual and politician Lucas Alamán, minister of Interior and Exterior Relations of Mexico during Leona Vicario's lifetime, openly diminished her heroism in public, stating that she was moved by romantic passion and became an insurgent only to follow Quintana Roo (Galí Boadella 57; García 142). In response to his attacks, Leona Vicario published an argumentative letter in *El Federalista Mexicano*, which Pascual includes in his novel, stating in her defense:

> Mi objeto en querer desmentir la impostura de que mi patriotismo tuvo por origen el amor, no es otro que el muy justo deseo de que mi memoria no pase a mis nietos con la fea nota de haber sido una atronada que abandoné mi casa por seguir a un amante . . . En la correspondencia interceptada no apareció ninguna carta amatoria, y el mismo empeño que tuvo el gobierno español para que yo descubriera a los individuos que escribían con nombres fingidos prueba bastantemente que mi prisión se originó por un servicio que presté a mi patria. Si cree Ud. que el amor fue el móvil de mis acciones, ¿qué conexión pudo haber tenido éste con la firmeza que manifesté ocultando, como debía, los nombres de los individuos que escribían por mi conducto, siendo así que ninguno de ellos era mi amante? Confiese Ud., Sr. Alamán, que no sólo el amor es móvil de las acciones de las mujeres: que ellas son capaces de todos los entusiasmos, y que los deseos de la gloria y de la libertad de la patria no les son unos sentimientos extraños.
>
> (I want to clarify that my patriotism was not born out of love because I do not want my grandchildren to think that I was crazy and that I abandoned my home just to follow my lover . . . None of the letters that were intercepted dealt with love, and the fact that the Spanish government wanted me to reveal the names of the people who signed their letters with

> pseudonyms proves that I was imprisoned because I was at the service of my fatherland. If you believe, Sir, that I behaved as I did because I was in love, what logical connection do you find between my love and my determination to not reveal the names of the individuals who sent their letters my way, if none of them were my lovers? Accept, Mr. Alamán, that women are not simply moved by love, that they are capable of feeling enthusiasm, and that they also desire the glory and liberty of their fatherland.) (158)

To further prove her genuine heroism in Pascual's fiction as she did in real life using words as weapons, Leona Vicario continues:

> En todas las naciones del mundo ha sido apreciado el patriotismo de las mujeres: ¿por qué, pues, mis paisanos, aunque no sean todos, han querido ridiculizarlo como si fuera un sentimiento impropio en ellas? ¿Qué tiene de extraño ni ridículo el que una mujer ame a su patria y le preste los servicios que pueda para que a estos se les dé, por burla, el título de heroísmo romancesco?
>
> (Women's patriotism has been appreciated in all the nations of the world. Why is it, then, that some of my own people have ridiculed their participation saying that such patriotic expressions are inappropriate in women? Why does a woman's love for her country and service to her fatherland have to be considered romantic heroism?) (159)

Years later, in defense of her deceased mother, a fictional María Dolores Quintana Vicario confronts Lucas Alamán on the second day of testimonies, recalling Leona's hardships during the War of Independence or the terrible living conditions in which Leona gave birth to Dolores's sister, Genoveva. Offended by Alamán's insistence on treating Leona's heroism as a mere romantic impulse, Dolores asks him:

> ¿Insiste usted en la idea de que mi madre vivió, por un mero gusto romancesco, hambre, persecuciones y se refugió en cuevas y en establos tan sólo para emular a las heroínas folletinescas? . . . Bien poco romántico debe ser el vivir en

> medio de los bosques y los campos, con las ropas desgarradas, oliendo a sangre, a sudor, a orines, deponiendo los estómagos al aire libre, entre los matorrales y las zarzas. ¿Qué tendrá de romántico o de aventurero comer higos, zapotes o changungas verdes, robadas de algún árbol, para después largar el cuerpo en diarreas interminables?
>
> (Do you insist on saying that my mother endured, out of romantic passion, hunger and persecution, and that she sought refuge in caves and barns just to emulate some melodramatic heroines? . . . It cannot be all that romantic to live in the woods and the country with torn clothes, with the smell of blood, sweat, urine, having to empty your stomach out in the open, in the midst of scrubs and bushes. What is so romantic about eating figs, sapodillas, green nances stolen from a tree that will later give you endless diarrhea?) (165)

I mention these instances—historical and fictional—in which Leona and her daughter respond to Alamán's misogynist judgment in Pascual's novel because they confront head on the nineteenth-century belief that women were not capable of having disinterested patriotic feelings and could only be moved by emotions and not reason (Macías, *Contra viento* 22). In the novel, a retired soldier calls Leona a hysterical woman who acts according to the weakness of her gender. The famous journalist Guillermo Prieto, who knew her personally, considers that she was above all an outstanding wife whose noble service to the country did not prevent her from going back home as soon as the war ended. Simply put, she did what any noble woman would have done in her situation: she helped her husband free the nation, but after several years of hardships and struggle, she was happy to take care of her daughters at home. After highlighting her maternal instinct, he begs the Audiencia to remember before anything else her sacred role as a woman, wife, and mother, using a powerful argument within a male-dominant society: "Hacer lo contrario sería traicionar el relicario de virtudes de las mujeres mexicanas que de manera entusiasta han confundido el amor y deber, y así, henchidas de pasión, abrazaron de manera vehemente las causas de nuestra tierra" (Otherwise, we would betray the many virtues of all Mexican women who have enthusiastically confused love for duty, and, in this manner, full of passion, have fought with vehemence for our fatherland) (112–13).

Interestingly, in this novel it is not Leona Vicario but the character of Andrés Quintana Roo who delivers a pathetic lover's discourse, tainted by the anguish, pain, endless suffering, and extreme anxiety that Roland Barthes observes in similar discourses that seek to reveal the secrets of a broken heart (*Lover's* 29–30). After expressing in various ways that Leona is dead, Quintana Roo asks the Audiencia to go on with their deliberations indefinitely so he may keep her by his side without having to bury her. Defeated by the absence of the loved one, he feels empty and worthless:

> No deberían los maridos enterrar a sus esposas y menos cuando éstas han sido compañeras, cómplices, amigas. Jamás habría pasado por mi mente, ni en mis peores pesadillas, vivir este infierno . . . El infierno se ha asentado en las manos de mi Leona de las que todo nacía, crecía y florecía. El infierno es el silencio en los labios de Leona, y el silencio habla porque un ser maligno ha colocado un candado en sus labios y después ha tirado la llave en el más profundo y obscuro pozo del vacío . . . Tan sólo suplico, ruego, imploro de rodillas que no me quiten a mi Leona, a mi Leona, mi esposa amada.
>
> (Husbands shouldn't have to bury their wives, especially not when they were our companions, accomplices, friends. The idea of living this hell never crossed my mind, not even in my worst nightmares . . . Hell has taken possession of Leona's hands, where everything grew and flowered. Hell is the silence on Leona's lips, and silence speaks because an evil being has put a lock on her lips and has thrown the key into the deepest and darkest well . . . I only ask, beg, and implore on my knees that my Leona is not taken away from me. My Leona, my beloved wife.) (184)

It is hard to recognize the illustrious figure of Quintana Roo, the patriot who served as a member of the Congress of Chilpancingo, the man who presided the Constitutional Assembly in charge of drafting the Declaration of Independence in 1813, the senator, the legislator. Historically, as Barthes argues, the discourse of absence has been carried on by women: they give shape to absence and elaborate its fiction, while the men who wait and suffer, on the other hand, are "miraculously feminized" (*Lover's* 14). By attributing these supposedly "feminine" words to a male hero such as Quintana Roo, intratextually the novel kills two birds with one stone: it banishes the idea that Vicario was a mere follower of her husband and simultaneously places any hints of romance, passiveness, longing, desperation, and domesticity usually attributed to women in the discourse of a man who represents hegemony.

In Eugenio Aguirre's novel, in contrast, all of Leona's patriotic actions seem to be fueled by her love for her future husband. True to her fictional role as a romantic character (Sotelo 17), at the beginning she cannot help but fall in love with the young Quintana Roo. Although the lovers care about the future of Mexico and discuss politics, the narrator sends the message that they are, above everything, genuinely in love with each other. Leona is not afraid to share this information with some of her friends and tells Doña Gertrudis del Castillo that she cannot wait to become Andrés's wife to find happiness in a home of her own: "Quiero casarme con Andrés tan pronto como sea posible, a pesar de la oposición de mi tío Agustín; soy mujer y tengo derecho a la felicidad de un hogar" (I want to marry Andrés as soon as possible, regardless of my uncle's disapproval; I am a woman and have the right to be happy at home) (34). Soon after, when Andrés is about to join the dissident movement, an enamored Leona assures him that she will wait for him, declaring: "Yo te esperaré, Andrés. Dispón tu partida, y que la Virgen te cuide" (I will wait for you, Andrés. Arrange your departure, and I hope the Virgin takes care of you) (61). It is easy to see why this novel has been criticized for its lack of experimentation. In his introductory note, Aguirre promises to reveal the story of a woman whose intelligence and heart found love and hope in the midst of a chaotic world. He gives us just that without any kind of suspense or interior development, relying on romantic clichés that are predictable: the devoted woman who loves her man, the heroine who prays for her lover, the future wife who knows how to wait and when to be there for her husband (García Argüelles, "Leona" 122).

Months later, when Leona escapes from the Colegio de Belén and joins the insurgents, Andrés also behaves like the romantic lover we expect in this type of novel. Desperate to open his heart to Leona, he does not leave any room for the reader's imagination to wonder outside the limits of the written page. "Si supieras cómo sueño con estar juntos, con que formemos nuestra propia familia, construyendo nuestro mundo" (If you only knew that I dream of being together, of having our own family and building our world), says the lover, using words that come from a script. "Si supieras cómo he esperado este momento para decirte que te amo y que ansío hacerte mi esposa inmediatamente" (If you only knew how much I've waited for this moment to tell you that I love you and that I want to make you my wife as soon as possible) (124). In sync with this unsurprising discourse, Leona answers like a soap opera star who has memorized her lines: "Lo sé, Andrés, por eso veo en ti a mi compañero" (I know, Andrés, that's why I see you as my partner) (124).

The love discourse we find here resembles that of Alexis Pola's 1982 soap opera, *Leona Vicario*, where Mexico's independence heroine is depicted as a beautiful and intelligent woman, tragically in love with Quintana Roo. Under the direction of Luis Guillermo Basurto and Wilebaldo López, Mexican actress Diana Bracho interpreted the role of Leona Vicario, and the soap opera, aired on Canal 4, attracted a large viewing audience. Like the typical romantic heroine of a *telenovela de época*, a young Leona appears in various scenes reading a book to her lover, discussing politics with other men, arguing about the future of the new republic, and expressing her thoughts on freedom and democracy. She is often reprimanded by men and women around her for being "demasiado enérgica" (too strong-willed), and "demasiado mandona" (too bossy). Ultimately, though, her courage does not prevent her from feeling afraid of entering a bloody war that takes the lives of many. As expected of this TV drama, Leona's husband provides her strength; he is the reason she fights for independence, and she follows him unconditionally.[10]

Similarly, the melodramatic undertones we find in Aguirre's novel weaken the portrayal of Leona Vicario as a heroine of Mexican independence. She is, as the author announces in his introduction, an honorable woman who deserves a literary homage for her services to the nation especially—if not exclusively—for her intimate association with a male patriot, Quintana Roo. This poor conclusion is to be expected from a bestseller that offers the story of a patriotic couple as "ejemplo de lo que puede ser una buena relación matrimonial, basada en el respeto, en la comunicación franca, en la espontaneidad, en la confianza" (an example of what could be a good marital relationship, based on respect, open communication, spontaneity, and trust) (10). Predictably, in the last three pages Leona Vicario is finally at home like a model wife and mother who has no political ambitions and is happy to be there after a long struggle—"¡Cuántos años, Andrés de mi alma, cuántos años soñando con este hermoso día!" (I've dreamt of this beautiful day for so long, Andrés, my love!) (168).

Certainly, a great deal of Del Palacio's novel sells the love story of Vicario and Quintana Roo. But at least the story that we find in the novel *Leona* is well rounded: it allows us to see the protagonists from an intimate perspective, and we feel their unexpected transformations, their inner dilemmas, and existential turning points (Alba Villalobos 55). The development of a romantic setting becomes apparent from the moment Del Palacio intertwines the lives of her characters with threads of the epistolary genre and the *novela de folletín* of typical romanticized scenarios (García Argüelles, "Leona" 120). The more the young Andrés spies on Leona, the more she becomes disturbed by his presence, to the point that they can no longer resist the temptation to be together:

> Andrés y Leona se las arreglaban para escapar hasta un rincón oscuro y beberse los labios, sorberse los sueños, buscarse la piel por encima de la tela que los cubría, para luego regresar jadeantes y ruborizados, escondiendo apenas la excitación entre los gritos de sus amigos en defensa de la patria.
>
> (Andrés and Leona would manage to find a dark corner to passionately kiss each other, to share their dreams, to grope at each other's skin through their clothes, before going back panting and flushed, trying to hide their excitement in front of their patriotic friends' shouting.) (56)

This type of sensual discourse that appears every so often in the novel allows us to imagine why Leona undergoes a series of hardships knowing that in the end Andrés will be there for her. As the torn protagonist becomes the emblematic body of a tormented country with painful blisters on her feet, a growing rash, and unimaginable sores of all types, what sustains her is the altruistic love for the nation and the love she feels for Quintana Roo, whose memory keeps her calm.

Leona's desire to see her lover grows as the insurgents become stronger, and the letters they write to each other during the war fuel the novel's romantic spirit. These letters, however, mimic the epistolary genre of the late eighteenth and early nineteenth centuries and therefore represent the space where individual psychologies are allowed to grow with discretion and audacity (Monsiváis, *Género epistolar* 17). In one of these letters, for instance, which Leona reads "para llenarse los ojos y el corazón con las noticias de su amado" (to fill her eyes and heart with news of her lover) (173), Andrés assures her that he can no longer live without her: "no dejo de pensar que deberías estar aquí conmigo, iluminando mis días y mis noches con la luz de tu inteligencia y de tu belleza, las que ni un solo día he dejado de tener presentes en mi corazón" (I cannot stop thinking that you should be here with me, illuminating my days and nights with the light of your intelligence and your beauty, which my heart hasn't forgotten all these days) (174). When they finally see each other, after two years apart, their love and passion are capable of erasing at once the troubles and pains suffered during the war. From Leona's romantic perspective, nothing has happened: no one had died, she had never been imprisoned, and she had not been hurt. Andrés experiences a similar sensation that combines their uncontainable passion with the country's optimistic hopes of liberation. When he makes love to Leona, he forgets not only that he was incarcerated by the viceroy but three centuries of slavery, all promises of equality, the high taxes, the cruelty of the governing class. To top it all off, their first sexual encounter after the extended absence echoes the success of the insurgents. While Leona is having passionate sex with Andrés, she recognizes herself as a sexual being and, in her climatic moment, remembers that the rebels have declared that Mexico will be a free country, independent, and sovereign.

What saves the foundations of Del Palacio's novel from rupturing, due to an accumulation of romantic and sensual scenes in which the lovers are consumed by their obvious passion, are the novelistic moments that portray them in a raw state, with no hints of romanticism and away from idealized scenarios. Leona's pregnancy, for instance, is described as a heavy burden; it slows her down; it is not a heavenly gift that symbolizes the fruit of her love, or a spiritual and sacred bond, according to Christian theology (Guerra 54), but a physical impediment. Unlike what we would expect from the protagonist of a *novela de folletín*, Leona is upset with the changes of a body that now fails her and reminds her that she has limitations. Absolutely humanized, when Leona's water breaks, she screams: "Ay, Andrés. ¡Cómo duele, carajo!" (Oh, Andrés. This fucking hurts!) (223). In a sense, the pregnant Leona that we see here contradicts the static and idealized images of a *mater dolorosa*; instead, she occupies a space of her own, "another space" that simultaneously destabilizes and alters her surroundings with a vibrant new life (Guerra 55–58). After hours of painful labor and desperation, Leona shows herself not as an altruistic heroine of abstract dreams and national ideals but as a woman who fears for her child's safety in an unprotected cave: "¿Y si nos atrapan? ¿Y si hay alimañas en esta cueva? ¿Si le pica un alacrán? ¿Y si se me muere mi niña, Andrés? . . . ¿Si se me seca la leche? ¿Si no le puedo dar de comer?" (What if they find us? What if there are vermin in this cave? What if a scorpion stings her? And what if my baby dies, Andrés? . . . What if my milk dries out? What if I can't feed her?) (228).

In tune with these humanized scenes, the puppy love that Leona and Andrés cultivate in the first pages of the novel becomes a full-blown carnal passion when they live as fugitives. In one instance, after Leona reminds Andrés that she joined the insurgent cause of her own initiative and not simply to follow him, the couple makes passionate love to overcome their personal differences and the misfortunes of war. As they find comfort in each other's bodies, and as we witness them biting their necks and scratching their backs until they end up "sudorosos y jadeantes" (sweating and moaning) (246), we get to know these characters in depth. Unlike most pornographic discourses whose protagonists generally are only seen from the outside, due to an intentional emotional flatness that requires a sexual response from the reader (Sontag, *Styles* 54), the erotic discourse here reveals the inner layers of two characters clearly in love and afraid of their future. Thus, their sexual scenes let us perceive their hopes and disillusion, their insecurities in regard to the nation, and their fear of a negative final outcome. Instead of the repetition and monotony that we find in books that are only erotic, the sexual activity that the main characters develop in this novel changes over time, in harmony with their humanity (Vargas Llosa, *La civilización* 114). In one last sexual scene, for example, the lovers have considerably aged. Andrés has lost the vigor of youth, and Leona's breasts and legs have lost some of their firmness and beauty. What matters, though, is not that they are still capable of making passionate love but the fact that in that precise moment, they are able to "read" each other intimately. Andrés tells Leona that he would love to stay in her arms forever, but as he says that, she reminds him that he will always be at the mercy of his country's politics: "Mentiroso—murmuró Leona medio dormida entre sus brazos. En cuanto te llame Santa Anna te irás de ministro o a cualquier encargo del señor presidente" (Liar—whispered Leona, half-asleep in his arms. As soon as Santa Anna calls you, you will work for his cabinet and you'll do whatever he asks you to do) (365).

Evidently, affect is in the heart of all these novels, which includes sexual desires, love, passion, feelings, mixed emotions, and sentimental conflicts. But only in the most convincing scenarios, such as those created by Del Palacio and Pascual, the display of affect reveals the protagonists' ethical and moral dilemmas, their political agendas, their fears and internal troubles. After all, affect allows us to simultaneously enter the realm of the real, the symbolic, and the imaginary; it moves carefully between control and excess, to construct and deconstruct preconceived ideas, transgressive behaviors, and dissident movements (Moraña, "El afecto" 323–24).

A Woman Who Knows Latin . . .

In 2010, Leopoldo Gómez produced for Televisa the series *Gritos de muerte y libertad* (*Shoutings of Death and Freedom*). The series was conceived as an in-depth reflection of the Mexican War of Independence, and the directors (Mafer Suárez and Gerardo Tort) were advised by such renowned historians as Enrique Krauze, Héctor Aguilar Camín, and Enrique Florescano. In the ninth episode, titled "Retrato de una Leona" (Portrait of a Lioness) Cecilia Suárez plays the role of Leona Vicario. Over the course of twenty-five minutes, we revisit what we already know about this heroine: that she served as an insurgent messenger, was imprisoned for her dissident actions, escaped with the help of the rebels (disguising herself as a black woman), and gave birth to her first daughter in a cave. In the opening scene, however, Leona appears in front of the camera writing a letter to the rebels in a coded language of her own. In a barn, she is surrounded by several pieces of paper, an inkwell, and a writing quill. She writes in secret and later undergoes trial for the letters she has written to the dissident Guadalupes, whose pseudonyms come from her favorite literature. When Morelos, during the Congreso de Chilpancingo, creates a constitution for the new republic with other men, he politely dismisses Leona after acknowledging her patriotism. However, in the last episode that ends in 1824, portraying Leona at home and taking care of her daughters and husband, she is sitting at her desk like an intellectual. This time she writes—a letter? an article?—about her services to free her nation from the Spanish monarchy.

The image of Leona Vicario as a woman intellectual who reads and writes is also present in García's biography, where she is recognized as an avid reader of adventure novels and a skilled writer and secret insurgent messenger. It is not an ordinary image of the early nineteenth century, especially if we consider that the education of the Spanish and criolla women of New Spain did not always include an exposure to selected literary readings or learning how to exercise and master the art of writing (Gonzalbo Aizpuru 353–54). The vast majority of women received a basic education, which consisted of memorizing devotional prayers and the catechism, reading fluently and writing poorly, embroidering, knitting, dancing, singing, and perhaps playing an instrument; in general, very few of them went to school and most of them were left ignorant (Flores Castillo 152). Consequently, as Castellanos recalls in *Mujer que sabe latín . . .* , most of the female characters that we find in nineteenth-century Mexican literature appear in the background so that a man can be neatly perceived as the sole protagonist, as the *caudillo* who executes plans and designs a better future (123). Leona, however, is not a quiet character in the background of all action, although history and popular tradition insist on selling the idea that "a heroine" is simply "the hero's lover" (Monsiváis, *Misógino* 107).[11] This is the empowered image of Vicario conveyed in Del Palacio's *Leona* and Pascual's *La insurgenta*.

In Del Palacio's novel, Leona exchanges letters with the insurgents, studies diligently of her own initiative, and shares her knowledge with numerous people around her. Besides instructing other women, as we have seen before, on the need to participate in their country's politics, she works at the press and finds time to teach the Indians, the blacks, and the mestizos how to read and write. Thanks to her frequent interactions with them, Leona wonders if they are all equal and, more important, if a new country could be built with people who believe in spells and pacts with the devil and spend most of their lives drinking mezcal and pulque. Later on, when she receives the founding charter from the Congreso de Chilpancingo, Leona behaves like a true intellectual who confronts power from a marginal position: "Leona se hizo oír. A gritos, enjugándose las lágrimas, leyó el discurso del generalísimo. Y la gente la escuchó en silencio referirse a las crueldades de los gachupines y cómo celebraban como salvajes, las desdichas y la desunión de los libertadores" (Leona made them listen to her. Screaming, wiping away her tears, she read the general's speech. And people listened to her in silence as she referred to the cruelties of the Spaniards and how they celebrated like savages the misfortunes and division of the liberators) (181).[12]

Unlike the other women around her, the soldiers' wives who complain about their harsh lives, in this novel Leona spends a great deal of her time acting as the children's teacher, even with a lack of books and school utensils. She gets up early each morning to supervise that the children are clean and ready to learn, and she teaches them the alphabet by drawing the letters on the ground. Reflexive at all times, Leona, a woman well versed in Greek mythology, cannot help but compare her life to that of the literary characters who inhabit her books. As a result, Del Palacio's novel fashions itself as a "pensive text" whose meaning surpasses the limits of the written page (Barthes, *S/Z* 216). I say this because Leona's arguments consistently invite us to think of the bigger picture at stake. At some point, for instance, when Leona and her family enter Toluca not knowing where to stay, she realizes that life is not the way it appears in her adventure novels:

> Mientras iban recorriendo las calles y perdiéndose entre el bullicio de los vendedores y transeúntes, Leona, sin saber por qué, pensó en Telémaco y en Ulises; se dio cuenta de que el viaje que ella había hecho era como los que emprendían los héroes míticos: un viaje de los que nunca terminan, un viaje en el que el héroe casi nunca puede regresar a casa. ¡Y ella que encontraba esas travesías tan atractivas! ¡Tan llenas de ilusión! Nunca se había puesto a pensar que Telémaco se llenaba de lodo y que también le dolía el vientre al quedarse sin comer durante muchos días. ¿Habría tenido que conformarse con un caldo de verdolagas sin sal en alguna de las islas que había visitado? ¿Le habría picado un alacrán? No era lo mismo leer las aventuras que vivirlas en carne propia.
>
> (As they walked through the streets, surrounded by noisy street vendors and passersby, Leona, without knowing why, thought of Telemachus and Ulysses. She realized that her journey was like the one that mythical heroes would undertake: a journey that never ends, a journey that almost always prevents the hero from returning home. And she had found those voyages so attractive! So full of hope! She had never thought that Telemachus got dirty and that his stomach hurt after not eating for several days. Did he have to satisfy his hunger with a soup of wild purslane without any salt in some of the islands that he had visited? Had a scorpion bitten him? Reading these adventures was not the same as living them). (241–42)

The knowledge presented here surpasses the limits of what is actually written and remains on hold as "supplementary" and "unexpected" information; its true meaning is revealed later as the protagonist's pensiveness flourishes over the course of the novel and surprises us when we least expect it (Barthes, *S/Z* 216). When Andrés treats her like a woman who does not understand that they have to give up part of their original dreams and hopes to be a free nation, Leona loses her temper and distances herself from the women who are ridiculed in several political pamphlets: "No me hables así. No me trates como a esas mujeres que caricaturizan en los panfletos: lerdas y estúpidas que no entienden nada de nada. ¡Claro que me doy cuenta! ¡Me doy cuenta de todo!" (Don't talk to me like that. Don't treat me like one of those women who are portrayed in the pamphlets as dumb and stupid. Of course I understand what's going on! I understand everything!) (262). That Leona speaks like this is indeed revolutionary. Throughout Mexican history, the few complex women who have entered the discourse of literature have done so as mere abstractions that follow previously conceived models and reflect inherited patriarchal mythologies (Monsiváis, *Misógino* 28).

When the press makes fun of Leona and calls her Quintana Roo's agent and wife, or a "quijote con enaguas" (Quixote wearing a skirt) (337), she writes combative responses and publishes them in *El Federalista Mexicano*. She is, as she declares to a man in the last pages of the novel, a woman who defends herself with the word. We believe her because Del Palacio manipulates various historical archives, recontextualizes them, and transgresses their form and content to set forth a particular type of documentary writing, one that renovates the past in the present, giving us the impression that history is just happening as we move through the pages of the book (Rivera Garza, *Los muertos* 114). Consequently, the letter Vicario writes to Lucas Alamán in real life, tactfully included at the end the novel, only confirms what we have seen since the very first pages: the portrait of a woman unafraid to defend herself in a misogynist world or, more precisely, a woman writer who becomes the scribe of her own body and constructs with her words and actions an autonomous identity (Guerra 51). This fearless woman writes:

> Confiese usted, señor Alamán, que no sólo el amor es el móvil de las acciones de las mujeres: que ellas son capaces de todos los entusiasmos y que los deseos de la gloria y la libertad de la patria no les son unos sentimientos extraños, antes bien,

suelen obrar en ellas con más vigor, como que siempre los sacrificios de las mujeres, sea cual fuere la causa por quien los hacen, son más desinteresados y parece que no buscan más recompensa de ellas, más de la que sean aceptados.

Si Madame de Staël atribuye algunas acciones de patriotismo de las mujeres a la pasión amorosa, esto no probará jamás que sean incapaces de ser patriotas, cuando el amor no las estimula a que lo sean.

Por lo que a mí toca, sé decir que mis acciones y opiniones han sido siempre muy libres, nadie ha influido absolutamente en ellas y en este punto he obrado siempre con total independencia, y sin atender a las opiniones que han tenido las personas que he estimado. Me persuado de que así serán todas las mujeres, exceptuando a las muy estúpidas y a las que por efecto de su educación hayan contraído un hábito servil. De ambas clases hay también muchísimos hombres.

(Accept, Mr. Alamán, that women are not simply moved by love, that they are capable of feeling enthusiasm, and that they also desire the glory and liberty of their fatherland more vigorously than men. After all, women's sacrifice, regardless of who they do it for, is more selfless: they don't want to be rewarded; they just want their sacrifices to be accepted.

If Madame de Staël attributes certain female patriotic actions to amorous passion, this will never prove that they are incapable of being patriots, when love doesn't encourage them to be patriotic.

As for me, I can say that my actions and opinions have always been free, that nobody has influenced them, and, in this regard, I have always been very independent, without taking into account what other people have thought of them. I want to believe that all women are like this, except for the very stupid ones or those who have adopted servile habits due to their education. There are plenty of men who represent both types.) (343)

Leona's words—historical, indeed—revamp her gendered self-defense in the twenty-first century, allowing us to scrutinize, from a contemporary feminist perspective, several forms of oppression and the social subordination of women that has negatively affected the construction of female subjectivities in colonial and postcolonial Mexico (Gargallo 34).

Working as a writer of documentary fiction who approaches historical facts and archives with the utmost creativity and sensibility, as if he were playing a musical instrument or creating a higher form of art that nonetheless echoes the original source (Rivera Garza, *Los muertos* 128), Pascual presents Leona Vicario as a multifaceted woman intellectual. In his novel, the servant María de Soto Mayor recalls that the soon-to-be Benemérita de la Patria wrote many letters and spoke with wisdom and prudence. During the first day of testimonies, when Don Domingo Ortiz protests the fact that Leona was allowed to publish vane and unimportant articles in the newspaper, the Audiencia reminds him that the nation has greatly benefited from Leona's lucid liberal arguments published in national newspapers, for which she is considered Mexico's first woman journalist. Although Doctor José Moreno Jove tries to convince the Audiencia that Vicario was insane—"¿No son las mujeres, débiles, enfermizas e histéricas el vehículo ideal para las obras del Maligno?" (Aren't the weak, sickly, and hysterical women the ideal vehicle to transport the work of Evil?) (93)—in view of the many cryptic documents of strange signs that she sent to the insurgents, her work as a journalist is undeniable. Don Víctor Bravo argues that Leona Vicario wrote numerous anonymous articles for *El Ilustrador Americano* (*American Illustrator*), an insurgent newspaper. She was, according to him, not just Quintana Roo's wife and collaborator but "la amanuense, la correctora, la tipógrafa y, ciertamente, la autora de muchos de los textos" (the scribe, the editor, the typographer and, certainly, the author of many of those texts) (123). Vicario's elegance, Bravo further claims, was her trademark, and her arguments resembled Sor Juana's writing.

His words, evidently hyperbolic, reveal the portrait of a learned woman, an intellectual who thinks without restrictions and expresses her conception of the world with a heroic attitude, within established limits (Castellanos, "Esplendor" 369, "La corrupción" 198). The conception of Leona as a woman intellectual is solidified when Manuel de la Concha asserts that both Quintana Roo and Vicario used words as weapons: "Sus armas eran las palabras; sus pensamientos, sus bayonetas y sus preclaros razonamientos eran esgrimidos con la misma maestría con la que un espadachín maneja el florete" (Their words were their weapons; their thoughts were their bayonets and their clear arguments were applied with the skill of a swordsman) (174–75). Unlike other witnesses who depict Leona as a hysterical woman in love or a hollow heroine who simply followed her husband, De la Concha does not make any distinctions between her and Quintana Roo. Rather, he presents both of them as free thinkers who fought for an altruistic ideal: “la idea más peligrosa y al mismo tiempo más grandiosa que pueda existir: la idea de la libertad” (the most dangerous and at the same time the greatest idea that could ever exist: the idea of liberty) (175).

The Leona that Pascual reconstructs here, as he declared in an interview, is a woman of ideas, a self-taught journalist, and one of the most important ideologists of Mexico’s independence (Montaño Garfias). We close the book feeling that she was, as Pascual explains in his final “Habeas Corpus,” a complex woman who was not liked by everyone and yet became a national symbol, a female icon associated with Mexican independence:

> Porque nació como hija de la Ilustración y murió como símbolo del Romanticismo. Porque es la primera mujer periodista de México, la primera que habló ante el Congreso Nacional y porque creo que es la única mujer mexicana—a menos de que algún avezado historiador me corrija—a quien se le han ofrecido funerales de Estado.
>
> (Because she was born as the daughter of Enlightenment and died as a symbol of Romanticism. Because she was the first female journalist of Mexico, the first one who spoke at the National Congress and because I believe that she is the only Mexican woman—unless a shrewd historian corrects me—who received a state funeral.) (242)

Here, too, as in Del Palacio’s novel, Leona’s open letter to Lucas Alamán is included in the narrative, and her feminist thinking is refurbished as if it had been written for us in the twenty-first century:

> En todas las naciones del mundo ha sido apreciado el patriotismo de las mujeres: ¿por qué, pues, mis paisanos, aunque no sean todos, han querido ridiculizarlo como si fuera un sentimiento impropio en ellas? ¿Qué tiene de extraño ni ridículo el que una mujer ame a su patria y le preste los servicios que pueda para que a estos se les dé, por burla, el título de heroísmo romancesco?

> (Women's patriotism has been appreciated in all the nations of the world. Why is it, then, that some of my own people have ridiculed their participation saying that such patriotic expressions are not acceptable in women? Why does a woman's love for her country and service to her fatherland have to be considered romantic heroism?) (159)

Her words, already powerful in the early nineteenth century, today represent the contestatory speech of a woman who empowers herself and other women with multiple and contradictory experiences that reject the norm and challenge masculinist habits and worldviews (Olivares 60).[13]

In Aguirre's novel, Leona is also an educated woman who reads *Las aventuras de Telémaco, hijo de Ulises* (*The Adventures of Telemachus, the Son of Ulysses*) and translates it from French to Spanish. She sends letters, as the story goes, to the insurgents whom she calls Telémaco, Robinson, Nemoroso, Lavoisier, and so on. But Leona's intellectual capacity and her potential as a woman of letters are not developed at all in *Leona Vicario: La insurgente*. In fact, in one of the last chapters, the narrator highlights her exemplarity stating that all the women involved in the War of Independence fed the soldiers, cured the wounded, and gave them comfort with lovely words: "Sus palabras, siempre tranquilas y alegres, se hicieron oír para confortar a los moribundos, a los abatidos, a todos aquellos que, como fantasmas, erraban siguiendo la luz de la libertad y que el destino llevaría a la prisión o al cadalso" (their words, always serene and cheerful, would comfort the dying, the miserable, those phantom-like individuals who went after the light of freedom but ended up in prison or in the scaffold) (134). Because of the absence of Leona Vicario's intellectual characterization in the novel, it is hard to believe that she was, as the narrator argues in the final two pages with a sensationalist statement, "indiscutiblemente la mujer más destacada entre las heroínas de la causa libertaria" (indisputably, the most prominent among the heroines of the liberation movement) (167). We never see her in action here; nor do we know how exactly she becomes, over the course of the narrative, the most distinguished woman of the insurgent movement.

Evidently, Pascual and Del Palacio work with Leona's intellectuality to craft the complex portrait of a feminist thinker who contests the demands of femininity, proving that she is, like other historical women in similar situations, a subject, although the world around her insists on seeing her as a mere object (Marso 70). Del Palacio goes the extra mile as she reconstructs Leona's emblematic figure to save her, in a feminist way, from history's ashes. In her book *Adictas a la insurgencia: Mujeres en la guerra de Independencia* (*Addicted to Insurgency: Women in the War of Independence*) (2010), a hybrid work that combines history and a few poetic licenses, Del Palacio succinctly writes of Vicario's education: "Recibió una educación esmerada. Su padre le enseñó a escribir y la acostumbró a nutrirse de su biblioteca: adelantos científicos, obras filosóficas y literarias, libros de oraciones . . . Su voracidad no tenía límites. Con él aprendió francés y un poco de latín, y fue él quien insistió en que fueran a la casa maestros para enseñarle matemáticas y filosofía" (She received an excellent education. Her father taught her how to read and introduced her to his library, where she nourished herself with scientific developments, philosophical and literary works, devotional books . . . Her voracity had no limits. With him she learned French and some Latin. And he hired teachers to teach her math and philosophy at home) (24). In her novel, however, she manufactures a round character of the late eighteenth and early nineteenth century. Indeed, over the course of almost 400 pages, Del Palacio convinces readers that her protagonist must fight gender inequality with an autonomous, complex, feminine, and feminist "I" made up of multiple and contradictory experiences. This is something we continue to find in several literary reconstructions of historical characters carried out by women writers of the late twentieth and early twenty-first century. Such works, argues María Teresa Navarro Salazar, reveal the feminist desire to rewrite the hidden histories of unknown or less popular female characters representative of female empowerment (201).

The fact that Leona received an education is extraordinary, as I have stated already, especially if we consider that she devoured novels, devotional books, *comedias*, poetry, and perhaps picaresque and adventure texts that entered New Spain throughout the colonial era (Gonzalbo Aizpuru 344). What is remarkable, though, is that in a world of limited and censored sources for men and even more restricted texts for women (Adams 115),[14] Leona Vicario used her letters and articles as her best allies to combat gender discrimination and dismantle the silence that men impose on women. She writes, as she expresses in a letter addressed to the editors of *El Sol* (*Sun*) dated February 7, 1831, to clean up her reputation, "para que el público se imponga de todo y falle como le parezca justo" (so that the people understand everything and judge for themselves) (Martínez Pichardo 158).[15] On a different occasion, Vicario refers to her good manners and pardons the government journalists for portraying her as an uneducated woman, capable of offending the president of Mexico (Martínez Pichardo 164). With affected modesty, she tells Lucas Alamán, in the letter that Del Palacio and Pascual reproduce in their fictional texts, that her patriotic actions were not heroic but simply "unos servicios tan comunes y cortos" (small and normal services) (Martínez Pichardo 165). But she quickly attacks Alamán with elegance and determination, saying that she does not want her family to remember her as a madwoman who sacrificed her life only for the love of a man (Martínez Pichardo 165).

In many ways, Leona's public and private letters attract such writers as Celia del Palacio and Carlos Pascual inasmuch as they demolish the conception that women are inferior to men; that they lack initiative, agency, endurance, and determination; or that they are overall passive agents of history. Fictionally re-created in an era of heated gender debates, they confront sexism, that distorted mirror (in the words of Monsiváis) that legalizes the gestures of the *caudillos*, invents disproportions, and assures women that they are safe (or better off) at home, taking care of their children and supporting their husbands, those men whose primary mission in life is to change the world with their actions, unequaled intellectuality, and aggressive behavior (*Misógino* 22). Undeniably, Leona's historical writing explains how women of her social status and education were able to write themselves into history in the early nineteenth century, creating a fruitful dialogue between the private and public spaces of the newly formed Spanish American nations (Masiello 12; Rodríguez and Szurmuk 97–98). But their participation, as expected in a patriarchal society, created friction and discomfort among the educated men of their time. This is something that Del Palacio and Pascual rearticulate in their fictions. Both novels are written from a gendered perspective, one that takes into account women's association with the historically oppressed, a wide variety of voices that highlight the problematic construction of a lettered woman and, more important, the articulation of the word in a sexist world that divides everything into masculine and feminine, male and female, or heroes and heroines.

Speaking of gendered heroes, in his graphic novel, *Sensacional de héroes* (*Sensational Heroes*), not coincidentally published in 2010, Francisco Haghenbeck devotes a brief chapter to Leona Vicario. Interestingly, the story promotes the idea that a woman's intellectuality, political compromise, and agency are virtually unthinkable in the absence of a man. Leona Vicario appears as a brave heroine of Mexican independence, but, above all, as a woman in love with her husband: "antes que nada, enamorada de su esposo" (34). The graphic story we find over the next four pages includes her romance with Quintana Roo; his passionate love declaration, kneeling in front of other people; and a violent scene that portrays Leona's tutor, Agustín Pomposo, kicking Andrés out of their house when he proposes to marry her. Leona does appear as a brave woman who risks her life for the insurgent movement, as the messenger that we all know, and as the author of important articles. She is also depicted in other scenes surrounded by the small press that she carries "entre sus faldas" (under her skirt) to print "noticias de los insurgentes" (news about the insurgents) (36). At other times, the drawings show Leona hiding with her husband and her daughter in a cave or walking with Genoveva in her arms after receiving the royal pardon. In one of these scenes, she reassures Andrés that she will wait for him "hasta el fin del mundo" (until the end of the world) (37).

After independence is won, Leona is portrayed in the graphic novel as a housewife, knitting in front of Andrés and her baby in a comfortable living room. Even though a few printed lines say that "Leona se dedicó a actividades intelectuales al lado de su esposo" (Leona was dedicated to intellectual work alongside her husband) (37), and that her knowledge was outstanding, "sorprendente para una mujer de su época" (surprising for a woman of her time) (37), the last drawing depicts her as a mythical silhouette that is about to disappear like an *alma en pena*, or a wondering ghost. It is the same shadow of Leona Vicario that vanishes in Laureana Wright de Kleinhans's *Mujeres notables mexicanas* (*Notable Mexican Women*) (1910), where the heroine, depicted as an exceptional virtuous woman, wife, and mother, returns home after several years of insurgence to take care of her husband and the poor, donates money to several churches, lives an exemplary Catholic life, and finally dies away from public affairs on August 24, 1842 (268).

Mujer que sabe latín . . . we might be tempted to think that even if Leona Vicario finds an honorable husband and is recognized posthumously as the mother of a modern nation, her multiple transgressions in real life do not always guarantee her a good ending in contemporary Mexican fiction.

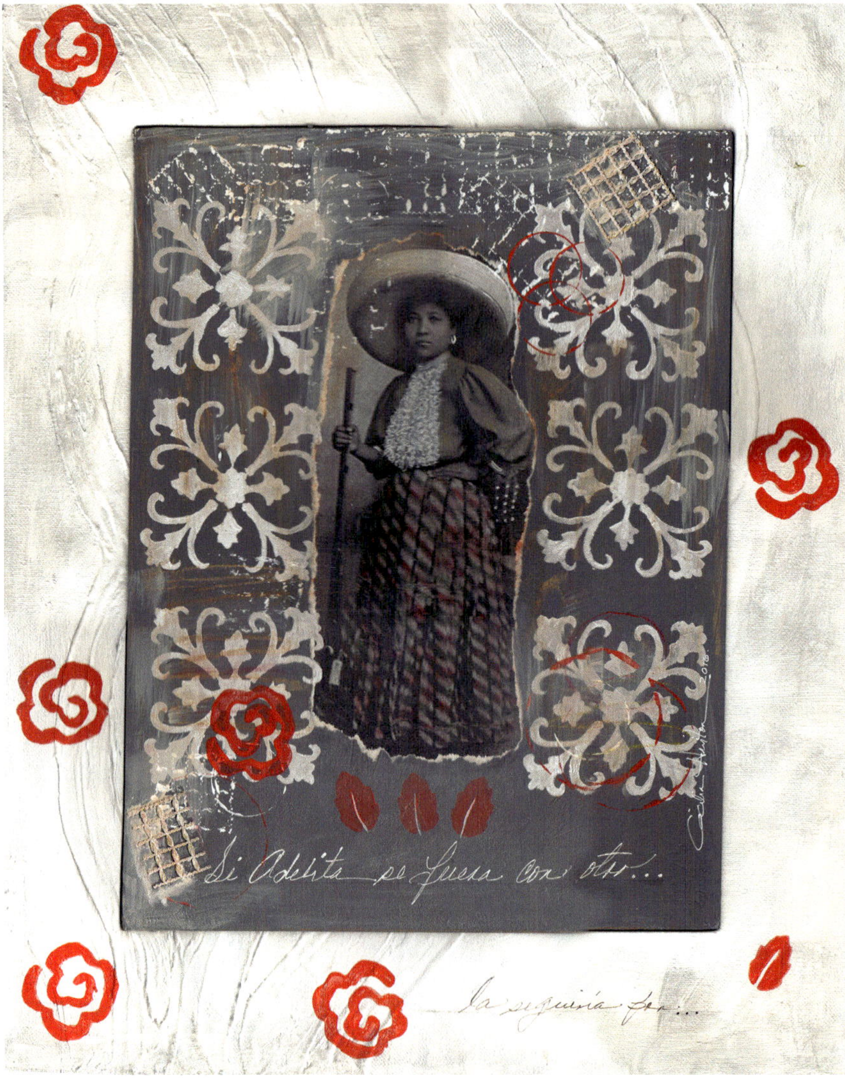

Soldadera. *Si Adelita se fuera con otro . . .*, mixed media collage by Cecilia Hinton, 2016.

4

Si Adelita se fuera con otro . . . *Soldaderas* of an Unfinished Revolution

Si Adelita se fuera con otro
la seguiría por tierra y por mar.
Si por mar en un buque de guerra,
si por tierra en un tren militar.
(If Adelita were to leave with another man,
I'd follow her over land and sea.
If by sea, in a warship,
if by land, in a military train.)

—"La Adelita"[1]

Thanks to the wonders of myth, invention, and publicity, many people remember the Mexican Revolution as a historical event that has remained fixed on a stereotyped canvas. The revolutionary image that the world has inherited over time is that of the brave Juanes and their enormous sombreros, worn-out jackets, and cartridge belts, accompanied by their loyal Adelitas, the women who form a shady army of their own, unthinkable without their typical *rebozos* (shawls) and *huaraches* (sandals), torn skirts (Monsiváis, *Imágenes* 301). Because of this, the men and women who participated in the revolution beginning in 1910 share a common marginal space within the spectrum of a mythical Mexicanness. But the *soldaderas* of diverse experiences and multiple family backgrounds, class affiliations, ethnic identities, military roles, and personalities are even less fortunate than their male counterparts (Salas 69). Over the past fifteen years, numerous novels and short stories have been published on the lives of Pancho Villa, Emiliano Zapata, Felipe Ángeles, Francisco I. Madero, Porfirio Díaz, and other men involved in the revolution. But the women of the Mexican Revolution are almost always mentioned in passing or in a slim footnote. In the meantime, their idealized presence remains unaffected in the *corridos* (ballads) of the Mexican Revolution or in the black-and-white photographs, postcards, and posters that continue to sell their image in and outside of Mexico as a national relic in a globalized and postmodern era.

In 1913, American journalist John Reed, who was commissioned to cover the Mexican Revolution, paid close attention to several camp followers or *viejas* involved in the conflict. In his *Insurgent Mexico*, published the following year, he described several women who crossed their chests with cartridge belts and fought the enemy simply because their partners were revolutionaries. Some of these women, he noticed, carried and loaded their men's rifles, cooked for them, carried their *chamacos* (babies) on their back and their *metates*, those "heavy little stones" used to grind corn (104). The women who appear in his chronicle travel by foot or on top of train cars, along with their half-naked children. Some remain silent, "after the custom of [their] sex and country" (104), and others smoke their corn-husk cigarettes and complain about multiple hardships and uncertainties.

Through several historical accounts, however, we know that women joined the Mexican Revolution not just as wives and lovers but also as soldiers. Many of them participated in some of the battles, and a few of them led armies and became colonels. As Elizabeth Salas explains in *Soldaderas in the Mexican Military*, these women came from all over Mexico. Originally from Oaxaca, Morelos, Guanajuato, Zacatecas, Sonora, and Chihuahua, among several other states, the majority of them were working-class women from rural villages and haciendas or from well-populated towns.[2] Some volunteered to fight and others followed their partners, fathers, or brothers. Others joined the revolution because they had been raped and abducted by the revolutionaries (Salas 67–72).[3]

Some scholars have separated the *soldaderas* or camp followers from the women soldiers who participated in the Mexican Revolution. Anna Macías, for instance, notes that female soldiers were decisive and courageous, while camp followers were self-sacrificing and only took care of their partners (*Against* 40–42). Following this distinction, Andrés Reséndez Fuentes also separates those women who served as true soldiers from the women who simply followed the men from one battle to the next, arguing that their simultaneous portrayal as loyal camp followers and fierce warriors "makes it exceedingly difficult to reach general conclusions about why these women decided to join the revolution and what was their contribution in the battlefield" (114). Although this may be the case, several historical testimonies show that the differences between female soldiers and *soldaderas* are not that clear. "Because of the changing configurations of battle lines," Salas notes, "many times camp followers by necessity had to perform as soldiers with all the skill, resourcefulness, and aggression that survival required. On the other hand, female soldiers sometimes took a decidedly motherly attitude toward the welfare of their fellow male soldiers" (73).

Ultimately, as Elena Poniatowska recalls in her chronicle *Las soldaderas*, trapped in a misogynist society, most of the women who participated in the Mexican Revolution, even those involved in important battles as soldiers or their partners' assistants, remained nameless and were referred to as cockroaches, sloppy workers, gossips, sluts, captain's pets, blabbermouths, robbers, and Adelitas, as if they all shared the same identity (22). A brief overview of a few narratives of the revolution indeed confirms this pejorative attitude.[4]

In Mariano Azuela's *Los de abajo* (*The Underdogs*) (1915), Camila is portrayed as an ignorant woman of vulgar features; the one-eyed María Antonia seems to have slept with most of Demetrio Macías's men; and La Pintada is presented as a loose woman who kills Camila to keep her position as the general's lover. Overall, one could say that the few *soldaderas* of this novel are depicted almost like animals, as "perros callejeros entre los grupos [revolucionarios]" (street dogs among the revolutionaries) (146). Martín Luis Guzmán's *El águila y la serpiente* (*The Eagle and the Serpent*) (1928) also revolves almost entirely around the men of the revolution; the few women mentioned in a handful of passages appear as wise girlfriends who do not expect much from their temporary lovers. The Güera Carrasco appears briefly right next to her man, General Juan Carrasco, but she lacks any characterization. Along these lines, women are virtually nonexistent in *¡Vámonos con Pancho Villa!* (*Let's Go with Pancho Villa*) (1931) and *Se llevaron el cañón para Bachimba* (*They Took the Cannon to Bachimba*) (1941) by Rafael F. Muñoz. Francisco Rojas González's *La negra Angustias* (*The Black Angustias*) (1944) could be considered an exception, as the eponymous character becomes a brave and somewhat masculine colonel of the revolution. But when Angustias falls in love with the ambitious Manuel, she becomes a submissive woman destined to inhabit "la casa chica" (the second house) (219).

In view of these and other works, Debra A. Castillo points out that "the war's multiple traumas have been discussed obsessively in Mexican literature since 1920, but seldom have women of any sort appeared in more than a token role" (*Easy Women* 5). This is understandable, especially within a patriarchal literary tradition that over the course of the twentieth century has mostly depicted women as traitors like Malinche or as reincarnations of the Virgin Mary, as faithful wives and devoted mothers, or as old maids, nuns, overly religious women and inoffensive schoolteachers (Leal, "Female Archetypes" 231–35). As has been noted on numerous occasions, Nellie Campobello's *Cartucho* (1931) and *Las manos de mamá* (*My Mother's Hands*) (1937), and certainly Poniatowska's *Hasta no verte Jesús mío* (*Here's to You, Jesusa!*) (1969), provide fine examples of a few *soldaderas* who stand out for their courage and actions. In the end, however, they return to a state of invisibility, domesticity, and conformism, as if their literary representation was not capable of overcoming their real historical impediments or the hegemonic forces that even today relegate women and other minorities to the outskirts of power.

The fact that the *soldaderas* of the Mexican Revolution have been represented in this fashion is closely related to the disappearance of female corporality in the midst of the turbulent movement. I speak, like Tabea Linhard, of the hundreds of female bodies that literally and figuratively vanish from the revolution and become ghost-like silhouettes that cannot transcend an unfortunate literary exoticism or their perennial subaltern status (6). In *Cartucho*, for example, colonel Nacha Ceniceros is executed by Pancho Villa's soldiers after she accidentally killed her lover, the young colonel Gallardito. In the original version of 1931 we read: "Hoy existe un hormiguero donde dicen que está enterrada" (Today there is an anthill where they say she was buried) (Campobello 107). But in the edited version of 1940, Campobello adds that Nacha did not really die: "Nacha Ceniceros vivía. Había vuelto a su casa de Catarinas, seguramente desengañada de la actitud de los pocos que pretendieron repartirse los triunfos de la mayoría" (Nacha Ceniceros was still alive. She had gone back to her home in Catarinas, undoubtedly disillusioned by the attitude of those few who tried to divide among themselves the triumphs of the majority) (107). Although the narrator empowers Nacha, stating that she "domaba potros y montaba a caballo mejor que muchos hombres" (tamed ponies and rode horses better than any man) (107), in the end she is relegated to an ambivalent space of excluding historiographies or a world of myths and legends that either eliminate or blur the truth of female histories (Linhard 170).[5] We see a similar process of female disappearance in *Las manos de mamá* when Campobello transforms her mother into a divine-like figure, quite distant from other human beings.

In *Hasta no verte Jesús mío*, Jesusa Palancares participates in the Mexican Revolution, first as her father's *soldadera* and later as her husband's *soldadera*. In the novel, the Mexican Revolution empowers her momentarily as she learns to defend herself from her husband's beatings, and she recalls with pride, "Pedro se volvió más bueno desde que lo balacié. Pero entonces yo fui la que me emperré [. . .] La bendita revolución me ayudó a desenvolverme [. . .] Y le doy gracias a Dios" (Pedro was nicer after I tried to shoot him. But afterward I'm the one who got stubborn [. . .] The blessed revolution helped me grow up [. . .] And I thank God) (101–2). Unlike what we see in other narratives of the revolution, Jesusa is a brave *soldadera* and not just a passive follower: "Yo siempre usé pistola al cincho [. . .] A lo que yo me dedicaba era a cargarle el máuser a Pedro, el mío y el suyo; mientras él descargaba el que tenía en las manos, yo estaba cargando el otro cuando ya él me pasaba el vacío" (I always carried a pistol [. . .] My job was to carry Pedro's rifle, mine and his; while he unloaded one, I was loading the other one for him) (110). She has a foul mouth, fights with other *soldaderas*, and drinks more than other male revolutionaries. At some point, she is in charge of an entire troop but leaves the movement when she finds herself alone, arguing, "andaba en la bola siguiendo a mi marido más de a güevo que de ganas" (I was in the movement following my husband more because I had to than out of pleasure) (132). Unfortunately, her accomplishments are ephemeral, and she returns to an unchangeable condition of invisibility. The government does not recognize her participation in the revolution, and at the end of her life she can conclude that she did not gain anything as a *soldadera*, that she will always be the other in a country that is definitely not hers.

Taking into account this historical and literary background, here I argue that the *soldaderas* of the Mexican Revolution are still fighting an unfinished gender battle in today's literature. The few *soldaderas* we find in the twenty-first century still resemble the stereotyped and familiar characters that we see in a handful of literary works of the twentieth century—including Carlos Fuentes's *Gringo Viejo* (*Old Gringo*) (1985) and Laura Esquivel's *Como agua para chocolate* (*Like Water for Chocolate*) (1989)—or in such films as Ismael Rodríguez's *La Cucaracha* (*The Cockroach*) (1958), Miguel Zacarías's *Juana Gallo* (1961), or José Bolaños's *La soldadera* (1966). Only in some cases, and usually in works penned by women writers, do we see real acts of female empowerment, gender transgressions, and convincing rearticulations of women as complex historical subjects and key agents of the Mexican Revolution. Although the revolution allows thousands of women to move across the battlefields from one side of the country to the other by train, foot, or horse, most of them have entered various historiographic discourses or archives as mere cultural icons of a distant historical past.

Part of the problem here, as Gabriela Cano argues, is the fact that popular culture has idealized the *soldaderas* of the Mexican Revolution as emblematic "Adelitas," without considering their multiple roles. Furthermore, because Adelita is an anonymous woman with no last name, no concrete geographical origin, and no political affiliation, her popularity has greatly contributed to the invisibility of the *soldaderas* who participated in the revolution as propagandists, spies, messengers, journalists, and nurses (Cano, "Historia de las mujeres" 13). By virtue of this invented or inherited cultural tradition, the majority of the *soldaderas* I analyze here remain trapped in an ambivalent zone, on the bridge of history and literature, facts and fiction, popular fantasy and oral testimonies (Linhard 31). Because of their anonymity, they are even less fortunate than Malinche, Sor Juana, and Leona Vicario. Their mythification, however, strengthened by the black-and-white photographs of the Casasola archive, reinforces a long chain of female archetypes that from Malinche onward, instead of representing a historical truth, personify an anxiety generated by the active participation of women in crucial moments of Mexican history (Latorre 100).

Ambivalent Gender Battles and Invisible Others

In her biographical novel *Itinerario de una pasión: Los amores de mi general* (*Itinerary of Passion: My General's Lovers*) (1999), Rosa Helia Villa, one of Pancho Villa's granddaughters, reconstructs a sentimental history of the renowned general, taking into account about eighteen women who were either his wives or lovers. The novel, however, builds its foundation on the cold ashes of magical realism. We perceive this from the moment that three of Villa's widows, Luz Corral, Austreberta Rentería, and Manuela Casas, drink a mysterious passion flower tea that allows them to daydream about "los días de contradictoria feliz angustia, de dolorosa alegría, de emocionado pesar, de esperas interminables e inenarrables congojas al lado del hombre de leyenda que yacía inerte frente a ellas" (the days of contradictory happiness and anguish, of painful joy, of excited sorrow, of endless waiting and inexpressible anxiety with the legendary man who laid still before them) (48). If the most endearing figures of the Mexican Revolution are the women who join the movement as mere shadows or phantoms that have nowhere to go (Monsiváis, "La Revolufia" 17), *Itinerario de una pasión* echoes this unfortunate representation, especially when one of Villa's women—Luz Corral—summarizes her life with him in the following terms: "Las mujeres no somos importantes en su vida [. . .] Somos, si acaso, el consuelo, el reposo, la paz, la alegría, qué sé yo; el desfogue de la pasión que lo consume cuando toda su energía no está concentrada en planear el combate siguiente, la campaña próxima o la batalla en turno" (Women are not important in his life [. . .] If anything, we give him comfort, peace, happiness, who knows; we're the outlet for the passion that consumes him when he's not planning the next battle) (128).

Consistent with this portrayal, Villa appears in his granddaughter's novel as a brave and courageous male hero surrounded by numerous women who try to make his life easier. The *soldaderas* of this novel hardly ever speak. Only toward the end of the novel, in less than two pages, the author allows a group of *soldaderas* to confront him when he tries to get rid of them to build a professional army. In this isolated episode, a nervous Baudelia Reséndez covers her mouth with her *rebozo*, as she explains to Villa their determination to continue fighting with him: "Aquí nomás, mi General, con la molestia de que nos permita usté seguir partiéndonos la madre junto a usté y a nuestros señores en las filas" (Here we are, General, bothering you to let us stay and serve you and our men) (362). But Villa dismisses them with condescending words:

> Miren, muchachitas, yo les agradezco todos los sacrificios y sufrimientos que les ha costado andar siguiéndonos con la

> impedimenta de anafres, carabinas, chilpayates y hasta panzas preñadas a la hora de los chingadazos, como dice usted, Baudelia; pero como les digo, la División del Norte es ya un ejército profesional, y me cabe la satisfacción de que sea el más alegre y mejor organizado de la Revolución, pero en él las mujeres ya no tienen cabida.
>
> (Look, young ladies, I thank you for your sacrifices and suffering, for following us with your stoves, weapons, children and even your pregnant bellies when we were fighting, as you say, Baudelia; but as I've told you, the Division of the North is now a professional army, and I'm pleased to say that it is the happiest and best organized of the Revolution, but it doesn't have room for women). (362–63)

We know quite well that the narratives of the Mexican Revolution, extended over several decades, successfully created unprecedented characters within a national culture that wanted to sell the movement as a symbol of otherness. Thanks to these narratives, the revolution came to be known as something that happened to others, in another historical moment, and within other social environments (Monsiváis, "La narrativa" 63–65). Regrettably, Rosa Helia Villa's novel perpetuates this sense of otherness. Her blind admiration for her grandfather relegates women to the margins. In *Itinerario de una pasión*, Villa disarms women with his watchful eyes, and he sends them home when they are not needed anymore. Only then, "sin el lastre de las soldaderas" (without the burden of the *soldaderas*), we read, "el ejército villista se constituy[e] en la fuerza armada más profesional e importante del país" (the Villista troops became the most professional and important army of the country) (363).

Apparently, this *machista* setup allows women to be included in the construction of history as long as they let their male heroes shine in front of the cameras and is what propitiates the successful production and commercialization of the film *Itinerario de una pasión* (*Itinerary of Passion*) (2013). In confirmation that a story of passionate encounters, multiple sexual affairs, and scandalous intimacy sells in a globalized neoliberal era, the film originally produced by Juan Andrés Bueno and Lourdes Deschamps is currently available on Netflix in seventeen countries. The film has not received the best reviews by recognized film critics, yet the story of a hypersexual revolutionary hero still markets Latin American exoticism as a cultural commodity.

This marginal portrayal of women also appears in the biography *Pancho Villa* (2006), penned by the renowned Spanish-born Mexican novelist Paco Ignacio Taibo II. In his nearly nine hundred-page volume, subtitled *Una biografía narrativa* (*A Biographical Narrative*), the legendary Villa is described as an extraordinary man involved with at least twenty-seven women, some of whom became his wives. The narrator explains that Villa married these women almost simultaneously, not so much because he liked weddings or priests but because he loved "las fiestas, el baile y, sobre todo, los compadres" (parties, dances and, especially, *compadres*) (10). Similar to other Villas who appear in historical and fictional narratives, this Pancho Villa tells women not to approach the battlefields. Although in real life the *soldaderas* helped him tremendously during many of his battles, on his way to Parral Taibo's Villa threatens his men: "El que suba una vieja a los trenes, se muere con ella" (the man who takes his woman on the train will die with her) (671). The *soldaderas* only appear tangentially in the lyrics of "La Adelita," the famous *corrido* that popular bands play for Villa when his troops enter a new town or village. In most cases, the *soldaderas* are mentioned when the narrator lists the number of casualties after a particular battle, but they remain nameless, part of an anonymous whole.

Only in one of the endnotes of chapter 29, which covers the Battle of Torreón, Taibo explains that Adelita, whose real name was Adela Velarde, a native of Ciudad Juárez, participated in that battle. In one brief sentence he summarizes her vitae: "era enfermera de las tropas de la brigada Domingo Arrieta en la División del Centro, de Durango" (she was a nurse for the troops of Domingo Arrieta, in the Division of the Center, in Durango) (337). We do not know for certain whether Adelita was Adela Velarde from Ciudad Juárez or, according to other accounts, a fourteen-year-old girl who nursed a soldier back to health, a twenty-one-year-old from Chihuahua who attracted Villa's attention (and love), or a courageous *soldadera* who told soldiers that she would wound or kill cowards (Salas 92). Taibo's theory of Adelita's origin is, after all, one among many that abound in Mexico, where people from different regions would argue that Adelita was from their town and lived across the street from them (Monsiváis, "Las mujeres" 18). The point here is that Taibo reduces Adelita's participation in the Revolution to a couple of lines. Also in passing, the author mentions that Valentina, "era según algunos Valentina Ramírez, una soldadera de la División del Noroeste en las tropas de Ramón Iturbe; según otros se trataba de Petra Herrera" (was, according to some, Valentina Ramírez, a *soldadera* in the Division of the Northeast, with the troops of Ramón Iturbe; according to others, she was Petra Herrera) (337). In regard to the protagonist of the *corrido* "Marieta," the author simply writes in one discreet sentence: "se llamaba María del Carmen Rubio, era natural de Oaxaca, nacida en 1896, y la hirieron dos veces en la batalla de Torreón" (her name was María del Carmen Rubio, from Oaxaca, born in 1896, and she was injured twice in the battle of Torreón) (337).

As we read these brief notes, where women are virtually ignored, it is hard to believe that the *soldaderas* of the Mexican Revolution were, as Rafael Torres Sánchez observes in a study, loyal companions to the soldiers and revolutionaries, nurses, messengers, informants, and spies (189–90). In fact, Taibo pays more attention to Pancho Villa's mare than to any *soldadera*. He writes about the legendary Siete Leguas, as if she were closely related to the Cid's Babieca or Don Quijote's Rocinante:

> La entrada de la *Siete Leguas* en esta historia, es como todo, sujeto de múltiples versiones. Según unos era hija de la *Muñeca*, una yegua que Villa había secuestrado de un establo de Lanza y Escandón en la calle Guerrero, a su paso por la ciudad de México, y de *Fripón*, un caballo árabe fino que había tomado en la escuela de Agricultura y que lo ayudó a encontrar a la *Muñeca* en el establo ya mencionado, porque relinchaba al estar cerca de ella. Pero de ser así, cuando la historia se narra sólo tendría dos años y medio. Otros dirán que se trataba de la misma *Muñeca*. Y habrá incluso quienes digan que era una yegua que le cambió a un soldado que la usaba como animal de carga. Según Estanislao Prieto, incorporado a la escolta de Villa como caballerango después de la batalla de Zacatecas, simplemente no existió [. . .] Y el novelista estadounidense William Lansford dirá que fueron muchas, porque "a partir de cierta época siempre dio a su montura favorita el nombre de *Siete Leguas*."
>
> (The introduction of *Siete Leguas* into this story has, like everything, different versions. According to some, she was the daughter of Muñeca, a mare that Villa had stolen from a

> stable on Guerrero street, while passing through Mexico City, and of Fripón, a fine Arabian horse that he had taken from the school of Agriculture and that helped him find Muñeca in the aforementioned stable. But, if this is true, the horse would have been only two and a half years old at the time that the story was told. Others will say that it was the same Muñeca. And some will even say that it was a mare that he got from a soldier who used her as a pack animal. According to Estanislao Prieto, a stableman who joined Villa's army after the battle of Zacatecas, she didn't exist [. . .] And American novelist William Lansford will say that she was multiple horses, because "he always called his favorite horse mount Siete Leguas.") (713)

In this biography, not a single *soldadera* merits as much characterization as the general's horse. Siete Leguas, on the other hand, is developed as a round character and her story has a literary conclusion. After 150 pages of her initial appearance in the narrative, the mare's life has a happy ending when, as a symbol of friendship, Pancho Villa lets Adolfo de la Huerta have her. Since then, we read:

> La *Siete Leguas* vivió en las caballerizas de Palacio Nacional. Como allí nadie la montaba se estaba volviendo arisca; al final del interinato de De la Huerta, Lázaro Cárdenas, que se entrevistaba con De la Huerta, quiso conocer al animal y Adolfo se lo regaló. Un día, un viejo cardenista le pasó al autor de este libro una nota en la que decía que la *Siete Leguas* sobrevivió a Villa y terminó apaciblemente sus días en una cuadra de un rancho del general Lázaro Cárdenas, donde murió de vejez. ¿Los mitos se toman de la mano con un caballo como intermediario?
>
> (*Siete Leguas* lived in the stables of the National Palace. Since nobody was riding her, she was becoming wild; at the end of De la Huerta's interim term, Lázaro Cárdenas, who was visiting De la Huerta, wanted to see the animal and Adolfo gave it to him as a present. One day, an old Cardenista passed me a note stating that Siete Leguas outlived Villa and spent her last days peacefully in the ranch of Lázaro Cárdenas, where she died of old age. Do myths use horses as intermediators?) (772)

Evidently, little seems to have changed since Jesusa Palancares in Poniatowska's *Hasta no verte, Jesús mío* tells us that horses always received better treatment, more water, and more protection from inclement weather than did any of the Indians—women included, of course—involved in the revolutionary conflict (94). Not much has changed from the time when Gustavo Casasola decorated the *soldaderas*' true marginality with an idealized, *costumbrista* description:

> Nada tan pintoresco en la vida militar de gruesos contingentes como los carros del ferrocarril destinados a las soldaderas, sobre todo cuando la campaña tiene ya algunos meses. Esos carros—casas sobre ruedas—son una maravilla en que al amor se une el sacrificio, a la brutalidad los gestos de una belleza jamás vista, a la urgencia de la vida, episodios de un desinterés tal que solo puede concebirse en almas superiores. En los techos de los carros, cuando el cupo no corresponde con el contingente, se hace lumbre, se hace corrillo, las mujeres en el centro y los soldados con los pies colgantes hacia los lados del convoy.
>
> (There is nothing as picturesque in the army as the train cars assigned to the *soldaderas*, especially when the troops have been out for a few months. Those wonderful cars—houses on wheels—bring together love and sacrifice, brutality and the gestures of unseen beauty, the urgency of life and episodes that come from superior souls. On the roofs of the train cars, where there's hardly any room for everyone, they make a fire and form a circle around it; the women in the center and the soldiers with their feet hanging on the sides of the convoy.) (720)

In his novel *Zapata* (2006), Pedro Ángel Palou does present a few *soldaderas*, after stating that "a Emiliano le gustaban las mujeres, los trajes y los caballos, sin importar el orden. O mejor sí: los caballos y los trajes para tener más mujeres" (Emiliano liked women, suits and horses, in no particular order. Or perhaps: horses and suits in order to have more women) (19). Like Pancho Villa in most narratives, in this novel Emiliano Zapata appears as an irredeemable conquistador who kidnaps the adolescents of the region and has multiple affairs with the women of his native town, Anenecuilco. Unlike Villa, as a young man Emiliano has a few homosexual encounters with his master, Ignacio de la Torre, and these homoerotic passages strengthen Zapata's legend as a revolutionary hero (Price 50–52). Ultimately, Emiliano marries Josefa Espejo, maintains a solid relationship with Gregoria Zúñiga (alias La China), and continues having other women around him until his death. The few *soldaderas* we find here remind us that numerous Zapatista women participated in the Mexican Revolution, either following their men or providing food and other provisions for the troops from their homes. We do not know how many found themselves in the actual battlefields as true soldiers, but we know, for instance, that Esperanza Echeverría of Yautepec, upon Madero's victory, entered Mexico City dressed as a man and caught the attention of several reporters and photographers. We also know that in the company of her son and her husband, Rosa Bobabilla worked as a woman soldier under the command of General Francisco Pacheco and became a colonel. It is also well known that Margarita Neri was one of the cruelest *soldaderas* of the Liberation Army of the South (Salas 42; Reséndez Fuentes 124).

In Palou's novel, the narrator mentions that Zapata has children with "una soldadera de nombre Dolores" (a *soldadera* named Dolores) (160) and affairs "con las coronelas, particularmente con las hermanas Robles, Carmen y Amelia" (with the colonels, particularly with the Robles sisters, Carmen and Amelia) (171). For sure, splitting the identity of a *soldadera* whose real name was Carmen Amelia Robles entertains readers who might know something about this brave colonel from Guerrero (Cross and Miles 190), more so if they realize that she lived most of her life as a man under the name of Amelio Robles (Cano, "Inocultables" 63).[6] Leaving aside the possibility that Zapata's relationship with the Robles "sisters" could be read between the lines as a subversive hint of his homoerotic desires, we never get to see the *soldaderas* participating in any battles or important military affairs. Only toward the end of the novel do we see an anonymous group of them crying inconsolably when Zapata dies.

In his novel *No me dejen morir así* (*Don't Let Me Die Like This*) (2014), Palou gives a deceased Pancho Villa the opportunity to reflect on his many accomplishments and failures from the objective perspective of the afterlife. As Villa recalls his love affairs, he names a few of the women who accompanied him during the revolution. Besides naming two of his wives, Austreberta Rentería—who would have made a great "generala" (79)—and Luz Corral, he mentions several women with revolutionary blood in their veins like "Chonita," Soledad Seáñez Holguín, and Manuelita Casas Morales. While Villa recalls the many children he had with these and other women, his narrative momentarily revives a community of women who participated in the revolution:

> Ahora que si me apuran, pues a nadie se le niega un beso y así puedo contar a María Isabel Campa, mamá de Reynaldita; me apresuré con María Leocadia y con Petra Espinoza, que me dio a la Micaela. Esther Cardona me dio de a dos, Esther y Francisco; Agustín vino de la relación con Asunción Villaescusa, y Águedo de Piedad Nevárez. La memoria me falla pero estoy seguro de que se llamaba Guadalupe Coss la madre de Octavio, y Macedonia Ramírez la de Ernesto. Antes de ellos, Juana Torres, mamá de Juana María, y Librada Peña, de Celia. De María Dominga Barraza me quedó Miguel. Luego, Francisca Carrillo tuvo como hijo a Francisco. Paula Alamillo me dio a Evangelina. Otros hijos tuve con Cristina Vázquez, Dolores Delgado, con Aurelia Severiana y con Gabriela Villescas, Otilia Meraz, María Amalia Baca, Pilar Escalona, María Anaya.
>
> (Now, if you want me to, and because I believe that no one should be denied a kiss, I can think of María Isabel Campa, mother of Reynaldita; I rushed things with María Leocadia and with Petra Espinoza, who gave me Micaela. Esther Cardona gave me two children, Esther and Francisco; Agustín came from my relationship with Asunción Villaescusa, and also Águedo de Piedad Nevárez. My memory fails me but I'm sure that Guadalupe Coss was Octavio's mother, and that Macedonia was Ernesto's. Before them, Juana Torres was Juana María's mother, and Librada Peña was Celia's. With María Dominga Barraza I had Miguel. Later, Francisca Carrillo had a son, Francisco. Paula Alamillo gave me Evangelina. I had other children with Cristina Vázquez, Dolores Delgado, with Aurelia Severiana and with Gabriela Villescas, Otilia Meraz, María Amalia Baca, Pilar Escalona, María Anaya.) (80)

As readers, we can only imagine their multiple roles as women, mothers, soldiers, messengers, and accomplices; only tangentially can we think of their plural experiences, personal conflicts, and political dilemmas in times of war.

Can we blame these authors for not developing the lives of the historical *soldaderas* in greater detail? Of course not. But the fact that they have chosen to focus their attention primarily on the men of the Mexican Revolution, or that revolutionary women in general have been less appealing to editors and writers, reflects Mexico's current gender divisions and sexism in the realm of literature. Again, what we have here is a clear example of how the mythification of Adelita or the invention of her as an idealized woman in the collective memory of the revolution has contributed to the invisibility of numerous *soldaderas* (Cano, "La invención"). This is not a new situation by any means. Over three decades ago, Carlos Monsiváis observed that a great deal of his country's literature expresses an unequal cosmovision that denies women the possibility of an organic and wholesome representation (*Misógino* 22).[7] Considering the works discussed so far, the situation does not look much better in today's literary spectrum, in which only a few *soldaderas* are mythologized and hardly ever receive the same fictional treatment as men.

Returning *Soldaderas*

Some stories come back, as José Ramón Ruisánchez argues in the study *Historias que regresan* (*Stories That Come Back*), to modify the past and question official versions of history, the legitimacy of historical archives, and the lack or excess of knowledge. As he examines such canonical texts as *Pedro Páramo* (1955), *La muerte de Artemio Cruz* (*The Death of Artemio Cruz*) (1962) or *La noche de Tlatelolco* (*Massacre in Mexico*) (1971), Ruisánchez points out their reiterative spirit, or an urgent and multifaceted need to retell, contradict, and reassert the past (25). This need to rearticulate the past from a dissident, problematic, or sometimes conformist perspective persists in the twenty-first century, thanks in part to several episodes of the Mexican Revolution that continue to come back. This is what happens, in fact, with a well-known revolutionary scene in which Pancho Villa apparently orders the execution of at least sixty *soldaderas* immediately after one of them tries to kill him. It is a fascinating story that evolves throughout the twentieth century and manages to enter the twenty-first with problematic undertones and questionable depictions of gender and marginalization.

Relying on the biographical testimony of the revolutionary José María Jaurrieta, author of *Con Villa (1916–1920), memorias de campaña* (*With Villa [1916–1920], A Military Memoire*), in 1934 Rafael F. Muñoz solidified some of the stereotyped images typically associated with the *soldaderas* in the history of Mexican literature. In the short story "Un disparo al vacío" ("A Shot in the Dark"), included in his collection *Si me han de matar mañana* (*If They Kill Me Tomorrow*), after a brief summary of a battle that leaves the soldiers exhausted, sick, and wounded, "con más deseos de levantar un paño en la punta de los fusiles, que de acertar los disparos en el pecho de los rebeldes" (more willing to hold a white flag up to the ends of their rifles than to shoot the rebels in the chests) (155),[8] the narrator presents the *soldaderas* with the romantic undertones we see in several stories without any specific names and sharing a common identity:

> Sesenta soldaderas, bravas mujeres que eran para los federales esposas, proveedoras de alimento, cocineras, ayuda a toda hora, compartían la inquietud de los hombres, quizá con más carácter. Eran las mujeres del pueblo, acostumbradas a las vicisitudes de la campaña militar, a las fatigosas caminatas, a la continua falta de alimentos, al peligro de los combates y la angustia de las retiradas; mujeres que muchas veces combatían al lado de sus hombres, los veían morir o morían con ellos.
>
> (Sixty *soldaderas*, brave women who served as wives to the federals, provided food, cooked; they helped them, shared the worries of their men, perhaps even with a better attitude. They were humble women, used to the difficulties of the army, the tiring walks, the continuous lack of food, the dangers of combat, and the threat of the retreat; these women oftentimes fought right next to their men, they would see them die or died with them.) (155)

This exoticizing description sacrifices the individuality of the *soldaderas* and is reinforced in the text when the narrator insists, with admiration, that the women kept their spirits up, even more than any of their men. Subsequently, the narrator depicts the *soldaderas* as a unified whole, as "una sola masa hostil y enérgica" (a hostile and energetic mass) (158). Apparently, from this human bundle came the bullet that almost killed Pancho Villa. Since none of the *soldaderas* confess who did it, the general orders their immediate execution. The women are tied up, "en diez o doce mazos de carne humana, unos verticales, otros tirados en el suelo como bultos de leña, como barriles" (in ten or twelve bundles of human flesh, some lined up vertically, and others thrown on the floor like firewood, like barrels) (159), and they curse Villa until the fire consumes their voices. The story ends with the grotesque image of their massive burning, just as one of them screams: "¡Perro, hijo de perra! ¡¡Habrás de morir como perro!!" (You mongrel, son of a bitch! You will die like a dog!) (161). Indifferent, Villa walks away satisfied and simply replies that these worthless women talked too much: "¡Qué diantres de mujeres tan habladoras! . . . Ya me comenzaba a dar coraje" (These damn women talked so much! . . . They were beginning to piss me off) (161).

The main argument of Muñoz's story is revealing because it shows how very soon the individualities of the Mexican Revolution become emblems of national identity, and/or cultural icons that reflect a problematic gender division (Linhard 31). More than sixty years after this story was published, precisely because stories do come back—and they come back because the Zapatistas are alive and active, or because Mexico's peripheral zones are still ignored—in her chronicle *Las Soldaderas* (1999), Poniatowska comes back to this and other early representations of Mexican revolutionary women. She employs a feminist perspective that attempts to unveil the discursive strategies used by a misogynous culture to describe and constrict the female body (Richard, "La crítica" 77). Drawing from oral and written testimonies that combine politics and aesthetics, Poniatowska rewrites the episode of the victimized *soldaderas* but thickens the plot with other narratives. Consequently, her chronicle expresses multiple worlds of experience that incorporate vague and fragmented incidents and the discontinuities of subjectivities in the process of becoming (Richard, "La crítica" 80).

Poniatowska takes Muñoz's story as a point of departure. As it happens in other chronicles, she borrows various fragments of the original story and intertwines them with other versions that confirm the massacre of the sixty or perhaps even ninety *soldaderas*. Although at first her chronicle reiterates the anonymity of the women murdered by Pancho Villa, Poniatowska provides us with a list of *soldaderas* who carried on their shoulders "la peor parte de la Revolución" (the worst of the Revolution) (11/13). Guided by a feminist perspective that is also present in the writings of several women whose literature challenges the marginal place that has been historically assigned to them (Lorenzano, "Mujer y narrativa" 351), the chronicler recovers the lost identity of Amelia Rodríguez Soriano, better known as La Leona, who tells her fellow *soldaderas* not to dance with other soldiers while their men are fighting. She restores the life of Elisa Zambrano, the woman who gathers an army of women and children armed with rocks and sticks to defeat the enemy. Thus, Poniatowska reconstructs, as she does in her urban chronicles, heterogeneous personalities silenced by a cultural and political tradition that discriminates against the marginal and dispossessed (Bencomo 75).[9] In many ways, she follows the example of several women historians who have done extensive research on the *soldaderas* since the mid-twentieth century, like Ángeles Mendieta Alatorre, Anna Macías, and Elizabeth Salas, among others.

Most *corridos* of the Mexican Revolution are filled with romantic and idealized Adelitas, whose military presence is practically nonexistent (Herrera-Sobek 104–5; Linhard 75). In view of this unfortunate situation, Poniatowska subverts the domesticity and mythification of the female space to portray gender transgressions that successfully rearticulate women's marginality and reconfigure an imposed silence. This is how the chronicler attempts to heal the open wounds caused by official history, not only rescuing a number of otherwise anonymous or forgotten women but also the portrait of others previously mythified, such as Adela Velarde Pérez, who might have been the real Adelita (Rueda-Acedo, "*Las Soldaderas*" 424). Instead of portraying women as an integrated and unified whole, Poniatowska re-creates, for instance, the figure of a strong, fearless, dangerous tortilla maker, better known as La China, in charge of an army made up of widows, wives, daughters, and sisters from all walks of life. Through this creative process, the chronicler rewrites historical facts gathered by Salas (67–81) and thus vocalizes a noncorporeal discourse within a story that corrects previous versions of official history.

Poniatowska began rewriting women's participation in the Mexican Revolution in 1969, when she fictionalized in her testimonial novel, *Hasta no verte, Jesús mío*, the life of Jesusa Palancares and the experiences of other *soldaderas*. Based on Josefina Bórquez's testimony, Poniatowska re-created, for example, the revolutionary profile of Lucía, General Genovevo Blanco's daughter, an extraordinary *soldadera* who was feared by men and women alike: "Todos la obedecían. Revisaba la puntería de los hombres. Entrenaba la caballería. Conocía el calibre de las balas y con su papá planeaba ataques y defensas" (All of them obeyed her. She checked their aim. She trained the soldiers. She knew the caliber of the bullets, and with her father she planned attacks and defenses) (80–81). In the novel, Jesusa asserts that her husband dressed her like a man and took her to the battlefields: "me puso mi pantalón de montar, mi chaquetín, mi paliacate rojo y mi sombrero tejano y nadie se dio cuenta si era hombre o si era mujer" (he gave me riding pants, a jacket, a red bandanna and a hat, and nobody noticed whether I was a man or a woman) (90). She explains in great detail the role of other women like and unlike her:

> Casi no iban mujeres en campaña; a mí me llevaba Pedro sin orden del general Espinosa y Córdoba; por eso me vestía de hombre para que se hicieran de la vista gorda. Me tapaba la cabeza con el paliacate y el sombrero. Por lo regular, unas iban como yo, porque sus maridos las obligaban, otras porque le hacían al hombre, pero la mayoría de las mujeres se quedaban atrás con la impedimenta.
>
> (Very few women participated in the battles; Pedro took me without permission from General Espinosa y Córdoba; that's why he dressed me like a man, so they wouldn't say anything. I covered my head with a bandanna and a hat. Usually, there were some women just like me there because their husbands forced them to, others were there because they were like men, but the majority of the women stayed behind.) (109–10)

In *Luz y luna, las lunitas* (*Light and Moon, Little Moons*), Poniatowska continues the task of reinserting women's historical presence in the Mexican Revolution and writes that one of Jesusa's fellow *soldaderas* "tuvo a su chilpayate en una trinchera" (had her baby in a trench), while another one gave birth in the desert "y se le murió por falta de agua" (and the baby died due to lack of water) (47). As she retells the life of Jesusa, once again Poniatowska takes the opportunity to depict the *soldaderas* as brave women and soldiers that without any fear "se lanzaban atrabancadas a desafiar a la muerte" (openly defied death) (47). She also writes, without giving any particular names, that the *soldaderas* in general, besides carrying their pots and pans, chickens, pigs, blankets, ammunition, kettles, riffles, and grinding stones, played the guitar and sang their songs at night. In *Las Soldaderas*, however, the chronicler goes the extra mile: she writes lengthy descriptions of some women who distinguished themselves for their unique actions.

In addition to retelling the story of Jesusa Palancares, who confronts Venustiano Carranza when he refuses to pension her as the widow of Captain Pedro Aguilar, Poniatowska writes about Carmen and Natalia Serdán and points out, most likely drawing from Mendieta Alatorre's *Las mujeres en la Revolución Mexicana* (53–56), that these sisters distributed revolutionary pamphlets and transported weapons for the rebels. In *Las soldaderas* we meet the famous Colonel Carmen Amelia Robles, "más plana que una tabla" (flatter than a board) (15/19). This woman who accentuated her masculinity wearing a shirt and a tie, Poniatowska writes, "ni dormida dejó de acariciar su pistola que pesaba sobre su muslo derecho. Si con la mano derecha disparaba, con la izquierda sostenía el cigarro" (even in her sleep she wouldn't stop caressing the pistol she carried on her right thigh. She'd shoot with her right hand and hold her cigar with her left) (15/19). Poniatowska informs us of Petra Ruiz, who dressed up as a man and worked as a soldier for Carranza's army. She was so courageous and violent, we read, that she was better known as "el Echa Balas" (The Shooter) (16/20). She highlights the life of the legendary Petra Herrera, who became Pedro Herrera and led an army of her own. Recognized as an excellent soldier, Petra/Pedro "en las madrugadas fingía rasurarse la barba" (at dawn she pretended to shave her beard) (17/21), until she finally reveals her braids, asserting in front of everyone: "Soy mujer y voy a seguir sirviendo como soldada con mi nombre verdadero" (I'm a woman and I will continue to carry out my duties as a soldier using my real name) (17/21).

Many other *soldaderas* fill this chronicle with copious details about the varied lives of women during the Mexican Revolution. In a clear attempt to recover their image from the lost archives of history, Poniatowska writes *in extenso*:

> Rosa Bobadilla viuda de Casas, coronela zapatista, fue una figura indispensable en más de 168 acciones armadas; Juana Ramona viuda de Flores (la Tigresa) participó en la toma de Culiacán, Sinaloa; Carmen Parra de Alanís (la Coronela Alanís) se unió al movimiento antirreeleccionista, fungió como correo de Madero, peleó contra las tropas de Huerta, formó

parte de las filas villistas en la toma de Ciudad Juárez, fue convencionista y correo de Emiliano Zapata. Clara de la Rocha, comandante de guerrilla, tuvo un papel importante en la toma de Culiacán, Sinaloa; Carmen Vélez (la Generala) destacó por comandar más de trescientos hombres en los distritos de Hidalgo y Cuauhtémoc en Tlaxcala. Catalina Zapata Muñoz (capitán primero zapatista) se encargó de proveer pertrechos de guerra e informes de actividades federales. Ángela Gómez Saldaña (agente confidencial de Zapata) llevaba y traía información a los jefes zapatistas sobre las acciones de los federales; conseguía y repartía armas a los campamentos revolucionarios. María Esperanza Chavira, coronela zapatista, combatió en los sitios de Cuautla, Puebla y Chilpancingo. Florinda Lazos León, enfermera y correo del Ejército Libertador del Sur, cuidó a los heridos hasta que cayó exhausta y murió. Nada le espantaba, ni las manos arrancadas de cuajo, ni los huesos pelados, ni el vientre destripado, ni la cabeza ensangrentada. Encarnación Mares (Chonita) se incorporó al lado de su marido al décimo regimiento de Caballería Constitucionalista, en 1913. A lo largo de su carrera militar obtuvo los grados de cabo, sargento segundo, sargento primero y subteniente. Destacó en diversas batallas. Muy hábil en el manejo de animales briosos, domaba potros al igual que la Nacha Ceniceros de Nellie Campobello. Se vestía de hombre y engrosaba la voz al hablar.

(Rosa Bobadilla, a Zapatista colonel and the widow of Casas, played an indispensable role in more than 168 armed encounters. Juana Ramona ("The Tigress"), Flores's widow, participated in the capture of Culiacán, Sinaloa. Carmen Parra de Alanís ("La Coronela Alanís") joined the anti-reelectionist movement, acted as Madero's messenger, fought against Huerta's troops, was part of the Villista ranks during the Battle of Ciudad Juárez, became a Convencionista and a messenger for Emiliano Zapata. Clara de la Rocha, guerrilla commander, played an important role in the capture of Culiacán, Sinaloa. Carmen Vélez ("La Generala") distinguished herself by leading 300 men in the Hidalgo and Cuauhtémoc districts in Tlaxcala. Catalina Zapata Muñoz, Zapatista First Captain, took charge of distributing battle gear and obtaining

> reports of federal activities. Ángela Gómez Saldaña, Zapata's confidential agent, carried dispatches back and forth reporting on federal movements; she was also charged with finding and distributing weapons among the revolutionary camps. María Esperanza Chavira, a Zapatista colonel, fought at the sieges of Cuautla, Puebla, and Chilpancingo. Florinda Lazos León, nurse and messenger for the Liberation Army of the South, took care of the wounded until she collapsed and died of exhaustion. Nothing frightened her, not severed hands, nor exposed bones, nor disemboweled abdomens nor heads bathed in blood. Encarnación Mares ("Chonita") joined up with her husband's Tenth Regiment of the Constitutionalist Cavalry in 1913. During the length of her military career, she attained the rank of private, second sergeant, first sergeant, and sublieutenant. She distinguished herself in several battles. Extremely skillful in handling wild animals, she tamed colts much like La Nacha Ceniceros whom Nellie Campobello wrote about in her book. She dressed like a man and spoke with a deep, husky voice.) (16/19–20)

In each case the *soldaderas* represent a "multi-differentiated plural," one that challenges the common labels of "woman" or the erroneous essence or substance of the female body with a complex discourse that intersects power, hegemony, culture, and resistance (Richard, "La crítica" 83). Not all of them are brave or feared by others. Some passively follow their men because they have no other option, and this fact does not exclude them from an openly feminist work. As she writes their lives in a hybrid text that combines creativity and the testimonies gathered by women historians such as Salas, Poniatowska creates several literary certificates of citizenship for them, even if they are only temporary, even if these acts of female empowerment do not always change the mythical presence of *soldaderas* in popular culture. Metaphorically speaking, Poniatowska obtains these certificates of recognition for an entire group of women in desperate need of reinvention. At least within this chronicle, the women who have hardly entered any official records have a place of their own, even if during their lifetime they were disrespectfully referred to as gossips and cockroaches, blabbermouths and sluts. As Mendieta Alatorre noted in her 1961 study, during the revolution many women worked as nurses, founded newspapers, and joined the army as *soldaderas*, and some even signed public manifestos, but their ultimate reward was death, misery, imprisonment, persecutions, violation, and derision (174).

As a contemporary chronicle that is not a novel or a short story, Poniatowska's work presents itself as "liminal literature" (Corona and Jörgensen 1–21) but, more important, as an oblique discourse that challenges hegemonic discourses. Thus, *Las soldaderas* represents women within a reality that tends to exclude them from any in-depth cultural reflections or artistic manifestations. Most *soldaderas*, as we have seen so far, enter a limited number of literary spaces, and their portraits reinforce various patriarchal structures of power. Only in a handful of fictional spaces do some authors give the *soldaderas* the opportunity to speak, the central role, or the kind of interior development or complexity usually reserved for the male characters of the Mexican Revolution.

Ignacio Solares's short story "Las soldaderas," for example, included in his collection *Ficciones de la Revolución Mexicana* (*Fictions of the Mexican Revolution*) (2009), has more to do with the men of the revolution, such as Pancho Villa or Jesús Cárdenas, than with any *soldaderas*. Only at the beginning of the story, when a young soldier wants to take his partner with him, we read that Pancho Villa will not allow that. Villa

> cree que un ejército moderno debe estar formado únicamente por hombres que ocupen todos los puestos de línea, sin la monserga de traer atrás a las viejas corriendo desaforadas, tropezándose y volviéndose a levantar, con sus escuincles moquientos, sus ollas, sus cacerolas, sus peroles, sus aperos para dormir sonándoles como cencerros.
>
> (believes that a modern army should be composed of men that serve in all ranks, without having to drag their women, who follow the troops with their children, pots, pans, and mats, making noises like cowbells.) (93)

The entire story focuses on Villa's cruelty and the negative transformation of this Mexican Robin Hood who becomes a robber and a heartless villain. His cruelty is summarized in the last pages of the story, as we reread the episode in which he orders the murder of ninety (rather than sixty) *soldaderas*. This time his soldiers do not burn them; instead, they shoot them one by one. The conclusion is practically the same. The *soldaderas* are still portrayed as "viejas tercas" (stubborn women), "pinches viejas" (fucking women), and ultimately as a "bola de viejas" (a bunch of women) (98) who can only accept their deterministic life and death.

Women Rebels of the Twenty-First Century

History tells us that a good number of women participated in the Mexican Revolution not only as *soldaderas* but also as true intellectuals. I speak, for instance, of journalist Juana Belén Gutiérrez de Mendoza (1875–1942), who edited the anti-Díaz newspaper *Vésper*; schoolteacher Dolores Jiménez y Muro (1848–1925), whose poems and controversial articles appeared in several newspapers and in the feminist journal *La Mujer Mexicana* (*The Mexican Woman*); and the private secretary of President Venustiano Carranza, Hermila Galindo de Topete (1896–1954), author of several feminist and political tracts and editor of the feminist journal *Mujer Moderna* (*Modern Woman*).[10] In many ways, the character of Diamantina Vicario, in Cristina Rivera Garza's *Nadie me verá llorar* (*No One Will See Me Cry*) (1999), honors these women. Diamantina attends revolutionary meetings and discusses politics; speaks of justice; makes fun of the editorials that appear in *El Imparcial* (*The Impartial*), the journal controlled by Porfirio Díaz; and publishes her own articles in *Vésper* or other polemical venues. Accordingly, her house is presented as a center of dissidence and political activism:

> Hombres y mujeres entran con cifras alarmantes en la boca, noticias de nuevos atropellos, papeletas con letras negras y rojas. El periódico que les deja manchas negras en las yemas de los dedos no es *El Universal* o *El Imparcial*, sino *El Hijo del Ahuizote* donde, bajo el nombre de Tina Vica, Diamantina publica comentarios críticos y bromas contra don Porfirio. Los esqueletos juguetones de Posada los hacen reír. La palabra huelga es una llave maestra en sus labios, todo lo abre y todo lo cierra.
>
> (Men and women enter with alarming figures on their lips, news of new outrages, pamphlets printed in red and black. The newspaper that leaves black stains on their fingers is not *El Universal* or *El imparcial*, but *El Hijo del Ahuizote*, in which, under the name Tina Vica, Diamantina publishes a column of

> criticism and jokes against the country's president, don Porfirio Díaz. Posada's playful skeletons make them laugh. The word "strike" is a passkey on their lips—it opens everything and closes everything they say). (126/136)

Tireless, Diamantina travels across the country for days at a time, transporting "papeletas y panfletos en su maleta negra" (papers and pamphlets in her black suitcase) (127/136). Thus she teaches Matilda Burgos, the novel's protagonist, a lesson that changes her life: "El cuarto que debes limpiar está detrás de tus ojos, de tu cabeza. Las mujeres deben entrar al cielo con libros, con música, no con escobas y trapos viejos, damita. Ponte lista" (the room that you must claim is behind your eyes, inside your head. Women should enter the kingdom of heaven with books, with music, not with brooms and dust rags, little lady. Wise up) (127/137). Matilda does not become an activist or a *soldadera*, but she carries out gender transgressions of her own when she works as a prostitute at La Modernidad or during the twenty-eight years she spends within the walls of La Castañeda, an insane asylum where she writes diplomatic letters denouncing her unjust living condition.[11]

In the play *Soles en la sombra: Mujeres en la Revolución* (*Suns in the Shade: Women in the Revolution*) (2011), playwright Estela Leñero also pays attention to Juana Belén, who became a Zapatista colonel, and Dolores Jiménez y Muro, the leader of the Tacubaya plot against Díaz. In addition, she traces the life of María Talavera (1867–1946), an anarchist, and highlights the political actions of Leonor Villegas (1876–1955), a political activist, journalist, and founder and director of the White Cross under the orders of Venustiano Carranza. The play revolves around these women and demystifies the male figures of the Mexican Revolution (Flores Magón, Zapata, Carranza) who are privileged in most historical rearticulations. Thanks to a *corrido* that depicts her life for the audience, we know that Juana Belén "luchó contra don Porfirio / con alma, tinta y papel" (fought against don Porfirio / with her soul, ink and pen), and that "Allá en mil novecientos / a la cárcel fue a caer / porque defendía a los mineros / y huelgas se puso a hacer" (Back in 1900, / she ended up in jail / because she defended the mine workers / and began to organize strikes) (39). In the play, Juana Belén wants to change the country, fights for her democratic ideals and uses her articles as weapons against social injustice. As Zapata's colonel, she punishes other soldiers who take advantage of women, arguing, "en mi tropa nadie abusa de las mujeres" (under my command, nobody abuses women) (72) and appears as the real author of the Plan de Ayala.

In the same vein, María Talavera is not portrayed simply as Ricardo Flores Magón's lover and companion in El Paso, Texas, but as a brave woman of political conviction who transports weapons to Ciudad Júarez. As proof of her courage, at one point María "*Se levanta la falda y muestra cartucheras, municiones y armas desarmadas, colgando de un cinturón. Se abre la capa que trae puesta y muestra alrededor de la cintura cartuchos y un revolver; abre su blusa y dentro de su corsé tiene un par de bombas de dinamita como si fueran senos*" (*lifts up her skirt and shows cartridge belts, ammunition, and unloaded weapons hanging from a belt. Under her jacket, she has more cartridges and a revolver; she unbuttons her blouse and her corset holds two dynamite bombs as if they were breasts*) (52, emphasis in original). In the play, she kills for her man and confesses to writing propaganda, manifestos, and all sorts of revolutionary flyers. In one of her final speeches, the play moves forward to the twenty-first century and Talavera confronts the president of Mexico with a discourse that speaks for those who are permanently silenced:

> ¿Habrá justicia para mi Ricardo, señor presidente? ¿Habrá justicia para todos estos muertos? ¿para los que lucharon por la libertad? ¿para los que lucharon denunciando tanta infamia? ¿para los que se mueren de hambre? ¿para los que no tienen con qué curar a sus hijos? ¿para los que están encerrados en la cárcel sin haber cometido un crimen? ¿Habrá justicia señor presidente? (Pausa) ¿Por lo menos sabe usted qué es justicia? ¿Puede contestar a mi pregunta? . . . Contésteme señor presidente . . . ¿Es usted capaz de hacer justicia? Contésteme . . . Porque si usted no es capaz de darle justicia a la Nación nosotros lo haremos con nuestras propias manos.
>
> (Will there be justice for my Ricardo, Mr. President? Will there be justice for the deceased? For those who fought for freedom? For those who denounced so much infamy? For those who are starving? For those who cannot cure their children? For those who are imprisoned without having committed a crime? Will there be justice? (*Pause*) Do you at least know what justice is? Can you answer my question? . . . Answer me,

> Mr. President . . . Are you capable of doing justice? Answer me . . . Because if you're not capable of doing justice to our Nation, we will take the matter into our own hands.) (90–91)

Talavera speaks with the urgency of an unjust present of unpunished crimes and from the perspective of a contemporary Zapatista leader, such as the late Comandante Ramona or the Mayor Ana María.

In *Soles en la sombra*, Dolores Jiménez y Muro is in jail for her revolutionary ideals and mainly serves as an interlocutor to the other female characters. Leonor Villegas, on the other hand, is portrayed as a fearless nurse: "Salí a las calles impulsada porque me dolía ver tantos heridos. Quería curarlos a todos. Aunque iba tan de prisa que lo primero que encontré fue una toalla" (I went out to the streets because it hurt me to see so many wounded people. I wanted to cure them. And I was walking so fast that the first thing that I found was a towel) (70). "Ahí entre enfermos" (There, among the wounded), according to the *corridista*, "la rica Leonor brilló / y de ser mujer elegante / en líder se convirtió" (the rich Leonor shone, / and, after being an elegant woman, / she became a leader) (64). Like the historical Villegas, this one leaves her husband and children to lead the White Cross and warns the women who work under her direct supervision: "antes que el amor está el deber" (duty comes before love) (67). Surrounded by a community of strong women, Leonor behaves like a true leader throughout the play. Thanks to her activism, we meet Teresa, a brave colonel who wears men's clothing and calls herself Guillermo Martínez Celis; Araceli, an important nurse; and María de Jesús, another colonel. Through their voices and actions, Leñero effectively displays subtle gender transgressions. As the *corridista* summarizes toward the end of the play, "Esta historia de mujeres / una enseñanza nos dio / la lucha no ha terminado / sigue la Revolución" (this story of women / has taught us a lesson / the struggle has not ended / the Revolution continues) (88). While Leonor realizes in contemporary times that she will have to take care of the wounded in an uncontrollable new battle, María is convinced they will be able to defeat the powerful, and Juana Belén takes this opportunity to reaffirm her political agenda: "Yo publicaré *Vésper*. Si servía en tiempos de don Porfirio, seguro que podremos darle algunos madrazos al dictador actual" (I will publish *Vésper*. If it worked in times of don Porfirio, I'm sure we can use it to attack the current dictator) (92).

Focusing on these women, Leñero's play confirms that the Mexican Revolution had a profound impact on their lives. As Shirlene Ann Soto observed in an in-depth study on several revolutionary women who also joined the women's rights movements in the early decades of the twentieth century, during the Mexican Revolution they undertook new responsibilities and participated in the fighting, plans, and attempts to implement the revolutionary goals; they also traveled throughout the country and became politically active, although mostly they were neither recognized for their efforts nor granted the political equality promoted by revolutionary ideology (106). Mexican women, as Monsiváis argued on several occasions, have consistently been portrayed in Mexican literature as distant and admirable, serene, passive, and delicate, thanks in part to a sexist rhetoric that sells their image as a vaporous spirit that could be, at best, loyal and gracious, entertaining and brave, but hardly ever anything more than that. Although women gained a considerable amount of agency during the revolution, Mexican culture has kept the oppressive structures of a sexist family system, one that, supported by the Mexican Revolution, promotes the admirable vision of a *soldadera* who follows her Juan and thus ratifies her unalterable submission (Monsiváis, *Misógino* 32–40). Indicative of this attitude is, in fact, the famous revolutionary *corrido* of "La rielera," in which the female protagonist, armed with a couple of pistols, sings: "Yo soy rielera y tengo mi Juan, / él es mi vida y yo soy su querer. / Cuando me dicen que ya se va el tren, / adiós mi rielera, ya se va tu Juan" (I am a train rider and I have my Juan, / he is my life and I am his love. / When they tell me that the train is leaving, / goodbye my *rielera*, your Juan is leaving).

In her play, Estela Leñero subverts this romanticized idea of the revolutionary woman who appears in Mexican literature and in some *corridos* of the Mexican Revolution.[12] Writing against the grain, in *Soles en la sombra* Leñero confronts head-on the fact that the world of politics has been historically reserved for men. Here, the heroine of the revolutionary movement is no longer perceived simply as "la mujer del héroe" (the hero's woman) (Monsiváis, *Misógino* 107). On the contrary, through the actions of Gutiérrez de Mendoza, Talavera, and Villegas (among others), we are asked to recognize the revolutionary woman as the real precursor of today's feminism. As a colonel, for instance, Juana Belén openly challenges Emiliano Zapata when he commands her to go to Huautla. At her refusal, he insults her: "No me chingue" (Don't fuck with me), only to hear her unforgiving reply right away: "Usted tampoco, general Zapata" (Likewise, General Zapata) (75). She and the rest of the women who fight for him are just "pinches viejas" (fucking women) (75), according to the leader, but soon these "viejas" prove that "La Revolución está todavía por venir" (the Revolution is yet to come) (89) and that it needs women of their strength and political ideals.

The play, then, confirms that women of all sorts—not just those *soldaderas* who followed their Juanes—participated in the Mexican Revolution within different systems of authority and made an impact socially and politically, while their bodies were simultaneously transformed by the emergence of new social and political relations across the country (Kaplan 407). Due to Mexico's sexism, women's participation in the revolution has mostly been considered "ahistorical," as if their real historical interventions occurred at the margins of political and social prestige or in the domestic—and therefore "inferior"—realm of everyday life (Monsiváis, "De cuando" 16). This, in fact, is the reason someone like Elena Arizmendi (1884–1949), founder of the Cruz Blanca Neutral at the beginning of the revolution, has been remembered not as a pioneer of feminism and Madero's supporter but simply as José de Vasconcelos's lover or as an erotic female character in his autobiographical works. Only now, thanks to Gabriela Cano's timely biography, *Se llamaba Elena Arizmendi* (2010), do we begin to see her under a new light: as the courageous nurse who challenged male doctors and soldiers with a firm attitude that contests imposed ideals of feminine sacrifice, maternity, and submission.

Why else does Mexico remember Adela Velarde Pérez (1900–1971) not as a nurse of the Cruz Blanca formed by Leonor Villegas but as a romantic and idealized lover? Thanks to the famous *corrido* that supposedly immortalizes her, we can imagine that "Popular entre la tropa era Adelita, / la mujer que el sargento idolatraba, / que además de ser valiente era bonita / y hasta el mismo coronel la respetaba" (Popular among the troop was Adelita, / the woman that the sergeant idolized, / and besides being brave she was pretty, / so that even the colonel respected her). She is allowed fame and popularity only as a desirable and irresistible woman and because she is adored by an important soldier who will follow her if she tries to go away with someone else: "Si Adelita se fuera con otro / la seguiría por tierra y por mar, / si por mar en un buque de guerra, / si por tierra en un tren militar" (If Adelita were to leave with another man, / I'd follow her over land and sea, / if by sea, in a warship, / if by land, in a military train). "La Adelita" becomes the great text and melody of the Mexican Revolution because her image does not represent a threat to the social order (Monsiváis, "De cuando" 18). Furthermore, she is loved for her potential to become, in a matter of seconds in the midst of the song, someone's girlfriend, someone's lover: "Si Adelita quisiera ser mi novia, / y si Adelita fuera mi mujer, / le compraría un vestido de seda / para llevarla a bailar al cuartel" (If Adelita wanted to be my girlfriend, / and if Adelita would be my woman, / I'd buy her a silk dress / to take her to the barracks' dance).

In Mexican popular culture, the romantic story we find in this *corrido* will always win over any historical truth. It is safe and beautiful. It sounds appealing, and it is noncombative. Interestingly, a committed writer such as Poniatowska continues to rearticulate, well into the twenty-first century, Adelita's life and myth with seemingly nonthreatening narratives that attempt to give a historical dimension to this and other *soldaderas*. In one of her children's books, titled *La Adelita* (2006), instead of repeating the same old story that most parents would want their children to memorize, Poniatowska, as she has done in the past, thickens the familiar lyrics of the *corrido* with details that disturb the original plot. After recalling a number of uncertainties around Adelita's life and the eponymous *corrido*, Poniatowska tells her "young" audience that she probably ran away from home at the age of fourteen in 1913 and joined the troops of Colonel Alfredo Breceda. Subsequently, she writes, "Se hizo enfermera de las tropas constitucionalistas y atendió a los heridos en los combates de Camargo, Torreón, Parral y Santa Rosalía" (She became a nurse for the constitutionalist troops and tended the wounded in the battles of Camargo, Torreón, Parral and Santa Rosalía).[13] Like a good storyteller, Poniatowska includes several fragments of an idealized story that undoubtedly her readers expect: "En Tampico, Tamaulipas, un joven capitán, Elías Cortázar Ramírez, tocaba en una armónica la canción en su honor" (In Tampico, Tamaulipas, a young captain, Elías Cortázar Ramírez, played her song on the harmonica). Along these lines, she writes, "Según otra de las leyendas, la canción fue compuesta por un sargento villista, Antonio del Río Armenta, con quien Adela, supuestamente, tuvo un hijo cuando ambos militaban en la División del Norte" (According to another legend, the song was composed by a Villista sergeant, Antonio del Río Armenta, with whom Adela, supposedly, had a child when both of them were serving in the Division of the North). Just as we begin to recognize what we already know of Adelita's legendary profile, Poniatowska writes with her unfailing tone of denouncement:

> La Adelita de carne y hueso y un pedazo de pescuezo trabajó durante treinta y dos años en la Secretaría de Industria y Comercio, en un puesto burocrático. En 1963, a duras penas, se le concedió una pensión como veterana de la Revolución. Otras famosas, como Juana Gallo y la Cucaracha, nunca alcanzaron la popularidad de la Adelita.
>
> (The flesh-and-blood Adelita worked for thirty-two years at the Ministry of Industry and Commerce, occupying a bureaucratic position. In 1963, she was granted a pension as a veteran of the Revolution. Other famous women, like Juana Gallo and La Cucaracha, never gained Adelita's popularity.)

This is the story of Adela Velarde Pérez, but not necessarily the story of the real "Adelita," whose identity is still unknown to us.

Is the outcome for the other women rebels any better? Not really. After fighting all her life for justice and liberty as the editor of *Vésper* and *Alba Mexicana* (*Mexican Dawn*), or as a Zapatista colonel, the creator of worker unions, and the founder of the Club Político Femenil Amigas del Pueblo, Juana Belén Gutiérrez de Mendoza died in poverty and was soon forgotten by her country. As historian Alicia Villaneda recalls in her recent edition of the rebel's biography, "Cuando Juana Belén murió el 13 de julio de 1942, a la edad de sesenta y siete años, su hija no pudo solventar los gastos de su entierro y tuvo que vender su máquina de escribir, esa máquina donde Juana Belén pasó horas y horas, procurando la *Justicia* y persiguiendo la *Libertad*" (When Juana Belén died on July 13, 1942, at the age of sixty-seven, her daughter couldn't pay for her funeral and had to sell her typewriter, the typewriter that Juana Belén used for endless hours, fighting for *Justice* and seeking *Liberty*) (125). María Talavera, the outspoken anarchist, political activist, and loyal supporter of *magonismo*, died in an adobe house in Ensenada and was also forgotten by her people. These endings are unfortunately predictable. Women involved in politics are condemned to face not only the problems of the nation but also gender violence and the double standards of their misogynist work environments (Monsiváis, *Misógino* 164). Only in the Mexican *corrido* do the soldiers glorify the women involved in the revolution: "Una pasión me domina / y es la que me hizo venir, / Valentina, Valentina / yo te quisiera decir" (A passion dominates me / and it's made me come here, / Valentina, Valentina / I'd like to tell you). Only the men in those songs deserve a courageous and dignified ending: "Valentina, Valentina, / rendido estoy a tus pies, / si me han de matar mañana, / que me maten de una vez" (Valentina, Valentina, / I surrender at your feet. / If they're going to kill me tomorrow, / let them kill me now).

Nurses of the Mexican Revolution

In tune with Leñero's play, in her novel *Las rebeldes* (*The Rebels*) (2011), Mónica Lavín focuses her attention on the women of the Cruz Blanca Constitucionalista. Unlike her bestseller *Yo, la peor*, this novel has not received critical attention, perhaps because it revolves around the life of Leonor Villegas instead of Sor Juana, who has become not only an iconic figure but a true Mexican tradition. This seems to be the destiny of many women cataloged as "secondary characters" in the vast majority of historical formulations (Beltrán 119). Sor Juana's fame saves her from oblivion, Gabriel Zaid would note, because it allows her to become a cultural commodity and a popular "object" that substitutes the real "subject" (126). This is why culture uses her in infinite ways, remembers her on important occasions, and attributes to her impossible love affairs in contemporary literature, a masculine personality, and an alternative sexuality or feminisms that are not always coherent with her true historical context. With the exception of Adelita and a few others, however, most of the women involved in the Mexican Revolution remain invisible in the twenty-first century. They are treated as invisible social agents, incapable of having a positive impact on their communities, thanks to an ancestral and inherited disdain toward them. Not surprisingly, their actions and words are perceived as irrelevant; their names, dates of birth and death are forgotten; their lives are recorded with inaccuracy; and quite frequently, their printed documents are destroyed or just happen to disappear (Cano, "Las mujeres" 22).

We know how this story goes, but women did actively participate during the Mexican Revolution: they took care of their children and provided sexual pleasure to their companions; they served as wives, victims, and accomplices but also as mothers, spies, and cooks; they transported mail and illegal weapons, they looked for water and food and even provided medical assistance to the wounded after every battle (Lau Jaiven 102). Nursing in particular was a major occupation for the women of the Mexican Revolution. The *soldaderas* treated the injured on the spot before transporting them to the nearest hospital, which could well be a train car, or they simply took them to the camp, where often they had to tear up their clothing to make bandages for the wounded (Reséndez Fuentes 130). Precisely because the troops involved in the conflict were unable to provide proper sanitary services to their wounded, numerous humanitarian women formed groups of medical aid and thus promoted the professionalization of nursing (Cano, *Elena Arizmendi* 75). In this context, Leonor Villegas de Magnón, following Arizmendi's legacy, founded the Cruz Blanca Constitucionalista as part of Venustiano Carranza's army in Laredo, Texas, in 1913. The fictionalization of her life in Lavín's *Las rebeldes* in many ways combats silence and invisibility, as it reconstructs the profile of a historical woman who actively participated in the political and cultural changes of her country at the onset of the Mexican Revolution (Cano, "Las mujeres" 21).

The life of Leonor Villegas is reconstructed in the novel from the perspective of Jenny Page, an American reporter who came in contact with the revolution in her youth and has inherited Villegas's unpublished memoirs. As the metafictional aged writer restores the experiences of the woman responsible for the foundation of the Cruz Blanca Constitucionalista, readers are invited to revisit the revolution from the perspective of several women whose activism redefined male sovereignty and male historical privilege. At the beginning of the novel, Leonor comes across as a strong woman who believes in Madero's ideals of democracy and writes articles supporting him for several newspapers. After Madero's death, she transforms her living room in Nuevo Laredo into a hospital, aided by other women who have left their families to help the revolutionaries, like the historical nurses Areceli (García) or Eva and Trinidad Flores Blanco. She also works with Jovita Idar, a reporter whose military communiqués published in *La Crónica* (*The Chronicle*) are written with the soldiers' firsthand testimonies; and she finds a true friend and supporter in another nurse, Lily Long, who happens to be Jenny Page's aunt.

Moved by the urgency to change her country, Leonor becomes the president of the Cruz Blanca after leaving her husband in Mexico City and her three children in Laredo. She invests her personal fortune in uniforms, medicine, and trips to help the wounded and form new branches of the Cruz Blanca, even though she is criticized by other respectable women who would never sacrifice their families for the revolution. The cost of her endeavors is very high. Behind the facade of the successful fighter, Leonor hides her own insecurities, caused in part by what others—like her sister-in-law—say of her:

> ¿Qué clase de madre era Leonor, que dejaba a ese trío por atender heridos que no eran familia suya? ¿Qué clase de mujer era esa que quería andar haciendo cosas de hombres, montar a caballo, merodear las batallas, hablar con los más importantes, organizar, participar? ¿Qué no le bastaba con organizar su casa?
>
> (What kind of mother was Leonor if she left her children to tend the wounded who weren't her family? What kind of woman would want to do manly things: ride horses, hang around the battles, talk to the most important men, organize, participate? Wasn't she happy taking care of her house?) (231–32)

Suddenly, these words on the page reactivate Rosario Castellanos's denunciation of how Mexican society expects their women to be abnegated and maternal, virtuous and oppressed, sacrificed, exclusively devoted to their husbands and children, and ignorant of all issues outside the household (19–32). Fortunately, in the novel Leonor's political ideology and humanitarian commitment to the revolution is stronger than her personal inclinations and needs. She misses her children and misses intimacy with her husband; she longs for their meals together and their walks as a family. Yet "Subida en aquel tren, no cabía duda, ella era parte principal de la revuelta. Y los rebeldes iban ganando la partida" (On that train, without a doubt, she was an important part of the revolt. And the rebels were winning the game) (234). She feels valued serving under the orders of Venustiano Carranza and working with other admirable women for a common cause. After all, as her friend Lily Long recalls, "Las mujeres de México hacían cosas. Si eran pobres, acompañaban a sus hombres en la batalla o atendían en los hospitales de sangre improvisados en los pueblos; si eran ricas, algunas empeñaban su tiempo y su fortuna en servir a la batalla de los suyos" (The women of Mexico did a lot. If they were poor, they went with their men to battle, or they tended the wounded in improvised hospitals; if they were rich, some of them spent their time and fortune helping their men) (191).

Leonor knows what she wants, even if nobody else understands her: "Lo suyo era curar heridos" (she wanted to cure the wounded) (191). When a wounded soldier wants to know how to thank her for taking care of him, she replies with the voice of a warrior: "Peleando coronel" (Fighting, colonel) (154). However, not every nurse under her leadership shares her commitment and exclusive devotion to the revolution.

Aracelito, for instance, finds the time to write letters to her boyfriend, Guillermo, and Jenny Page cannot hide the forbidden love that she feels for Ramiro, a wounded federal soldier who happens to be her enemy. As tradition dictates, Adelita appears in this narrative as a young and beautiful nurse who catches the attention of the troops, and she is madly in love with Antonio, a sergeant who serenades her at night. Nevertheless, these women represent the human side of the revolution, one of sexual encounters and love affairs between soldiers and nurses, *soldaderas*, reporters, telegraphers. The Mexican Revolution disturbs the entire country not only at the national and political levels but also in the most personal and intimate spheres; it particularly changes how women relate to their own bodies and that of others of the same or opposite sex. This change in the perception of bodies is best exemplified in the novel when the three nurses talk maliciously about sex and sexuality, stating that "a los hombres les crece con lo que hacen pipí [. . .] y ya que está duro, pican a las mujeres para hacerles hijos" (men grow the thing that they pee with [. . .] and when it's hard, they poke women to get them pregnant) (168). Obviously these comments demystify the portrait of Adelita and other nurses and *soldaderas* found in the *corridos* of the Mexican Revolution. And Jenny Page reinforces the idea that the author wants to demystify Adelita when she pictures her being penetrated by one of the soldiers.

For better or worse, though, Adela cannot completely bury her mythical profile as the sensual woman of the revolution who disturbs the men around her with her beauty, "con sus pómulos y su piel cetrina, además de la elegancia espigada de su figura" (with her cheeks and olive skin, besides the elegance of her slim figure) (166). Like the legend requires her to be, she is "toda ojos y boca" (all eyes and mouth) (166), and these allusions to her physical aspect, sensuality, and sexual behavior, as we have seen with Malinche, Sor Juana, and Leona Vicario, make her more marketable in a neoliberal environment. Lavín, however, dramatically humanizes the icon's figure. When Adela's lover dies, she pulls her hair out of desperation and runs to his side to touch his body and close his eyes before the other soldiers drag him to his grave. Later, when Aracelito compares her loss to the loss of another nurse, Aurelia, she distorts her mythical figure. According to Page:

> Adela tomó un puño de arena y se lo lanzó a la cara. Aracelito, sobresaltada, se sacudió la arena, tosió y luego se le echó encima. Entre las enfermeras eran las más bonitas, y

> Adela, aunque en duelo, ya había aceptado alguno que otro cortejo de la tropa. Aracelito siempre marcaba su distancia. Por eso, por prudente que siempre fuera, me sorprendía verla ahora con el pelo revuelto y la cara enrojecida, intentando forzar a Adela para que cayera al piso. Empujones y rasguños. Los muchachos reaccionaron y fueron a separarlas.
>
> (Adela took a handful of sand and threw it at her face. Aracelito, shocked, shook it off, coughed and then attacked her. Among the nurses they were the most beautiful, and Adela, though in mourning, had already entertained possible suitors. Aracelito always established her distance. Because she was so cautious, I was surprised to see her with her hair tangled up and a red face, trying to push Adela to the floor. Shoving and scratches. The men reacted and separated them.) (202)

Adelita? Surely, this is not the Adelita who has survived the test of time in Mexican culture. In the famous Mexican *corrido*, the lover sings "Y si acaso yo muero en campaña / y mi cadáver lo van a sepultar, / Adelita, por Dios te lo ruego / que con tus ojos me vayas a llorar" (And if I happen to die at war / and they bury my body, / Adelita, by God, I beg you, / that with your eyes you cry for me). Accordingly, in the novel she enjoys telling her friends about her life with her deceased lover: "se defendía del dolor contando cosas, el cortejo de Antonio, la muerte de Antonio, su semblante aún tibio cuando lo fue a despedir. No se iba a quedar sin besar aquellos labios que murmuraron delicias, decía" (she protected herself from getting hurt by telling stories, Antonio's propositions, Antonio's death, his warm face when she said good-bye to him. She had to kiss those lips that murmured delights, she would say) (224). In this fictional space, Adelita knows that you only live once, "que esta muchacha se hará vieja" (that this young girl would become an old lady)—she reflects—"que el amor dura dos días, que en la batalla se mueren los hombres, que ayer Carranza era el mero mero y hoy Villa le está comiendo el mandado" (that love lasts a couple of days, that men die in battle, that yesterday Carranza was the man of the hour and today Villa is stealing his place) (226–27). In confirmation that at least some *soldaderas*, depending on their background, class affiliation, and individual personalities, could choose their own destiny, perhaps a new partner or a different occupation within the revolution (Salas 69; Poniatowska, *Las soldaderas* 21), Adelita begins to flirt with other men soon after Antonio's death. More important, though, she quickly decides to go with Pancho Villa, as she is convinced that good things happen where he is. In the novel, she is beautiful and wanted by the soldiers, but she is also intrepid and daring. Knowing that there is an opportunity to join the División del Norte with Felipe Ángeles and Pancho Villa, Adela begs her boss for permission to leave, arguing "Me gusta la acción, Leonor, y usted sabe que donde están esos dos, pasan cosas" (I like action, Leonor, and you know that things happen where those two are) (234). This determined Adelita does not need a man to promise her, as in the *corrido*, "un vestido de seda / para llevarla a bailar al cuartel" (a silk dress / to take her to the barracks' dance).

Considering that the women involved in the Mexican Revolution were not a single and unified subject but formed a diverse economic, ethnic, sexual, geopolitical, and cultural group (Cano, "Las mujeres" 23), in the novel Lavín fictionalizes all sorts of women. Her narrator, for instance, reflects on the generals' partners: "Carlota Miller, la mujer de González; Virginia Salinas, de Carranza; Luz Corral, la de Villa" (Carlota Miller, González's woman; Carranza's Virginia Salinas; Villa's Luz Corral) (253). We learn of the existence of influential and nonetheless marginalized women such as Leonor who could have become a general if she had been born a man. We are also asked to recognize the nurses who cannot help falling in love in times of war, as well as the *soldaderas* who follow their men from one battle to the next. In one of the chapters, for example, Leonor and Jovita visit one of the camps at night, and they see the *soldaderas* busy cooking for their men and serving their food. Leonor is moved by their solidarity, their abnegation, and their hard work and wonders with utmost honesty: "¿Cómo habrían de alimentar a los heridos que habían resguardado en esa vieja hacienda si no fuera por las soldaderas?" (How could they have fed the wounded in that old hacienda if it hadn't been for the *soldaderas*?) (271). The *soldaderas* in this particular scene hardly speak. They just offer food and serve it in silence. When one of them is asked if her husband comes with the troop, she simply replies: "En Charcas nos levantaron. Cuando el tren se detuvo. Queremos llegar a la capital" (They picked us up in Charcas. When the train stopped. We want to make it to the capital) (271). Acknowledging their vital mission within the revolution, as she eats the beans and tortillas one of them gives her, Leonor tells Jovita, the reporter: "Las soldaderas, Jovita, es todo un tema. Que no te acapare el trabajo de secretaria de la Cruz Blanca" (The *soldaderas*, Jovita, are something else. Don't let your work as secretary of the White Cross consume you) (273). And she asks Eustasio, the photographer, to take a picture of the *soldaderas* to keep a record of their fundamental work behind the scenes.

Evidently, the novel is not about this type of women but, as I have discussed, about the nurses of the Mexican Revolution, particularly Leonor Villegas de Magnón and her leadership in the Cruz Blanca Constitucionalista. Yet the novel as a whole deconstructs dominant discourses that marginalize, diminish, or obscure the participation of women in the revolutionary conflict. Furthermore, because it is written from a feminist and gendered perspective, *Las rebeldes* introduces the possibility of reading the Mexican Revolution from a different point of view, one that acknowledges the experiences of women from an authoritative stand. Like a good example of feminist writing, Lavín's novel exposes the female experience of the revolution in a way that disturbs and contests dominant, masculine discourses. This type of writing intersects today's political debates in regard to women, equality, and gender, especially as it redefines male sovereignty and privilege or as it confronts new oppressive structures and their literary representations in a new globalized era (Franco, *Ensayos* 38, 179).

Queer Revolutions

In *Las rebeldes*, there is a revolutionary woman who stands out from the rest. Her name is María de Jesús González, and she dresses like a man. Jenny Page notices that she is "muy desparpajada" (self-assured) (138), a brave soldier who drinks *aguardiente* and sleeps with her trousers on. During their brief lesbian encounter, Jenny pays attention not only to her feminine body in disguise but to the hard lifestyle that she has voluntarily chosen: "A la vista de esas plantas rosadas yo chupeteaba sus dedos, porque el aguardiente me había vuelto juguetona, mientras María de Jesús se retorcía cosquilluda. No podía creer que esa chica quisiera estar en lo más duro de la Revolución, en el campo, batiéndose" (I sucked her toes because the alcohol made me playful, while María de Jesús enjoyed my tickles. I couldn't believe that this girl would want to go through the hardships of the revolution, on the field, fighting) (140). Above all, Jenny admires María de Jesús because she can enter a world that is not accessible to other women; she can see what other women are unable to see, and she talks about the generals as if they were her close friends. This is understandable. Dressed as a man, Colonel María de Jesús is in close contact with Venustiano Carranza, General Murrieta,

General Maclovio Herrera, and other transcendental male figures of the Mexican Revolution. In fact, in recognition of her exemplary service to the revolution, General Felipe Ángeles saves her from being executed toward the end of the narrative, "Porque había sido valiente. Y porque no tenía la culpa de que los que éramos amigos fuésemos enemigos y se había jugado el pellejo" (Because she had been brave. And because it wasn't her fault that those of us who were friends were enemies, and because she had risked her life) (316).

The story of María de Jesús González is reminiscent of the brave Petra Herrera who became Pedro Herrera, the soldier, according to Poniatowska, who displayed "una enorme capacidad de liderazgo entre las fuerzas villistas" (extraordinary leadership abilities among the Villista troops) (Poniatowska, *Las soldaderas* 17/21). It is a story of gender transgression that has recently caught the attention of many Facebook and Twitter followers, thanks to animator Jason Porath, who includes an armed Petra Herrera in his collection of animated characters, titled *Rejected Princesses*: "Women Too Awesome, Awful, or Offbeat for Kids' Movies."[14] Together, the stories of María de Jesús and Petra remind us of other women who disguised themselves as men to be line soldiers and to become eligible for battlefield promotions (Salas 48). They also make us think of the lives of women like Oaxacan Ángela or "Ángel" Jiménez, who put on men's clothes to follow her father to the sierra, or women like "Chico," who enlisted with the Orozquistas after her mother and sister were killed by the federal troops (Reséndez Fuentes 117). In his 1994 novel *La negra Angustias*, Rojas González re-creates a similar story when the once-abused eponymous protagonist becomes a powerful colonel and orders Captain Güitlacoche to take off his clothes for she will wear them as part of her new identity. A good visual example of this kind of woman soldier is re-created in the film *La Cucaracha* (1958), directed by Ismael Rodríguez. In this film, renowned actress María Félix is dressed like a man, distinguishes herself from the *viejas* who passively follow their men, and leads her own army of women until the day she falls in love with Colonel Zeta and becomes his obedient *soldadera*.

One of the few women (dressed in men's clothes) praised in the *corridos* of the Mexican Revolution is the historical Petra Herrera, as evidenced in the "Corrido de la Toma de Torreón," the "Corrido del combate del 15 de mayo en Torreón," and "The Corrido de las hazañas del General Lojero y la Toma de Torreón por el ejército Liberador" (Herrera-Sobek 93). In reality, several women changed their identities during the course of the revolution, such as the Zapatista soldier María de la Luz Becerra or Petra/Pedro Ruiz, better known as "El Echa Balas" (Shooter), as Poniatowska recalls in her chronicle *Las soldaderas* (16). Others, such as Amelia Robles, became true transgendered subjects over the course of the revolution and defined themselves as men for the rest of their lives. Regarding Robles's case, Gabriela Cano explains:

> Por razones más vitales que ideológicas Amelio Robles, quien antes se llamó Amelia Robles, se unió a las fuerzas levantadas en el sur del país bajo la bandera agrarista de Emiliano Zapata y, en medio de las rudezas de la guerra, se forjó una identidad social y subjetiva masculina. Al término de la contienda armada, Amelio Robles continuó ostentándose como varón y sostuvo su identidad masculina a lo largo de su vida, en su actividad pública y en la esfera privada, durante la vejez y la enfermedad.
>
> (For vital more than for ideological reasons, Amelio Robles, who used to be Amelia Robles, joined the insurgent troops in the southern part of the country, under the agrarian flag of Emiliano Zapata and, in the midst of the cruelties of war, constructed for himself a masculine social and subjective identity. At the end of the armed conflict, Amelio Robles continued living as a man and kept his masculine identity throughout his life, in his public activities and in private, as an old man and in sickness.) ("Inocultables" 63)

Deeply unsatisfied with his biological gender assignment as a woman, Colonel Robles uses the revolution to his advantage, incarnates the ideal of the revolutionary macho, demands to be treated as a man, and even changes his birth certificate to be recognized as a *veterano* of the Mexican Revolution (Cano, "Inocultables" 69–76).

Apparently in sync with this spirit of self-determination that is possible thanks to the revolution, in the novel *Por debajo del agua* (*Under the Water*) (2001) Fernando Zamora re-creates the story of Hugo Estrada, a man who becomes a *soldadera* to embrace his true identity. Hugo joins the revolution, along with other women who carry all kinds of household goods and crockery, plus their children and pets, to be with the love of his life, the *Obregonista* cadet Pablo Aguirre, who will soon become a colonel and a general. With makeup and women's garments,

Hugo adopts a new identity as a woman and takes the name of his twin sister, Isabel, disappeared during the Decena Trágica. From the moment she rides the train—"yo soy rielera, tengo mi Juan" (I am a train rider, I have my Juan)—she and her friend Dolores work as courageous nurses for the rebels: "Entre las dos han dedicado tiempo y pericia a la Revolución, atendiendo enfermos y parturientas. Cuando el barbero no anda por ahí, saben también cortar el pelo, sacar una muela, desenterrar una uña o hacer infusiones para la reuma o el mal de ojo" (Both of them have dedicated time and expertise to the Revolution, tending the sick and the women who give birth. When the barber isn't there, they also know how to give haircuts; they pull teeth, remove ingrown nails, and make infusions for rheumatism or the evil eye) (47–48). Surrounded by other *soldaderas* who alternatively work as nurses and cooks, Isabel finds food—eggs, chorizo, anything—before the troops enter a particular town. At all times, she behaves as the colonel's wife, comforting him when he is afraid of his next military move and providing unconditional sexual pleasure for him, even when he mistreats her. Thus she repeats a story of gendered violence and female marginalization.

Toward the end of the novel, the meta-narrator analyzes one of Isabel's pictures where she is dressed as a woman and concludes: "Hay en ese pedazo de vida el tránsito de quien llega a ser su propio deseo. Como es evidente, Hugo se volvió más real en cuanto comenzó a llevar su propia máscara" (There is in that piece of life the transition of the person who becomes her own object of desire. Evidently, Hugo became more real when he began wearing his own mask) (143). Sadly, his gender transformation does not become a story of male or female empowerment. As soon as she joins the revolution, Isabel is treated like a *vieja* and *soldadera*, and she earns her living "cuidando niños y ancianas, echando tortillas, asistiendo a las parturientas, aprendiendo secretos de un cuerpo que no puede tener" (taking care of children and elderly women, flipping tortillas, helping the women who give birth, learning the secrets of a body that she cannot have) (179). Her physical transformation is so successful that at first Aguirre does not recognize her in women's clothing, and when he finally sees that she is Hugo, his secret adolescent love, he confirms with excitement: "¡Carajo, si eres una muchacha de verdad!" (Damn, you really are a woman!) (181). Ultimately, Pablo kills Hugo/Isabel after several years of a close relationship to destroy any rumors about his homosexual inclinations, which only confirms the power a man has over a woman or over a man who adopts a female identity.

As Zamora inverts the gender transformation of someone like Petra/Pedro Herrera, Amelio Robles, or the life of any other *soldadera*—as he declares in an interview—"que querían ser hombres, machorros" (who wanted to become men, manly) and consequently adopted male names and personalities (García Hernández), the novel confirms that male homosexuality is condemned because it is perceived as a rejection of masculinity. Pablo kills Isabel because other soldiers have found out, thanks to a child's testimony, that she has a penis and urinates standing up. In a violent bar scene, Pablo is publicly called a *maricón* (a fag), an effeminate man who threatens the masculinity of the troop and the overall masculine agenda of the revolution. To save his honor as a man, Pablo kills the aggressor in public, but he also kills Hugo/Isabel in private and lets others believe that "lo dejó la vieja" (his woman left him) (9). In the novel, there is not a single moment of female empowerment for Hugo/Isabel. Her gender transformation allows her to be perceived as a woman and behave like a woman, but that perception and adopted behavior forces her to live a story of misogyny and discrimination.

If we follow this logic, it makes sense that Amelio Robles is given the status of *veterano*, as his new gender identity highlights the overt masculinity that the revolution exalted (Cano, "Inocultables" 77). By the same token, it is understandable that in the "Corrido de las hazañas del General Lojero": "La valiente Petra Herrera / en el fragor del combate / aunque cayó prisionera / ni se dobla ni se abate" (The brave Petra Herrera / although she was captured, / in the midst of combat, is not defeated or bent). This overt display of masculine attributes—she is not bent—is also praised in the *corrido* "Juana Gallo," in which the protagonist "Siempre al frente de la tropa se encontraba / peleando como cualquier Juan" (At the front of the troops she would be found / fighting like any Juan). Only if we recognize this overvaluation of masculinity, do we realize why a *corrido* such as "La Chamuscada" honors a woman who becomes a general "porque sus manos la pólvora quemó, / entre las balas pasó la pelotera, / la 'revolufia' sus huellas le dejó" (because gunpowder burned her hands, / between the bullets she lived through the brawl, / the revolution left its mark on her). As a man who becomes a woman, however, Isabel occupies a lower place than Petra Herrera, Juana Gallo, or the anonymous Chamuscada, precisely because she adopts the "wrong" gender, emphasizing her chosen femininity and rejecting her assigned masculinity.

A queer novel such as *Por debajo del agua* acts as a double-edged sword. On one hand, it successfully destabilizes the heteronormative pattern we find in virtually all contemporary re-creations of the Mexican Revolution. The queer life that Pablo and Hugo share for seven years, living as a couple like any other Juan with his Adelita, fictionally deconstructs the allegedly masculine portrait of the revolution. Yet the more Hugo internalizes his role as Isabel, the more his new gender identity corroborates Mexico's sexism or the not-so-subtle ways Mexican culture empowers masculinity and marginalizes femininity. Thanks to this unjust division, the feminine is associated with tenderness and patience, sweetness, intuition, abnegation, resistance to pain, lack of initiative, inertia, and indecision, while the masculine is undoubtedly associated with the opposite (Monsiváis, *Misógino* 22). Is this not what Octavio Paz observed in *El laberinto de la soledad*? Has Mexican culture changed that much since Paz noted that women are considered "un instrumento, ya de los deseos del hombre, ya de los fines que le asigna la ley, la sociedad o la moral"? (an instrument, sometimes of masculine desires, sometimes of the ends assigned to her by morality, society, and the law) (39).

In the end, the *soldaderas* that we find in *Por debajo del agua*, including the transgendered Isabel, only confirm their marginality and subordination. When Isabel "disappears," nobody looks for her. She is just another *vieja*, and any other *soldadera* will soon replace her. Accordingly, after her death, she exits the narrative as a ghost, dressed in white and walking on air, representing in transgendered form the disappearance of the women in the turbulence of the revolution. Like Nacha Ceniceros, she is condemned to carry out her gender transgressions in the afterlife.

We might have to wait a while to see a well-rounded *soldadera* as the main protagonist of her own novel. Until now, only two popular fiction novels of the early 1980s—Carlos Isla's *La Valentina* (1980) and *La Adelita* (1981)—have attempted to reconstruct their historical figures, magnifying their positive relations with soldiers who treat them well and understand that they are their equal in the fight for social justice (Salas 88). Besides their partial reconstruction in Poniatowska's chronicles, Leñero's play, and Lavín's novel, most of them are standing still in one of the many photographs of the Casasola archive. Frozen in time and forever idealized in a number of Mexican *corridos*, they are waiting for somebody to take interest in their inner selves, their brief moments of empowerment, their victimization and historical invisibility. They are, as Monsiváis once argued, the dangerous force that the makers of History systematically ignore to avoid complications.

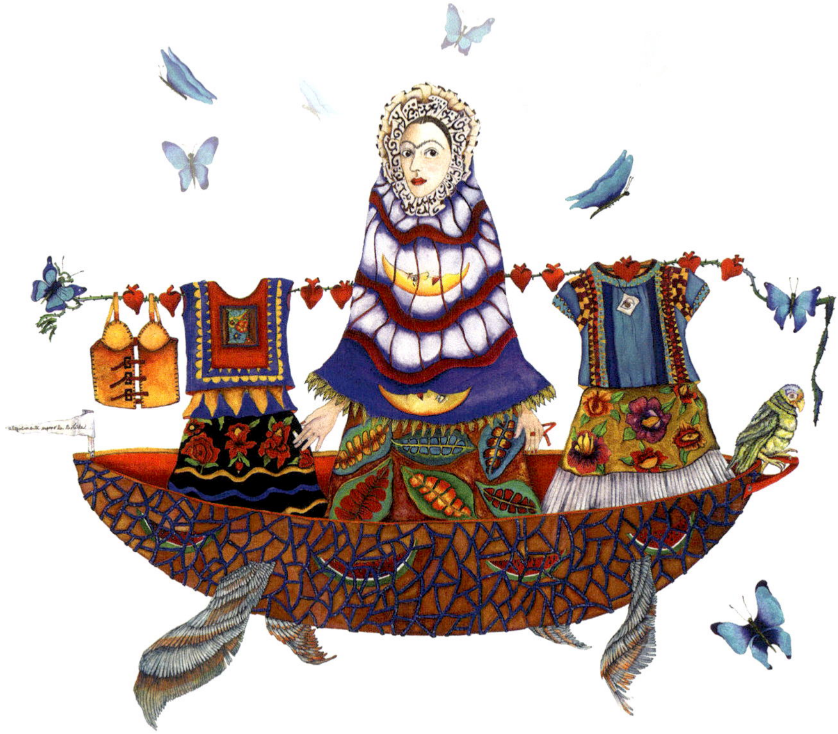

Frida Kahlo. *Frida Fashion*, painting by Perla Estrada.

EPILOGUE

ESPERO ALEGRE LA SALIDA

Frida Kahlo and the Never-Ending Torments of a Female Icon

Quieren que pinte yo unos retratos en el comedor del Palacio Nacional (son 5): Las cinco mujeres mexicanas que se han distinguido más en la historia de este pueblo. Ahora me tienes buscando qué clase de cucarachas fueron las dichas heroínas, qué jeta se cargaban y qué clase de psicología las abrumaba, para que a la hora de pintarrajearlas sepan distinguirlas de las vulgares y comunes hembras de México, que te diré que pa' mis adentros hay entre ellas más interesantes y más "dientonas" que las damas en cuestión. Si entre tus curiosidades te encuentras algún libraco que hable de doña Josefa Ortiz de Domínguez, de doña Leona Vicario, de . . . de Sor Juana Inés de la Cruz, hazme el favorsísimo de mandarme algunos datos o fotografías, grabados, etc. de la época y de sus muy ponderadas efigies.

(They want me to paint some portraits for the dining room of the National Palace (5 of them): The five most distinguished Mexican women in the history of this country. Now you have me trying to find out what kinds of cockroaches said heroines were, what they looked like, and what kinds of psychology oppressed them, so that when I paint them, the public will know how to differentiate them from the vulgar and common women of Mexico, although I'll tell you that in my heart I believe that there are more interesting, "cheekier" women out there than the ladies in question. If you happen to find a book on doña Josefa Ortiz de Domínguez, doña

> Leona Vicario, . . . Sor Juana Inés de la Cruz, please be so kind as to send me some information or a few photographs, recordings, etc., of their time and of their prudent figures.)
>
> —Frida Kahlo, *Escrituras* (197)

Little did Frida Kahlo know when she wrote this letter to her dear friend and doctor Leo Eloesser on July 18, 1941, that only within three to four decades after her death she would also be considered one of Mexico's most popular female icons of the twentieth century. Interestingly, though, she signed another letter to her "Queridísimo doctorcito" (Dearest doctor), as "La Malinche. Frida," adopting the personality of Hernán Cortés's interpreter, supporter, accomplice, mediator, and partner in crime. A couple of years earlier, in a letter addressed to her lover, Nickolas Muray, a famous Hungarian photographer, she called herself "Xochitl," after the legendary Toltec queen in charge of a battalion of women soldiers and presumably one of the five notable women she was asked to paint (Herrera 320).[1] As is well known, she changed her birth year from 1907 to 1910 so that it would coincide with the start of the Mexican Revolution. And she posed for several photographers—including her father, Guillermo Kahlo—wearing the typical *rebozos de bolita* commonly worn by the anonymous *soldaderas*.

As it turns out, Frida did not complete the portraits of any of the historical *cucarachas* (cockroaches) that would have ended up at the National Palace, perhaps because she genuinely believed that there were better role models out there than the heroines in question. Speculations aside, Magdalena Carmen Frida Kahlo y Calderón, the artist who used her own body in pain as an artistic object and mastered the art of performance and self-fashioning (practically until her death in 1954) has become a cultural commodity of her native Mexico. As Alfonso de Toro and René Ceballos explain in their introduction to the collective volume *Frida Kahlo "revisitada,"* thanks to a great number of art critics, cultural theorists, biographers, and all kinds of artists who continue rearticulating her unique gaze and artistic essence, eccentricities and indomitable spirit, public performances and transgressive attitude, we can now speak of a growing "Frida- or Kahlo-manía" (7–10). This cultural euphoria is fueled by several documentaries; essays; Julie Taymors's 2002 film, *Frida*, starring Salma Hayek and Antonio Banderas; Frida's successful appearance in the popular comic book *Viva México* (*Long Live Mexico*) in 2004;

and expositions of her art in London in 2005 or in Mexico's Palacio de Bellas Artes in 2007 (8).[2]

As a popular icon, Frida and her enigmatic image can be found in countless posters, T-shirts, postcards, necklaces, earrings, jewelry boxes, and souvenirs of all sorts, not only in Mexico but also all over the world. In response to these popular appropriations of the artist and her growing mythification, in 2001 the US Postal Service issued a Frida Kahlo stamp, and in 2010 she appeared on one side of the Mexican 500-peso bill, a privilege she shares with Diego Rivera on the other side of the banknote. In the meantime, her paintings have made history with skyrocketing auction prices, and her life continues a never-ending process of aesthetic construction in multiple plays and operas, books of all genres, and amateur songs that can be found on YouTube (Clifford 61). Frida has traveled a long way since she was represented as a conflicted artist by Ofelia Medina in Paul Leduc's 1983 film, *Frida Naturaleza Viva* (*Frida, Living Nature*), or since Barbara Mujica published in English the novel *Frida* based on her life (2001). By now Kahlo has been appropriated by Chicanos and feminists, nationalists and critics of postmodernism, radicals, independent artists, and the lesbian movement (Monsiváis, *Misógino* 260). She appears as a main character in Barbara Kingsolver's novel *The Lacuna* (2009), and in such revolutionary paintings as Trek Thunder Kelly's *The Suicide of Frida Kahlo* (2004), where the contemporary artist portrays her as an androgynous body that sells eroticism and fetishism in a neoliberal era, playing with a famous photograph taken by Nickolas Muray and a recognizable Calvin Klein ad for men's underwear (Schuchardt 94–95).

I end this book with a reflection on Frida Kahlo to show that her iconization and contemporary rewriting in Mexican literature reflects a set of cultural anxieties attached to the representation of other legendary women, like Malinche, Sor Juana, Leona Vicario, and the *soldaderas*, respectively bound to Mexico's history of conquest, colonization, independence, and revolution. What we see in most contemporary rearticulations of Frida's life—rearticulations that activate an already existing work of art like one of Frida's paintings, a page of her dairy, or even her overall everyday performance—is that the completed work "resembles a mosaic where each piece retains its own face and character" (Lévi-Strauss 7). This might have to do with the fact that the writer in question has not distanced him- or herself enough from the artist's biography to sketch her life "from memory," so to speak, instead of following a learned script. Only in the best literary scenarios created in the chronicles of Elena Poniatowska and Carlos Monsiváis, for instance, or in a handful of essays and short stories by Margo Glantz, Mónica Lavín, and Ana Clavel do we see a positive evolution that emerges from the historical rearticulation and gives us the impression that we are touching a higher work of art.[3]

When the aesthetic and conceptual evolution of a historical character is not fully developed, because it is too attached to a writer's literary obsessions and master plan (Carlos Fuentes) or because it follows the market demands of popular bestsellers (F. G. Haghenbeck), the exoticizing undertones take over the narrative. Ultimately, though, what several of these writings reveal is that even when it comes to a recent historical character such as Frida Kahlo, the representation of a woman seems unthinkable without her binding love story, her commitment to self-sacrifice, and her attachment to the domestic sphere. Pulled in different directions by feminist agendas, political views, and cultural agents, today's Frida appears in a series of gendered memories that pay attention to her physique and sexuality, her exceptionality and queerness. She is portrayed from an intimate perspective that almost invariably seeks to decipher the origin and destiny of her public paintings. Or she is forever divided between love and reason or between historical facts and myths. In one way or another, these literary pieces seek to find her a comfortable room of her own in the afterlife, but some reconstructions, as I discuss here, take her back to her bedroom in the Blue House of Coyoacán so that she can continue painting what people want her to paint: the bizarre face of a woman with a unibrow and a mustache, an exotic *tehuana* dress and elaborate braids that have a life of their own, a terrible accident that leaves her disabled, her three miscarriages, and her obsession with Diego Rivera.

Take, for instance, Carlos Fuentes's hyperbolic and quite dramatic description of Frida in his 1995 introduction to her now famous *Diario* (*Diary*). Enamored with her exoticism, the acclaimed *boom* writer recalls the only time he saw her from a distance, as she entered her box at the Palacio de Bellas Artes to enjoy a concert:

> Era la entrada de una diosa azteca, quizá Coatlicue, la madre envuelta en faldas de serpientes, exhibiendo su propio cuerpo lacerado y sus manos ensangrentadas como otras mujeres exhiben sus broches. Quizá era Tlazoltéotl, la diosa tanto de la pureza como de la impureza, el buitre femenino que devora

la inmundicia a fin de purificar al mundo. O quizá se trataba de la Madre Tierra española, la Dama de Elche, radicada en el suelo gracias a su pesado casco de piedra, sus arracadas tamaño rueda de molino, los pectorals que devoran sus senos, los anillos que transforman las manos en garras.

(It was the entrance of an Aztec goddess, perhaps Coatlicue, the mother deity wrapped in her skirt of serpents, exhibiting her own lacerated, bloody hands the way other women sport a brooch. Perhaps it was Tlazolteotl, the goddess of both impurity and purity in the Indian pantheon, the feminine vulture who must devour filth in order to cleanse the universe. Or maybe we were seeing the Spanish Earth Mother, the Lady of Elche, rooted to the soil by her heavy stone helmet, her earring as big as cartwheels, her pectorals devouring her breasts, her rings transforming her hands into claws.) (7/7–8)

Coatlicue? Tlazolteotl? The Lady of Elche? It is not hard to recognize in these lines the author of "Chac Mool," who believed throughout his long writing career that Latin America's "new narratives" were inevitably attached to its founding myths, Baroque language, and elaborate structures.[4] Fascinated by Kahlo—and Bakhtin's *carnival*, we might be tempted to add—in this essay Fuentes wonders if she was, instead, "un árbol de navidad" (a Christmas tree) or "a piñata," to finally conclude—again, with exotic undertones—that she was something else, an apparition difficult to describe, an impossible phantom that did not quite belong to this world:

Frida Kahlo era una Cleopatra quebrada que escondía su cuerpo torturado, su pierna seca, su pie baldado, sus corsés ortopédicos, bajo los lujos espectaculares de las campesinas mexicanas, que durante siglos han escondido celosamente las antiguas joyas, protegiéndolas de la pobreza, mostrándolas sólo en las grandes fiestas de las comunidades agrarias. Los encajes, los listones, las rumorosas enaguas, las trenzas, los huipiles, los tocados tehuanos enmarcando como lunas ese rostro de mariposa oscura, dándole alas: Frida Kahlo, diciéndonos a todos los presentes que el sufrimiento no marchitaría, ni la enfermedad haría rancia, su infinita variedad femenina.

> (Frida Kahlo was more like a broken Cleopatra, hiding her tortured body, her shriveled leg, her broken foot, her orthopedic corsets, under the spectacular finery of the peasant women of Mexico, who for centuries jealously kept the ancient jewels hidden away, protected from poverty, to be displayed only at the great fiestas of the agrarian communities. The laces, the ribbons, the skirts, the rustling petticoats, the braids, the moonlike headdresses opening up her face like the wings of a dark butterfly: Frida Kahlo, showing us all that suffering could not wither, nor sickness stale, her infinite variety.) (8/8)

The rest of the essay covers, in connection with the ancient Aztec world and Mexico's historical wounds, Frida's terrible accident in 1925, when a streetcar crashed into the bus she was riding and fractured her whole body, including her spinal column, ribs, and pelvis. Fuentes describes this tragedy in detail, stating, "Su pierna enferma [de la polio de la niñez] sufrió ahora once fracturas. Su hombro izquierdo quedó para siempre dislocado y uno de sus pies, irremediablemente lesionado. Un pasamano la penetró por la espalda y le salió por la vagina" (Her already withered leg [from childhood polio] now suffered eleven fractures. Her left shoulder was now forever out of joint, one of her feet crushed. A handrail crashed into her back and came out through her vagina) (12/12). Drawing parallelisms between Frida's painful existence and a tortured Latin American century of bloodshed, political turmoil, and revolutions, Fuentes highlights the fact that Kahlo transformed her agony into art:

> Sufrió treinta y dos operaciones entre el día de su accidente y su muerte. Su biografía consiste en veintinueve años de dolor constante. A partir de 1944, se ve obligada a usar ocho distintos corsés. En 1953, sufrió la amputación de una pierna gangrenada . . . Es el San Sebastián mexicano, atravesado de flechas.
>
> (She suffered thirty-two operations from the day of the accident to the day of her death. Her biography consists of twenty-nine years of pain. From 1944 on, she is forced to wear eight corsets. In 1953, her leg is amputated as gangrene sets in . . . She is the Mexican Saint Sebastian, slinged and arrowed.) (13/12–13)

Fuentes's writing here is elegant, as usual, full of rich intertexts and metaphors, parallelisms, clever connections. In the end, however, Frida comes across as more than just a mere human being. She is a Mexican *retablo*, a painted *ex-voto*, a broken body that becomes a temple. Fuentes does recall her passion for diminutives and *corridos*, her black humor and inappropriateness, her incomparable *carcajadas* (bursts of laughter) in the midst of pain, and her legendary foul mouth. In the long run, though, the Frida we find here is a theatrical disguise, a surrealist form of autoeroticism, an excess. She is depicted as a permanent mask that could also be worn in the afterlife, a *rara avis*; at best, she is one of Guadalupe Posada's skeletons or a living corpse permanently related to Death, otherwise known—at least in Mexico—as La Mera Dientona, La Tostada (a euphemism for La Chingada), La Catrina, La Pelona.

Four years later, in the novel *Los años con Laura Díaz* (*The Years with Laura Díaz*, 1999), Fuentes presents Frida as an unbelievable and unusual woman. In perfect agreement with his introduction to the *Diary*, the protagonist Laura Díaz wonders whether Frida is a real woman or an indigenous deity. At least this time we get the type of interior development that we expect in a good novel when an empowered and flirtatious Frida explains to Laura why she dresses like a *tehuana*: "Ya sabes que yo me disfrazo de piñata por fantasía personal pero también para disfrazar mi pierna enferma y mis andares de coja" (You know I trick myself out as a piñata because of my own fantasies but also to cover up my sick leg and my hobble) (222/185). The accident is revisited, as expected, but instead of portraying Frida as a fragile and broken woman, the narrator inserts doubts into the plot. When reflecting on the uneven relationship between Frida and Diego, the narrator asks:

> ¿Qué buscaba en un hombre así una mujer tan frágil como Frida Kahlo? ¿Cuál era su fuerza? ¿Le daba Rivera el poder que necesitaba su fragilidad, o lo importante era la suma de dos fuerzas para darle su sitio independiente y doloroso a la fragilidad física? Y el propio Diego, ¿era tan fuerte como su apariencia física, gigantón, robusto, o tan débil como ese mismo cuerpo desnudo, sin vello, color de rosa, gordinflón, con un pene infantil, que Laura descubrió una mañana al abrir accidentalmente la puerta del camarín? ¿No sería ella, Frida, la víctima, quien le daba fuerza a él, el hombre del vigor y las victorias?

> (What could a woman as fragile as Frida Kahlo hope to find in a man like that? What was his strength? Did Rivera give her the power her frailty needed, or was the important thing the sum of two strengths that would give her physical weakness its independent and painful place? And what about Diego: was he as strong as he physically appeared to be—huge and robust—or as weak as that same naked body—hairless, pink, puffy, with a tiny penis—which Laura saw one morning when she accidentally opened the door to the compartment? Might it not be she, Frida the victim, the one who gave strength to him, the man of vigor and victories?) (227/189)

From a similar intimate perspective, in the novel Frida has the opportunity to explain her sexual orientation and behavior to Laura. She tells her that she cheats on Diego just as much as he cheats on her, arguing that infidelity is a matter of establishing intimacy with another person and goes beyond a sexual act. Unlike the objective Fuentes, who writes in his introduction to Frida's *Diario* about the fetuses she loses in pools of blood, a more sensible narrator portrays her in the novel as a mother who is already in love with the baby who grows inside of her. Looking at a pregnant Frida in Detroit, where she will later lose her son at Henry Ford Hospital (as one of her paintings reminds us) Laura rightly observes that she has been deeply transformed: "Había una complicidad entre la madre y el hijo que se hacía en su vientre. Nadie podía entrar a ese círculo secreto" (There was a complicity between the mother and the child who was growing in her womb. No one could enter that secret circle) (232/194). Consequently, when Laura returns to the Blue House in Coyoacán, she leaves a doll on her friend's bed without a letter or a brief note, as a way of telling Frida that she remembers the child she lost.

Frida's interior development is short-lived, however. When she reappears in the plot, toward the end of the novel, she is already dead, and once again she is described as a mythical hermaphrodite, a goddess whose kingdom is not of this world:

> La espesura de las cejas pretendía, pero no lograba, disimular el bigote de Frida, el bozo notorio y notable que cubría su labio superior y hacía pensar que entre sus piernas un pene gemelo del de Diego pugnaba por brotar hasta completar en

> Frida la probabilidad, más que la ilusión, del ser hermafrodita, y, más aún, partenogenético, capaz de fecundarse a sí misma y generar, con su propio semen, el nuevo ser que ella misma, su parte femenina, pariría gracias al vigor de su parte masculina.
>
> (The thickness of her brows did not succeed in masking Frida's mustache, the notorious and notable down on her upper lip that made you think a penis, the twin of Diego's, was trying to spring up between her legs to confirm the probability, not just the illusion, that she was a hermaphrodite, and parthenogenic to boot, able to fertilize herself and generate with her own semen the new being that her feminine half would bear thanks to the vigor of her masculine half.) (505/433)

If unusual and disabled bodies in literature always have something to tell us, in the sense that their difference or "monstrosity" reflects hidden aspects of our human condition (Antebi 3), Frida's corpse in Fuentes's novel speaks of an ongoing tendency to see her as a mythological presence bigger than her human self, an eternal goddess who embraces death, or an extravagant deity who walks triumphant toward Mictlan, the underworld of Aztec mythology, "el averno indígena a donde sólo se llega guiada por trescientos perros ixcuintles, los perros pelones que Frida coleccionaba y que ahora aullaban desconsolados en los patios, las azoteas y las cocinas de la casa fúnebre, huérfanos de madre" (the Mexican Indian underworld you can reach only if you are guided by three hundred ixcuintles, those hairless dogs Frida collected which now, motherless, were howling disconsolately on the patios and in the kitchens and on the roof terraces of the funeral home) (506/433). When Frida is cremated, in the novel she acquires a miraculous second life that is only possible in a world of fairy tales and legends. Like Malinche, La Llorona, or La Catrina, she walks away from the world of the living "para irse con sus perros sin pelo al otro barrio, a la patria pelona, la mera dientona, la tostada, la catrina, la tía de las muchachas" (to go off with the hairless dogs to the other neighborhood, to the land of Madam Baldy, La Pelona, Miss Toothy, La Dientona, Lady Toasty, La Tostada, Mistress Fancy, La Catrina, Charley's Aunt) (507/434). Like Sor Juana, she is described as a "Fénix demasiado infrecuente" (too infrequent phoenix) (507/434). And like the *soldaderas* of the Mexican Revolution who are idealized in numerous *corridos*, Frida becomes another phantom. "Se fue vestida para una pachanga en el Paraíso" (She went dressed up for a party in Paradise) (507/434), imitating Adelita or perhaps Nacha Ceniceros.

Written as a "ventriloquist biography," on the other hand, Elena Poniatowska's 2000 chronicle "Diego estoy sola; Diego ya no estoy sola" ("Diego I Am Alone; Diego I Am Not Alone") allows Frida to express herself with a poetic voice made up of her own letters, biographical facts, and various documented sources that blur the lines between fact and fiction, a trait typically found in literary journalism (Rueda-Acedo, *Miradas Transatlánticas* 41).[5] Rearticulating the voice Sor Juana employs in her famous sonnet "Éste que ves, engaño colorido" (This object which you see, a painted snare), Poniatowska's Frida begins her story redefining herself from an intimate, grotesque, and even uncomfortable perspective: "Ésta que ves, mirándote a los ojos, es un engaño. Bajo los labios que jamás sonríen se alinean dientes podridos, negros" (This woman that you see, looking you in the eye, is an illusion. Underneath the lips that never smile there's a row of rotten, black teeth) (22). "Ésta que ves, mirándose en el espejo" (This woman that you see, looking at herself in the mirror), continues the narrator, "ésta que ves fumando, ésta que sale de la tela y te mira fijamente soy yo. Me llamo Frida Kahlo" (This woman that smokes, comes out of the canvas and looks at you is me, Frida Kahlo) (22).

On one hand, Poniatowka's words remind us that Frida used her own body to "act out" the story of her life, letting Frida "perform" Frida (Misemer 19). On the other hand, her use of Sor Juana's Baroque poem to create the portrait of a suffering Frida is not a minor detail or a lucky play on words. As Lois Parkinson Zamora argues in regard to "New World" Baroque and Latin American fiction, the Baroque insistence on the bodily expression of spiritual torment is omnipresent in Kahlo's self-portraits, where we find constant allusions to martyrdom and repeating selves that echo Baroque hagiography (182). In Poniatowska's chronicle, Frida appears, inevitably and understandably, as a woman in pain who uses her paintings not to exorcise her physical failures and emotional tragedies but to embrace them. As she reflects on her polio and solitude, the accident and her subsequent broken body, she immediately empowers herself, stating that she believes in love, in the human capacity to overcome tragedy, in her own strength to recover after losing "tres hijos y otra serie de cosas que hubieran llenado mi vida" (three children and other things that would have filled my life) (25). In the chronicle Frida defends her interiority, arguing that "La Frida que yo traigo adentro, solo yo la conozco. Solo yo la soporto. Es una Frida que llora mucho. Siempre tiene calentura. Está en brama. Es feroz. El deseo la embarga" (I am the only one who knows the Frida inside of me. I'm the only one who puts up with her. It's a Frida that cries a lot. She has a fever. She's angry. She's fierce. Desire consumes her) (26). Although she confesses her permanent desire to die, she quickly asserts her simultaneous need to fight tooth and nail for her own life: "Muchas veces me quise morir, pero también, con furia, quise vivir. Y pintar. Y hacer el amor. Y pintar era como hacer el amor. No tenía otra cosa más que yo. Yo era lo mejor para mí. Y Diego" (I wanted to die on many occasions, but I also wanted to live, furiously. And paint. And make love. And painting was like making love. I didn't have anything else but me. I was the best thing for me. And Diego) (27).

Consistent with Kahlo's paintings, which continue attracting new generations of admirers because they expose her interior self, her heart, and other internal organs (Franco, *Las conspiradoras* 145), Poniatowska's narrative voice surprises readers with the exposure of what could be Frida's true self. This contradictory Frida recalls Diego's infidelities and how she defends him when María Felix rejects him. She is cheated on but enjoys her own extramarital affairs just as much as she suffers when Diego finds a new lover: "Fui tras del que me gustaba o de la que me gustaba, fui una amante violenta y tierna. Yo nací para fregar pero la vida me fregó. Todavía creo en mí y en la vida. En mí mientras viva y en todo lo que vive" (I went after the ones I liked—male or female—I was a violent and tender lover. I was born to screw but life screwed me up. I still believe in me and in life, while I'm still alive) (28). This Frida proudly calls herself a great *chingona* and revives the historical one who wrote in her diary that she was thankful to her doctors and nurses but also to her own willpower.

In Poniatowska's chronicle, Frida recalls tongue-in-cheek that in France she was considered extravagantly beautiful, while in Mexico she was simply "una coja" (a lame) (29). She also remembers the glorious moment when her students, "los Fridos" (the Fridos), finished painting the *pulquería* La Rosita, and she celebrated with them the inauguration of this new type of popular art, getting rid of her corset so as to feel free and normal like everyone else. When she summarizes that moment as "El gran vacilón" (The great party) (30), we picture her triumphant that night of pure celebration and public recognition of her art and legacy. That night, history tells us, "all of Mexico" attended the opening, and Frida sang *corridos* with Concha Michel; there was dancing in the streets surrounding the *pulquería*, and Frida, "the pain in her back and foot dulled by excitement and tequila, danced *jaranas*, *danzones*, and *zapateados* with Diego" (Herrera 338). Thanks to a brief allusion to this party, Poniatowska's Frida smiles or laughs with all her might about her climatic moments as an accomplished artist and performer who had followers, admirers, friends, and lovers, even in view of her unstoppable disintegration.

Toward the end of the chronicle, we confirm that Frida has been speaking from the world of the dead:

> Ésta que ves, engaño tras engaño, murió el 14 de julio de 1954 y fue incinerada. La Frida de las calaveras de azúcar con su nombre escrito en la frente: "Frida," la del pincel de colores, la de los collares de barro y plata, la de los anillos de oro, la doliente, la atravesada por el pasamano, la que flameó, recuperó su cuerpo sano y grande en el momento en que lo envolvieron las llamaradas. La otra, la que yo inventé y pinté, la del rostro mil veces fotografiado, es la que permanece entre ustedes.
>
> (This woman that you see, deceit after deceit, died on July 14, 1954 and was incinerated. The Frida with the sugar skulls with her name written on her forehead: "Frida" and her colorful paintbrushes, her clay and silver necklaces, her gold rings. The suffering woman, pierced by the handrail, the one who went up in flames, and recovered her healthy body when she was consumed by the fire. The other one that I invented and painted, the one that was photographed a million times, is the one that remains among you.) (31)

Intertextually, her words again revive Sor Juana's on the printed page. This time there is an added element. Just as Sor Juana adds another layer of mystery to a description of herself in the poem that she wrote for her admirers in Europe, stating "No soy yo la que pensáis, / sino es que allá me habéis dado / otro ser en vuestras plumas / y otro aliento en vuestros labios, / y diversa de mí misma / entre vuestras plumas ando" (I am not at all what you think. / What you've done is attribute to me / a different nature with your pens, / a different talent with your lips. /

Borne on your feather-pens' plumes, / my flight is no longer mine; / it's not as you like to imagine, / not what your fancy depicts) (*Anthology* 102/103), Frida reminds us that only her multifarious painted self will survive divided among ourselves; we will make up our own versions of her, while the other one, the real one, extinguishes in the afterlife. This one, unlike Fuentes's, is not described as a goddess of the Aztec pantheon. She is aware of her human condition and knows better than anybody else that:

> Ésta que ven ha regresado al polvo. Han desaparecido sus olores, sus calzones, el espesor de su carne, el rojo de sus uñas, la brillantez, la fijeza de sus ojos, su única ceja ala de cuervo a lo largo de la frente, su bigotito, su saliva, sus aceites y sus juguitos, el grosor de sus cabellos, sus lágrimas calientes, sus huesos rotos, su paleta, sus cigarritos, su guitarra, su modo de ser canto y agua y carcajada.
>
> (This woman that you see has returned to the earth. Gone are her smells, her underwear, the thickness of her skin, her red nails, her brilliance, her eyes, her only brow like the wing of a crow across her forehead, her mustache, her saliva, her oils and juices, the thickness of her hair, her warm tears, her broken bones, her paint palette, her cigarettes, her guitar, her way of being a song and laughter.) (31)

This Frida is closely related to the one who writes in her diary: "Espero alegre la salida—y espero no volver jamás" (I hope the leaving is joyful—and I hope never to return). Following, furthermore, the Baroque tradition of employing doubles, divisions, and disjunctions to express the ambiguous instability of the self (Zamora 183), Poniatowska's Frida concludes her story reasserting her multiplicity: "Nunca he conocido a una mujer más cobarde que yo, nunca he conocido a una más valiente que yo, nunca he conocido a una mujer más viva, nunca más cochina, más cabrona, nunca una tan tirada a la desgracia" (I have never met a woman more cowardly than me; I have never met one braver than me; I have never met one more alive, or dirtier, *cabrona*, or as misfortuned) (31–32).

Poniatowska's voice as a chronicler appears only near the end of "Diego estoy sola; Diego ya no estoy sola," as is typical of her literary journalistic pieces, to state objectively that "El cuerpo de Frida envuelto en llamas fue cremado el 14 de Julio de 1954, mientras los asistentes entonaban *La Internacional*" (Frida's body wrapped up in flames was cremated on July 14, 1954, while the public sang "La Internacional") (32). All of Monsiváis's chronicle, "Frida Kahlo: de las etapas de su reconocimiento" ("Frida Kahlo: Stages in Regard to Her Recognition") (published originally in 2008), on the other hand, is written with the poetic distance, analytic gaze, informative report, sarcasm, and irony that we find in his texts (Egan, *Carlos Monsiváis* 16).[6] Like Fuentes, Monsiváis recalls the only time he saw her from a distance in the protest of June 2, 1954, against the Guatemalan coup d'état, and what a powerful presence she had. With admiration, he remembers her like a living *retablo*; nostalgic, he recalls her controversial funeral the following month, when the flag of the Communist Party was placed on her coffin, and how he felt, inexplicably, "la tristeza sin asideros, la de no haberla conocido" (the immense sadness, that of not having known her) ("Frida Kahlo" 257). Apart from these two brief moments in which the reporter personalizes his writing with a hint of intimacy, the rest of the chronicle delineates Kahlo's popular iconization in several stages that speak for her (re)valorization, public recognition, canonization, national adoption, and mythification.

For instance, observing the hundreds of people who wait outside the Palacio de Bellas Artes to see Frida's exposition in 2007, he concludes that her work is her life and that her life is an indelible popular memory. The visitors are there to see Frida, insists the chronicler, as if she had the capacity to come alive in her self-portraits. Sarcastic and well aware of a growing "Fridomania, Fridolatry, Fridaphilia, and Frida fever" (Lindauer 174), Monsiváis concludes that in 2007 Frida's presence grows thanks to TV programs, spectacular advertisements, and conferences where the artist becomes a cultural and emotional obligation. After playing the passive role of Diego Rivera's wife, he tells us, Frida becomes well known because of her own talent as a painter of numerous self-portraits, as a nationalist who is partially disabled, and later as a communist. Dressed as a *tehuana*, she is quickly associated with the indigenous essence of Mexico: "Frida es su aspecto, aretes que son templos o laberintos colgantes en miniatura, rebozos que son prodigios del arte textil, anillos de inspiración prehispánica que anticipan museos de la orfebrería" (Frida is her physical aspect: earrings that are miniature temples or hanging labyrinths, artistic *rebozos*, rings reminiscent of Prehispanic objects) ("Frida Kahlo" 251). She *is* Mexico, Monsiváis infers with his typical sarcasm, or at least that is what tourists want to believe—not only those who met her in person but also those who will see her in the murals of Diego Rivera as a symbol of exceptionality.

Like Poniatowska, Monsiváis recognizes the multiplicity of Frida, the fact that her legend sails off thanks to the controversial presence of her numerous selves. "¿Qué es Frida: nacionalista, comunista, surrealista, pintora fantástica, fabulista inesperada del yo?" (What is Frida: a nationalist, communist, surrealist, fantastic painter, an unexpected fable teller of her own self?) ("Frida Kahlo" 256), he asks rhetorically, before concluding that Frida's nationalism revolves around gastronomy, her colorful clothing, and her love for popular crafts and songs. Instead of repeating the story about her broken body and painful life that we find in most texts dealing with the iconic artist, Monsiváis pays careful attention to her political thought, strength, and dissidence, arguing,

> muy posiblemente por razones de misoginia, empecinada en no conceder valor político a las mujeres, la sociedad se desentiende del radicalismo de Frida en sus nociones antiimperialistas, su defensa conmovedora de la República española y su versión hoy explicable e inexplicable a la vez de la religiosidad comunista.
>
> (most likely due to misogyny, which doesn't recognize in women their political agency, society doesn't acknowledge Frida's radicalism, her anti-imperialism, her defense of the Spanish Republic, and her version of communist religiosity, understandable and still incomprehensible today.) ("Frida Kahlo" 256)

Monsiváis's Frida, then, is more in tune with the historical one who constantly criticized the United States and their gringos than the one we find on T-shirts that commercialize her figure regardless of her political thoughts. She is opinionated like the real Frida who writes to her doctor:

> Los gringos me caen muy "gordos" con todas sus cualidades y sus defectos que también se los cargan grandes, me caen bastante "gacho" sus maneras de ser, su hipocresía y su puritanismo asqueroso, sus sermones protestantes, su pretensión

> sin límites, eso de que para todo tiene uno que ser "very decent" y "very proper."
>
> (I can't stand Americans with their many virtues and faults. I can't stand their ways of being, their hypocrisy and their nasty puritanism, their protestant sermons, their boundless pretentiousness, the fact that you always have to be "very decent" and "very proper.") (*Escrituras* 189)

Monsiváis's Frida does not sell like one of her many postcards and souvenirs. Instead, the Frida that we analyze here wants to create discomfort, precisely because the chronicle is crafted, metaphorically speaking, like one of her own paintings: not as the product of the artist's dreams but as the painful result of her permanent state of "vigilia dolorosa" (painful vigil) ("Frida Kahlo" 256).

Irreverent as usual, Monsiváis notes that Frida is her best cultural agent, the person responsible for the process by which Mexico and the rest of the world fetishizes her and exports her legendary, commercial, extraordinary figure. Playing devil's advocate, Monsiváis enters Frida's mind and attempts to decipher it for us: "Me pinto, luego marco mi sitio en el espacio; me pinto, luego el tiempo me percibirá al cesar mis sufrimientos; me pinto, luego estos cuadros son la prolongación y la metamorfosis de mi figura, y son la figuración de las metamorfosis" (I paint myself, and time will depict my image when my suffering ends; I paint myself, so that these portraits prolong and transform my figure, so that they portray my metamorphoses) ("Frida Kahlo" 259). Leaving us with doubts in regard to Frida's personal agendas and forcing us to revisit our ideas concerning her self-portraits and the aesthetic and political representation of her traumatic life, Monsiváis wonders if "Frida-mania" is a cult of Christian origin, in the sense that it reflects the transmutation of an artist into a national, suffering, and gendered virgin. His conclusion, however, grounds Frida in a world of popular traditions:

> No escasean las vetas cristianas en la obra y el mito de Frida o, por lo menos, la artista se observa a sí misma con la piedad regocijada de uno de esos retablos que ella tanto observó, coleccionó y recreó. Pero nada en la fridomanía sugiere una translación efectiva de lo terrenal a lo celestial, sino más bien, la inercia de los métodos consagratorios de siglos de cultura

> cristiana y sus andamiajes de reproducción adoratriz. En lo básico, el mito de Frida es una realidad laica de la estética, y de allí el tránsito de la fridomanía a pasión popular.
>
> (There are several Christian leitmotifs around Frida's work and myth, or we can say that the artist observes herself with the joyful piety that we see in those *retablos* that she observed, collected and re-created. But nothing here suggests an effective transfer of earthly matters to a celestial reign; instead, we see consecrating methods from a long tradition of Christian culture and how they work to reproduce female adoration. Basically, Frida's myth is an aesthetic secular reality, and that is how Frida-mania has become a popular passion.) ("Frida Kahlo" 260–61)

The fact that Frida is a popular "passion" is reinforced in Monsiváis's chronicle when he writes, as if he were writing an epitaph for the artist, "Frida Kahlo carece de estatuas pero, a cambio, dispone de millones de nichos de la memoria" (Frida Kahlo doesn't have any statues but, instead, she is kept in a million niches of memory) ("Frida Kahlo" 262). He is right, in the sense that icons have afterlives and perpetuate their own iconology (O'Connor and Niebylski, "Afterlife" 187). What is rather unfortunate is that the image of Frida that we encounter today, as Jean Franco points out in one of her essays, behaves like the advocate or mediator of a "new" Mexico that appears to be "exotic," "wild," and seemingly "boundless" (*Ensayos* 84). This, indeed, is what we see in F. G. Haghenbeck's *El libro secreto de Frida Kahlo* (*The Secret Book of Frida Kahlo*) (2009), a sensationalist and magical-realist novel that has been translated into seventeen languages.

Throughout Haghenbeck's novel, Frida is presented as an exotic icon. She is described as the patron saint of melancholia, a woman of passion, a painter of agonies, or better yet, a "princesa prehispánica, musa artística hecha obra de arte" (a pre-Columbian princess, a muse transformed into art) (159/172). Sometimes, she is described as an Aztec ambassador, more precisely as "una versión roja de la Malintzin" (a communist version of Malintzin) (204), perhaps because the indigenous touch sells well in a neoliberal era that benefits the privileged and continues to marginalize the oppressed. Following the example of Laura Esquivel's *Como agua para chocolate*, the novel is composed as a cookbook that gathers Frida's favorite recipes. Thus, at the end of each chapter we find simple instructions on how to make Pico de gallo, Atole de piña, Pozole rojo, Pan de muerto, Caldo tlalpeño, Mole de olla, and so on. Like Esquivel's Tita or Malinalli, who establish strong bonds with their indigenous caretakers, nanas, or grandmothers, Frida maintains a close relationship with her godmother, Death, a mysterious lady from the underworld who haunts her throughout her life. In the novel Frida paints for her, and in return the ghost promises her—just as Death promises to Amaranta Buendía in *Cien años de soledad* (1967) that she will die when she finishes sewing her own shroud—that her life will end when the rooster to be born from a particular egg stops crowing. "Este será quien selle nuestro pacto" (This is what will seal our pact), Death tells Frida, as a phantom would tell the protagonist of a children's film. "El que nazca de este huevo te recordará con su canto al sol del nuevo día que seguirás viviendo porque así lo acordamos. El día que no cante al sol, morirás" (The creature born from this egg will remind you with its morning song that you'll live as we've agreed. But the morning that dawns without his song, you'll die) (150/162). Not surprisingly, when Frida realizes that it is time for her to die (during a magical conversation with the aged rooster), after 300 pages of loose recipes mostly unrelated to the plot, multiple sexual disclosures, the terrible accident that brings subsequent surgeries and promotes her self-portraits, she asks her loyal maid to kill and cook her dear Cui-cui-ri. As prophesied by Death, Frida does not live to see another day, and the novel ends, ingloriously, with a flat description of Diego eating the rooster.

Like several twenty-first-century novels on Malinche, Sor Juana, and Leona Vicario, Haghenbeck's *El libro secreto de Frida Kahlo* is more invested in portraying the protagonist's intimacy, her sexual experiences, and her cooking adventures than her political commitments or her originality as a painter. In the first part of the novel, Frida admits to have fallen in love with Diego as "una perfecta idiota" (a perfect idiot) (82). As if we were reading the CliffsNotes to Julie Taymor's *Frida*, we subsequently witness the complicity between Frida and Diego's second wife, Lupe Rivera, who tells her to learn how to cook for Diego if she wants to keep him happy: "Cuando pruebe el mole, haz que le guste tanto que prefiera quedarse para el recalentado antes que ir a cogerse una gringa" (When he tastes your mole, make it so he'll prefer reheated leftovers to fucking some gringa) (99/107). Likewise, the passion between Frida and Diego that most readers of this type of novel are expecting makes its big entrance in the tenth chapter with a detailed description of the couple's sex plays:

> Cada minuto que pasaba con él encontraba la pasión en las palabras, en su arte y en el cuerpo de su hombre. Desde el día de su boda las albas terminaban con el desalojo de su falda de holanes y los pechos descubiertos de su blusa del istmo para dejarse atragantar de lujuria . . . En el cuarto, al borde del majestuoso volcán Popocatéptl, donde pasaban sus noches de ímpetu, se olía la frescura del sexo y el cariño recién cocinado. Entre las tóxicas aves del valle se entonaba "La internacional" mientras se bañaban juntos, para luego volver a cubrirse de sudor, mordisqueando las frutas que cada mañana Frida colocaba en una gran vasija.
>
> (She found passion words, in her art, and in her man's body every minute she was with him. Since her wedding day, every dawn would welcome a lustful search through her frilly skirts and the revelation of her breasts at the isthmus of her blouse . . . Their bedroom at the foot of the majestic volcano Popocatéptl, where they spent their energetic nights, smelled of sex and new love. Over the sounds of the Internacionale and the exotic birdcalls of the valley, they bathed together, only to be covered in sweat later, snacking on fruits that Frida would set out every morning in a large bowl.) (103/113)

These descriptions of intimacy could be easily found in several contemporary novels that depict with voyeuristic insistence the sexual encounters between Malinche and Cortés, Leona Vicario and Andrés Quintana Roo, or Sor Juana Inés de la Cruz and one of her fictional lovers. What could be interpreted as a liberating scene, however, in the sense that it exposes Frida's intimacy, does not really do much for the protagonist's agency. We have a similar impression when the narrator recounts her New York affair with Georgia O'Keeffe. The narrator describes in great detail Frida's vagina, stating that "El sexo de Frida era pequeño, de labios apretados y vello extensamente ralo" (Frida had a small sex, with very tight labia and very fine hair) (196/210); we are told that Frida satisfies Georgia, who cannot control her intense moaning and contractions. But the description of these sexual scenes does not extend in the readers' imagination beyond the written page. The sexual scenes are just that: detailed descriptions of sexual acts that do not work as metaphors of something bigger; they attempt to show us a character naked, literally, but their state of nakedness does not reveal other worlds, symbols, or possible worlds.

Something similar happens when the narrator describes Frida's affair with Leon Trotsky. In one brief sentence, we are told that Trotsky writes passionate letters to Frida, while she communicates with him "con el sutil lenguaje de la comida" (through the exquisite language of food) (212/228). It is hard to imagine what Frida tells her lover, a revolutionary thinker, through her food when there is no further description of the dishes she cooked for him in any of the following pages. Only at the end of the chapter, in the prologue to one of her recipes Frida writes, "*Al Piochitas le gustaba que lo sorprendiera. No había mucho que decir, pues Diego me robaba la palabra a mí y a cualquiera que estuviera cerca de Trotsky, por eso yo sólo cocinaba, pues podía decirle más con mis sabores sobre mi visión de un mundo mejor, de lo que pudiera decirle con palabras*" (*Piochitas loved being surprised. There was not much to say because Diego would not let me or anyone near Trotsky to talk to him. That's why I just cooked; I could tell him more of my world vision through my cooking than what I could say to him with words*) (220, emphasis in original). Although what Frida says here is very moving, we actually have no idea how she is able to express her vision of a better world to Trotsky. What vision is she talking about? What exactly is she trying to tell Trotsky or the readers as she presents, immediately after, a recipe of Huachinango al cilantro?

In real life, Frida did use her get-togethers and parties to express her vision of Mexicanness, and she used the kitchen as a metaphor of Mexican culture (Rieger 26). This is the message that we perceive in Guadalupe Rivera Marín's *Las Fiestas de Frida y Diego* (*Frida's Fiestas*) (1994), where the artist's stepdaughter explains that Frida welcomed her friends into her house—artists, activists, revolutionaries—with meals that expressed her patriotism as she celebrated Fiestas Nacionales, El Día de los Muertos, Las Posadas, or La Santa Cruz (7). But Frida's cooking as an expression of something other than what is on the page—like the recipes for Chiles en nogada, Cochinita pibil, or Mole verde—is completely absent from Haghenbeck's novel. The links between the novel's descriptions of external behaviors and internal motivations are either weak or simply not there at all. Therefore, it is hard to extract any metaphorical or symbolic meaning from the recipes that make up a substantial part of the novel or from the sex scenes described with suspicious distance from Frida's interiority.

As of now, the most interesting works on Frida have appeared not in novels but in essays and chronicles or short stories that take one of her paintings or photographs, or perhaps one of her favorite songs, to re-create a possible world—and nothing else—that allows us to feel her pain and passion, her decisiveness and talent. Guadalupe Loaeza, in the chronicle "El venado . . . (¡herido!)" ("The [Wounded!] Deer") (2007), for example, analyzes the connections between Frida's painting *El venado herido* (*Wounded Deer*) and the *corrido* "El venadito" (Little Deer), which she sang passionately as an act of freedom, surrounded by friends and admirers, during the inauguration of La Rosita's murals. This *corrido*, argues Loaeza, inspired Frida to portray herself, three years later, as a "venadito herido en cuerpo y alma" (a wounded deer, physically and emotionally) (49), in an androgynous territory of classical allusions and mythical connotations. The intertextual links Loaeza draws between the two pieces is strengthen by her inclusion of the poem Frida wrote to accompany the painting she gave to Lina and Arcady Boytler. After stating her external sadness and internal happiness, Frida writes the poem—in the style of a *corrido*—and delivers the painting so that her friends remember her. Or so we infer when Loaeza ends her chronicle with Frida's lines:

> Gracias niños de mi vida
> gracias por tanto consuelo,
> en el bosque del Venado
> ya se está aclarando el cielo.
> Ahí les dejo mi retrato,
> pa'que me tengan presente,
> todos los días y todas las noches
> que de ustedes me ausente . . .
>
> (Thank you children of my life
> thank you for so much comfort,
> in the forest of the Deer
> a new morning begins.
> I leave you my portrait
> so that you remember me,
> every day and every night
> that I am absent from your lives . . .) (49)

Also in view of some of her paintings, such as *Lo que el agua me dio* (*What Water Gave Me*), in 2012 Margo Glantz studies how Frida fetishizes herself until she becomes a mythical character. With the inquisitiveness of the art critic, the writer observes Frida's deformed feet, her shoes (or the absence of them), and her prosthetic leg (adorned like the rest of her). Glantz's conclusions in this essay, appropriately titled "Diseminación y amplificación" ("Dissemination and Amplification"), amplify our understanding of the artist with a set of uncertainties. "¿Podremos concluir entonces que Frida Kahlo era surrealista?" (Can we conclude, then, that Frida Kahlo was a surrealist?), the critic asks. "¿O simplemente que fue una surrealista involuntaria?" (Or was she simply an involuntary surrealist?) ("Diseminación" 17). The answer comes several pages later, when she writes: "en Frida advierto más bien la perplejidad de no saber cómo enfrentar su alteridad, cómo salir de sí misma sin interrupción, constantemente, mirándose, retratándose" (in Frida I observe, instead, the perplexity of not knowing how to confront her own otherness, how to escape from herself without interruptions, constantly, looking at herself, painting herself) ("Diseminación" 19). Looking at her loose or braided hair and her unusual mustache, Glantz wonders if Frida paints her self-portraits to admire or to recognize herself, only to conclude that "La pintura se convierte en fetiche, y ella, la pintora, se vuelve el fetiche de sí misma: Madonna la idolatra, su familia le otorga la categoría de marca registrada y México existe muchas veces en la geografía mental del mundo gracias a Frida" (Her painting becomes a fetish, and she, the painter, becomes her own fetish: Madonna idolizes her, her family turns her into a trademark, and many times Mexico exists in the mental geography of the world thanks to Frida) ("Diseminación" 20). Later on, in view of Frida's *Autorretrato en la frontera entre México y los Estados Unidos* (*Self-Portrait on the Border between Mexico and the United States*) (where she depicts herself as the border), *Mi vestido cuelga aquí* (*My Dress Hangs Here*) (painted in New York), or *Las dos Fridas* (*The Two Fridas*) (created for an international Surrealist exposition in 1940), Glantz deduces with intellectual wisdom:

> Vestida o despojada de sus ropas, en sus pinturas Frida se nos ofrece casi desnuda a la mirada, pero cirquera y lúcida logra exhibir al mismo tiempo y en mágico malabarismo su historia personal, su obsesión con la fisiología del cuerpo humano donde ella es su propio conejillo de indias y asimismo un ejemplo viviente de la historia indirecta de su patria.

> (Dressed or her clothes stripped off of her, in her paintings Frida offers herself almost naked to our eyes, but she lucidly exhibits, at the same time, her personal history, her obsession with the human body where she is her own guinea pig and the indirect living example of her country's history.) ("Diseminación" 25)

Because of these in-depth reflections, the Frida we find in Glantz's essay is and is not the Frida we know. She is a woman in pain whose broken body fails her at all times, but she is also enigmatic and unpredictable, a collage of question marks, not a conclusion but a suggestive ellipsis that tells readers that there is more to Frida than what we see in her paintings.

Along these lines, one of my favorite rewritings of Frida in the twenty-first century is Ana Clavel's micro story, titled "Las dos Fridas" ("The Two Fridas") (2014), which reads: "De corazón a corazón—le dijo una Frida a la otra—el tuyo es más atormentado, pero el mío sangra más" (From heart to heart—one Frida said to the other one—yours is more tormented, but mine bleeds more) (17). In its brevity, Clavel's text invites us to revisit *Las dos Fridas* and Frida's painful life, inevitable ups and downs, complicated love affairs, miscarriages, and numerous operations. In this process that takes place inferentially on the blank space of the page, we reconsider the divisions of the self, the artist's doubles, and her intelligent appropriation of the Mexican Baroque and popular forms to present herself as a syncretic relic, a powerful talisman that must be kept close to the heart, or as a holy image that guards us against a cruel destiny (Zamora 207).

The Frida that we see in Mónica Lavín's short story "El rebozo magenta" ("The Magenta *Rebozo*") (2012)[7] is visiting her lover, Nickolas Muray, in New York. The story moves back and forth between the past and the present to show Frida behind the scenes as Muray softens her rebellious look with a camera that immortalizes her as "una madona" (a virgin) (80), according to Diego Rivera. The story portrays Frida unable to leave Diego to stay with Nick or unwilling to break up with Nick for Diego. As she looks at the photograph Muray sends to her when she is back in Coyoacán, we wonder if Frida is in fact the same extravagant and exotic woman we have come to know thanks to the lens of this photographer, or if the photograph is just an enhanced image that takes the place of the real, a beautified copy of the original, or a mask, a veil, a colorful *rebozo* that is there to partially cover a woman's soul. Frida sees her face in the photograph and realizes it has been transformed "por el éxtasis" (due to ecstasy) (80). Unhappy with a life of indecisions and ephemeral love affairs—we assume—torn between her Hungarian love in New York and her Diego in Mexico, Frida only wishes to rest away from her own image and her heart. After all, "¿ . . . a quién le importa quedar en una fotografía?" (. . . who wants to be immortalized in a photograph? (81).

Frida's life is a story to be continued. . . . She may have died, as she wrote in her diary, not wanting to come back. But writers, painters, playwrights, and filmmakers will make her return time and again. The world needs her broken body, her eccentricities, that long eyebrow and mustache that confirm her otherness, her paintings that speak of violence, torture, identity crisis. She is the exotic dot on the white canvas of modernity, the queer that defies heteronormativity, the colorful outsider, the disabled that societies need to reaffirm their normalcy. Ultimately, Frida is the symbol of Mexicanness or indigeneity, a "Third World" product that sells authenticity, uniqueness, or marginality, in a "First World" where contrasts and extremes are highly valued. She shares the fate of the other women studied in this book, those who await a wholesome representation within sensible worlds, coherent scenarios, and pensive texts whose metaphors extend beyond the written page.

NOTES

INTRODUCTION: ICONIC MEXICAN WOMEN AT THE THRESHOLD OF A NEW CENTURY

1. Throughout this book, I speak of national identity, nationalism, national icons, and national myths. Although such terms as *nation*, *nationality*, and *nationalism* are difficult to define, I treat them here (following Benedict Anderson's postulates) as the identity markers, signs, and symbols of an "imagined political community" (15). Ultimately, as John Charles Chasteen argues, "for nations to be united internally, they have to know who they are; they need a clear and positive sense of national identity" (*Born* 233). Nationalism in Latin America, Chasteen further argues, after four centuries of colonial and then neocolonial exploitation, fosters collective self-respect within a particular community by "positively reinterpreting the meaning of Latin American racial and cultural difference" (*Born* 234). On the other hand, when I speak of postnationalism, a postnational age, and postnational literary trends, I refer to the fact that national identities have lost their previous homogeneous value. In a globalized era, the concept of "nation" seems unfit to fully describe the identity of a particular state. According to Jürgen Habermas, "In contrast to the territorial form of the nation-state, 'globalization' conjures up images of overflowing rivers, washing away all the frontier checkpoints and controls, and ultimately the bulkward of the nation itself" (67).

2. David Harvey explains neoliberalism as a "theory of political economic practices that proposes that human well-being can best be advanced by liberating individual entrepreneurial freedoms and skills within an institutional framework characterized by strong private property rights, free markets, and free trade" (2). Mexico provides a fine example of its dark side. The North American Free Trade Agreement of 1994 only strengthened the attack on labor, on the peasants whose *ejido* lands were privatized, and on the poorest sectors of the country (Harvey 101–4).

3. In this study, I speak of postmodern subjectivities and a postmodern era to reflect on the literary and cultural construction of Mexican identities in the twenty-first century, marked by dispersion, absence, fragmentation, performance, superficiality, crisis, and incompleteness (Lorenzano, "Posmodernidad" 230–32). In many ways, postmodernism, as José Joaquín Brunner argues, can be read as a particular form of modernity that takes place in Latin America: "Condemned to live in a world where all the images of modernity and modernism come to us from the outside and become obsolete before we are able to materialize them, we find ourselves trapped in a world where not all solid things but rather all symbols melt into air. Latin America: the project of echoes and fragments, of past utopias whose present we can only perceive as a continuous crisis. This sensation of the permanent crisis of everything, of the economy, institutions, political regimes, universities, art, public services, private enterprise, the armed forces, poorly and barely hides the fact that we live and think in the middle of a modernity in the process of construction, whose dynamic is increasing the heterogeneities of our very perceptions, knowledges, and information" (53).

CHAPTER 1. FORGET ME NOT: MALINCHE'S STRUGGLES IN TWENTY-FIRST-CENTURY MEXICO

1. Throughout the book, I provide page numbers from the original sources in Spanish. The second set of numbers corresponds to the English translation, if it is available. Otherwise, all translations from the original Spanish are my own.

2. Sonia Rose de Fuggle analyzes Doña Marina as an epic and/or biblical character (939), and Julie Greer Johnson pays close attention to Bernal Díaz's intimate portrayal of the women of the conquest (16–20). In *La imaginación novelesca* (2009), I study in greater detail Bernal Díaz's unparalleled characterization of Doña Marina (93–101).

3. There are many theories regarding Malinche's name. Camilla Townsend argues: "Before she was twenty, the girl would be renamed Marina by Spanish newcomers and called Malintzin by other indigenous people. We do not know what name they gave her in the days following her birth. . . . It was most unlucky to be born under the sign Calli (House) or Malinalli (Grass), but these were rather theoretical misfortunes, as almost no one was ever really given an ill-omened name. . . . Some historians have loved to surmise that the Spaniards named the girl 'Marina' because her name had been the tragic 'Malinalli,' but this would never have been the case. The name would almost certainly have been avoided by her own people, and even if it hadn't been, the Spanish were not in the habit of interviewing their Indian slaves in order to come up with a European name that seemed particularly fitting. The girl's name is, quite simply, lost to us" (12).

4. In "Female Archetypes in Mexican Literature," Luis Leal gives us a good overview of several of these works that in one way or another reactivate the Malinche archetype. For an in-depth study of most of these works, see Cypess.

5. For a good overview of recent fictional works by Latin American women writers that approach the colonial past from an intimate perspective, see Alemany Bay.

6. Ryan Long notices something similar but only cautiously outlines Esquivel's shortcomings: "By imagining Malinalli's coming of age experiences, her encounters with the Spanish and Cortés, and the cultural and political negotiations of her life, Esquivel closes the narrative on what one might shallowly distill as a tale of true love and domesticity. Certainly Esquivel's feminism balances precariously between embracing patriarchy and resisting it" (202–3).

7. In his book *Tinta del exotismo* (2007), Gabriel Weisz rightly argues: "En el fondo la creación de lo exótico es una marca que distingue nuestra propia ficción de identidad. . . . Quizá el resultado de tanta inestabilidad, haga absolutamente necesaria la construcción de una ficción de otredad que me permita, por contraste, resolver lo que no puedo hacer yo mismo" (At its core, the creation of the exotic distinguishes our own identity fiction. . . . Perhaps the result of such instability makes absolutely necessary the construction of a fiction of otherness that allows me, by contrast, to resolve that which I can not do on my own) (36).

8. For a thorough discussion of "Chingona politics," see Gaspar de Alba (70).

9. His chronicle was most likely finished around 1560 but remained unpublished until the nineteenth century.

10. "Si su empeño en el cumplimiento de labores de adoctrinamiento estuvo motivado por su firme fe en la nueva religión o si los cometidos religiosos formaban parte únicamente de su estrategia política es algo imposible de clarificar y, en todo caso, un motivo no excluye a otro. No sabemos si el celo religioso de Marina quiere indicar que ésta había dejado de ser india, si su identidad sería indígena o española o una mezcla de ambas, pero sí parece que ella ha inaugurado un nuevo discurso, el de la transculturación o el mestizaje cultural. Si para actuar como agente aculturador le fue preciso interiorizar—y hasta qué punto—previamente los nuevos valores culturales es algo imposible de saber. Lo que sí se puede deducir de las informaciones de las fuentes históricas es que en Marina se operaron cambios considerables al menos en lo que a pautas de comportamiento se refiere" (Whether her motivation for complying with the efforts of indoctrination were motivated by her firm faith in the new religion or her religious commitments were just a part of her political strategy, it is impossible to know for sure and, in the end, one motivation does not negate the other. We do not know if Marina's religious zeal suggests that she ceased to be an Indian, if her identity would be Indigenous or Spanish or a mix of the

two, but it is clear that she has ushered in a new discourse, that of transculturation or cultural hybridity. If in order to act as an agent of acculturation it was necessary for her to first interiorize—and to what extent?—those new cultural values, it is impossible to know for sure. What is clear from the historical sources is that there were considerable changes that were taking place within Marina, at the very least in terms of her patterns of behavior) (González Hernández 240–41).

11. According to several historical accounts, the Virgin of Guadalupe first appeared to Juan Diego on December 9, 1531 (Cursio-Nagy 165), and by then Malinche could have been dead.

12. I borrow the phrase "possible world" from Lubomír Doležel's *Possible Worlds of Fiction and History*. The Czech literary critic argues that "fictional worlds are imaginary possible alternatives to the actual world" (vii). Fictional texts do call possible worlds into fictional existence, but they have to make sense at all times (42).

13. For more details on this debate, see Estrada "Crónica."

14. For a closer look at how Malinche appears in some of these texts, see Díaz's "Establishment" (55).

CHAPTER 2. IMPOSSIBLE NUN: SOR JUANA AND THE TRAPS OF REPRESENTATION

1. I refer here to Miguel Cabrera's famous painting, *Sor Juana Inés de la Cruz* (1750). Colección Museo Nacional de Historia, Instituto Nacional de Antropología e Historia.

2. See also Egan *Diosas*.

3. This painting appears as the book cover of *Sor Juana y su mundo* (1995), edited by Sara Poot-Herrera.

4. Oil painting on linen, 1995, collection of the artist. Interestingly, in the painting *Profesión de Sor Juana Inés de la Cruz*, Jorge Sánchez portrays the nun with an elaborate crown of roses and holding a lit candle. The oil painting is reproduced in Lavín *Sor Juana* (10).

5. See, for example, Bergmann and Mario A. Ortiz "Sor Juana."

6. See Paden's article on *Hunger's Brides*, where the critic discusses how the novel explicitly re-creates the work, life, and image of Sor Juana.

7. See Héctor Zagal's interview on YouTube.

8. For a closer look at Sor Juana's "final conversion" and current debates regarding her last years, see Soriano Vallès and Guevara-Geer.

9. For a thorough explanation regarding the controversy of this painting, see Pierce et al. (296).

10. In his study, Roger Shattuck proposes six categories of forbidden knowledge that range from inaccessible and destructive knowledge to delicate, dangerous, double-bound, and ambiguous knowledge (327).

11. "Monjas, frailes y clérigos se apropiaron con el flagelo del orgasmo que les estaba prohibido. . . . En el arrobo el hombre y la mujer recobran íntegra su animalidad, la trascienden y se vengan de sus sucias servidumbres. El furor genésico los transforma en la fiera poseída por la violencia. Es entonces cuando el abrazo se transforma en estrujón brutal, el beso en mordida, la palabra en grito y el deseo en orgasmo" (Nuns, friars and priests used their whippings to reclaim their forbiden orgasms. . . . In a trance, men and women could recover and transcend their animal instincts and avenge their filthy souls. The original fury transforms them into wild beasts possessed by violence. It is then that a hug becomes a brutal squeeze, a kiss turns into a bite, the word into a cry and desire into orgasm) (Benítez, *Los demonios* 63).

12. To further explore this metaphor, see Valdés's *The Shattered Mirror*, where the critic examines various representations of women in Mexican literature.

13. According to Pilar Gonzalbo Aizpuru, the *Amiga* schools were established rather early in the Americas with the first Spanish families that came to the New World. The women in charge of these schools taught their young pupils activities associated with the home, such as cooking, sewing, and knitting, within a quiet environment (322).

14. The short story can be found in Castellanos's *Album de familia*, first published in 1971.

15. For a closer look at these letters, see Estrada "Four Letters."

Chapter 3. Leona Vicario: The Sweet Mother of the Nation

1. Genaro García, as Carmen Ramos Escandón recalls, also wrote other books exclusively focused on women: *La desigualdad de la mujer* (1891), and *Apuntes sobre la condición de la mujer* (1891), as well as the essay "La condición jurídica de la mujer según Herbert Spencer" (1894).

2. In his "Advertencia," García mentions the biographies of Carlos María de Bustamante (1842), Francisco Sosa (1884), and Jacobo María Sánchez (1894). He does not mention Laureana Wright de Kleinhan's *Mujeres notables mexicanas* because it was published in 1910, the same year he published his biography.

3. In her *Foundational Fictions*, Doris Sommer rightly argues: "Romantic novels go hand in hand with patriotic history in Latin America. The books fueled a desire for domestic happiness that runs over into dreams of national prosperity; and nation-building projects invested private passions with public purpose" (7). Because of this relationship between erotics and politics, or between private and

political passions, Sommer argues, over the course of the nineteenth century eroticism and nationalism become figures for each other in numerous fictions throughout Latin America (31).

4. As Carlos Monsiváis recalls in his chronicle *Las herencias ocultas*, "el nacionalismo otorga coherencia interna, conciencia cultural (allí donde sólo había admiraciones diseminadas) y la identidad que es, en rigor, una propuesta de orientación vocacional: 'Así que soy mexicano ¿Y ahora qué? ¿Y qué parte de mi conducta memoriza y qué parte improvisa?' " (Nationalism creates internal unity, cultural consciousness (where once there were only scattered admirations) and an identity that is, at its foundation, an offer for vocational orientation: "So I'm Mexican, now what? And what part of my behavior do I memorize and what part to I improvise") (20).

5. I quote here from a book edited in 1955 under the title *Heroínas Mexicanas*, which reproduces Lizardi's *Calendario*. For a closer look at Lizardi's treatment of insurgent women, see Galván Gaytán.

6. For an in-depth discussion on how the Virgin of Guadalupe became a motherly icon during the colonial era, see Gruzinski: "Nadie duda de que la *imago* maternal, oculta en la Guadalupana, alimenta también la fascinación que ejerce sobre todos. Ejerce la seducción de una madre de piel cobriza como esas nodrizas mestizas, indias o mulatas que velaban sobre los pequeños españoles por toda la Colonia. La fetichización efectuada por los evangelistas mexicanos parece organizarse en torno a la producción de una *imago* única, femenina y protectora" (No one doubts that the maternal *imago*, hidden in the Guadalupana, also encourages the fascination that she instills in everyone. She practices the seduction of a mother with copper-colored skin like those mestiza, indian, or mulatta wet nurses that cared for the tiny Spaniards all over the colony. The fetishization created by the Mexican Evangelists seems to have been organized around the image of a unique *imago*, one that is feminine and a protector) (132–33).

7. In her study on historical women and melodramatic discourses of the nineteenth century and the present, Carolina Pizarro Cortés writes: "Las representaciones melodramáticas de las heroínas de las historias patrias, así como lo hacen las 'narraciones semanales,' ponen a la mujer y sus conflictos amorosos en el medio de la acción. Este centramiento, sin embargo, no es unívoco. Se trata de representaciones que, por una parte, reconocen al sujeto femenino, pero que al mismo tiempo lo incorporan en un discurso de 'segundo orden.' Contienen lo que no cabe en la historiografía patriarcal—probablemente porque no responde al modelo femenino instituido por esta—y simultáneamente lo traducen, reducen o regulan dentro de otros márgenes que sí parecen ser adecuados para comprender la función de la mujer en las historias nacionales de corte claramente belicista" (The melodramatic representations of heroines in stories of the fatherland, such as they appear in the "weekly reports," put the woman and her amorous conflicts in the center of the action. This centering, however, is ambiguous. They are

representations that, on the one hand, recognize the feminine subject, but, on the other, that incorporate it as a secondary discourse. They contain that which does not fit within the patriarchal historiography—probably because it does not correspond to the feminine model that it institutes—and simultaneously translates, reduces, and regulates the feminine subject to other margins that are seen as appropriate for understanding the function of the woman within the national histories of a clearly militaristic court) (415).

8. In an interview with Fabiola Palapa Quijas, Del Palacio admits: "Investigué libros de la época, historias del Congreso de Chilpancingo, en la propia historia de Quintana Roo, los testigos de la época, los diarios, en textos de viajeros para descubrir esa zona y recrear toda una época. Me fui a viajar por algunos de esos lugares para recuperar algunas de las tradiciones, de la música, incluso las enfermedades y curas para reconstruir y presentar en la novela a una Leona viva" (I researched books from the period, stories from the Chilpancingo Congress, Quintana Roo's own history, testimonies from the period, newspapers, traveler's logs in order to discover the region and to re-create a historic period. I traveled to some of those places to discover some of their traditions, the music, even the diseases and their cures so as to recreate and present a living Leona in my novel).

9. In regard to Leona's determinism and the fictionalization of her "destiny" within the novel, see Sánchez Robles.

10. Some episodes of this soap opera can be found on YouTube.

11. "Según la historia oficial" (According to the official history), Monsiváis reminds us, "muy escasas señoras merecen figurar en su seno, y eso en calidad de heroínas colaterales o complementarias: Josefa Ortiz de Domínguez, que le avisó al Tata Cura de que ya le sabían la maniobra; Leona Vicario, por arrimarse al buen árbol de don Andrés; Agustina Ramírez, que le subarrendó a la Patria todos sus hijos" (very few women deserve to be at the forefront, and even then they only appear as collateral or complementary heroines: Josefa Ortiz de Domínguez, who advised Tata Cura that they already knew his plans; Leona Vicario, who tied herself to the strong tree of Don Andrés; Agustina Ramírez, who sublet all of her children to the Fatherland) (*Misógino* 107).

12. Edward Said recognizes that intellectuals are in many ways exiles and marginal individuals, amateurs who nonetheless articulate a language that "tries to speak the truth to power" (xvi). Intellectuals, he further argues, use "one's rare opportunities to speak, catching the audience's attention, being better at wit and debate than one's opponent" (xviii).

13. "*Hablar-mujer*" (speaking-as-woman), Cecilia Olivares explains, drawing from Luce Irigaray's feminist theorizations, "sería, entonces, también un espacio en el que las mujeres se permitirían hablar como ellas hablan, 'sin dejarse distraer por la norma o por el hábito,' para no recaer en el mismo 'lenguaje que reproduce las mismas historias'" (would be, then, another space in which

women are allowed to speak as they speak, "without being distracted by rules and habits," to not fall into that "language that reproduces the same stories") (60).

14. Jean Franco also recognizes this. In her classic study on the representation of women in Mexico, the critic argues that even after independence was achieved, women did not have access to the same cultural capital as men, since they had not received the same type of instruction and could not, by any means, attend the university (*Las conspiradoras* 117).

15. This letter and the other ones that I quote in this paragraph have been transcribed by José Martínez Pichardo, keeping Vicario's original spelling. They appear at the end of his study, *Leona Vicario: Grandeza de una mujer*.

CHAPTER 4. *SI ADELITA SE FUERA CON OTRO . . . SOLDADERAS* OF AN UNFINISHED REVOLUTION

1. In his study, *Mujeres de armas tomar*, Francisco Ramos Aguirre analyzes different versions of this popular *corrido* and numerous legends about its origin (23–46).

2. I thank historian Francie Chassen-López for sharing an unpublished article of hers that has greatly enhanced my understanding of the *soldaderas* in the Mexican Revolution, "'No podemos ni debemos permanecer impasibles': las oaxaqueñas en la Revolución de 1910."

3. In the fifth chapter of her book, Salas analyzes nine cases of women who became *soldaderas* and represented most regions of Mexico. As part of her research, she consulted the Archivo de la Palabra del Instituto Nacional de Antropología e Historia in Mexico City, as well as the Library of Congress and the National Archives and Records Service in Washington, DC.

4. I refer to the "narratives" instead of the "novels" of the Mexican Revolution to highlight the plurality of experiences gathered by the narrators of the revolution in a series of hybrid texts. As Jorge Aguilar Mora points out in his most recent study on this topic, "los 'novelistas' de la Revolución más auténticos no se plantearon nunca la disyuntiva entre lo histórico y lo ficticio. De hecho, muchas obras tienen como objeto de reflexión justamente la convivencia ineludible, en las experiencias vitales de los revolucionarios, de lo real y de lo inventado o imaginado o mentido. Por eso, la discusión sobre el género "novela" no tiene sentido si se limita a ser una competencia retórica o una reivindicación de la moral clasificatoria" (the most authentic "novelists" of the Revolution never considered the difference between the historic and fictitious. In fact, many works reflect that unavoidable coexistence, in the dynamic experiences of the revolutionaries, in the real and in the invented or imagined or falsified. As such, the discussion surrounding the genre of the "novel" does

not make sense if it is limited to rhetorical competence or a revindication of moral standards) (15).

5. In the first chapter of *Ser mujer y estar presente*, I pay close attention to this passage of Campobello's *Cartucho*.

6. I revisit the story of Amelio Robles in the last section of this chapter.

7. I am paraphrasing from his chronicle "Soñadora, coqueta y ardiente. Notas sobre sexismo en la literatura mexicana." The text, originally published in March 1973 in *La Cultura en México*, appears now in *Misógino feminista* (2013), edited by Marta Lamas.

8. I quote from Rafael F. Muñoz's *Relatos de la Revolución* (*Stories of the Revolution*).

9. In the third chapter of *Ser mujer y estar presente*, I analyze Poniatowska's literary career, highlighting the multiple ways she uses her chronicles to expose Mexico's marginalized population.

10. Mendieta Alatorre's book focuses on these women intellectuals in the section "La participación de la mujer en el movimiento social de 1910." Anna Macías also studies them in her article "Women and the Mexican Revolution, 1910–1920."

11. For a closer look at Matilda's transgressions in the context of the Porfirian regime and the Mexican Revolution, see the eighth chapter of my book *Ser mujer y estar presente*.

12. According to María Herrera-Sobek, "Three types of soldaderas are represented in the corrido. These types vividly demonstrate the historical process in the fashioning of an archetypal image. Some corridos depict the soldadera in her true historical dimension. Some romanticize the soldadera and transform her into a love object. In others the soldadera is transformed into a mythic archetypal figure" (92–93).

13. *La Adelita*, illustrated by Fernando Robles, does not have page numbers.

14. The collection *Rejected Princesses* has its own webpage and is updated weekly. See http://www.rejectedprincesses.com. Petra's animated character appeared on July 2, 2014.

EPILOGUE: *ESPERO ALEGRE LA SALIDA*

1. In her 1983 biography of Kahlo, Hayden Herrera reproduces the letter that serves as my epigraph and finds among the famous women to be painted for the National Palace the name of Doña "Xochitl" written next to an illegible scribble (320). The letter she writes to Nickolas Muray on February 27, 1939, in which she calls herself Xochitl, can be found in *Escrituras* (148), an anthology of Frida's writings compiled by Raquel Tibol.

2. In his chapter, "Las 'nuevas meninas,'" De Toro further explains: "Frida Kahlo no era tan sólo una artista performativa que usaba su propio cuerpo como objeto artístico en su vida cotidiana y en sus intervenciones en la vida pública. Kahlo es una de las primeras personalidades artísticas que se mediatiza en forma absoluta, ya sea en su Diario, en su pintura o en las fotografías o eventos sociales" (Frida Kahlo wasn't just a performance artist who used her own body as an artistic object in her daily life and in her interventions in the public sphere. Kahlo is one of the first artistic personalities that absolutely takes control of her own work, whether that be in her Diary, in her paintings or in photographs or social events) (67).

3. In his in-depth discussion of aesthetic rearticulations, Claude Lévi-Strauss argues that the best ones show that "the seeds of transformation were perhaps already germinating" (17).

4. Fuentes coined this idea in his essay *La nueva novela hispanoamericana* (1969) and continued working on it throughout his prolific writing career.

5. Poniatowska's chronicle on Frida can be found in her book *Las siete cabritas* (2000).

6. Monsiváis had previously written on Frida Kahlo. For instance, see his piece "De todas las Fridas posibles," *Nexos*, January 1, 1992. The chronicle I study in this epilogue was first published in 2008, in *Debate Femenista*. After Monsiváis's death in 2010, Marta Lamas included it in the edited volume *Misógino feminista* (2013), which I use here as my primary source.

7. The story appears in the short story collection *La casa chica*. I quote from the 2016 edition.

Works Cited

Achugar, Hugo. "El lugar de la memoria. A propósito de monumentos (motivos y paréntesis)." *Cultura y globalización*. Ed. Jesús Martín Barbero, Fabio López de la Roche, and Jaime Eduardo Jaramillo. Bogotá: Universidad Nacional de Colombia, 1999. 141–67.

Adams, Jerome R. *Notable Latin American Women. Twenty-Nine Leaders, Rebels, Poets, Battlers and Spies, 1500–1900*. Jefferson, NC: McFarland, 1995.

Agren, David. "17 Months Later: Mexico President Visits Site of 43 Students' Disappearance." *The Guardian*. 24 February 2016. Web. 6 August 2016.

Aguilar Mora, Jorge. *El silencio de la Revolución y otros ensayos*. Mexico City: Era, 2011.

Aguirre, Eugenio. *Leona Vicario: La insurgente*. Mexico City: Planeta, 2010.

Aínsa, Fernando. *Los guardianes de la memoria: 5 ensayos más allá de la globalización*. Zaragoza: Sabara, 2013.

———. "Los guardianes de la memoria: novelar contra el olvido." *Cuadernos Americanos* 137.3 (2011): 11–29.

———. *Reescribir el pasado: Historia y ficción en América Latina*. Mérida: CELARG y El otro, El mismo, 2003.

Alba Villalobos, Ana María. "Leona Vicario, personaje femenino de ficción histórica y literaria." *Oficio: Revista de Historia e Interdisciplina* 1.1 (2013): 40–59.

Alemany Bay, Carmen. "Recuento de las aportaciones de las narradoras latinoamericanas a la historia colonial." *América sin nombre* 9–10 (2007): 7–11.

Anderson, Benedict. *Imagined Communities: Reflections on the Origin and Spread of Nationalism*. London: Verso, 1983.

Antebi, Susan. *Carnal Inscriptions: Spanish American Narratives of Corporeal Difference and Disability*. New York: Palgrave, 2009.

Aracil, Beatriz. "La Malinche: historia y mito en dos novelas mexicanas contemporáneas." *Mujeres novohispanas en la narrativa mexicana contemporánea*. Ed. Cecilia Eudave, Alberto Ortiz, and José Carlos Rovira. Alicante: Universidad de Alicante (Cuadernos de *América sin nombre* 33), 2014. 13–41.

Arenal, Electa. "Sor Juana and Company: Intellectuals and Early Feminists." *Approaches to Teaching the Works of Sor Juana Inés de la Cruz*. Ed. Emilie L. Bergmann and Stacey Schlau. New York: Modern Language Association of America, 2007. 37–46.

———. "Speaking the Mother Tongue." *University of Dayton Review* 16 (1983): 93–105.

———. "Where Woman Is Creator of the Wor(l)d: Or, Sor Juana's Discourses on Method." *Feminist Perspectives on Sor Juana Inés de la Cruz*. Ed. Stephanie Merrim. Detroit: Wayne State UP, 1999. 124–41.

Arenal, Electa, and Yolanda Martínez-San Miguel. "Refocusing New Spain and Spanish Colonization: Malinche, Guadalupe, and Sor Juana." *A Companion to the Literatures of Colonial America*. Ed. Susan Castillo and Ivy Schweitzer. Malden, MA: Blackwell, 2005. 174–94.

Azuela, Mariano. *Los de abajo*. 1915. Ed. Marta Portal. Madrid: Cátedra, 2002.

Bakhtin, Mikhail. *Rabelais and His World*. Trans. Hélène Iswolsky. Bloomington: Indiana UP, 1984.

Barrientos, Juan José. *Ficción-historia. La nueva novela histórica hispanoamericana*. Mexico City: Universidad Nacional Autónoma de México, 2001.

Barroso, Gabriela. "*La Insurgenta*." *Estudios sobre las Culturas Contemporáneas* 37 (2013): 179–81.

Barthes, Roland. *A Lover's Discourse*. Trans. Richard Howard. New York: Noonday Press, 1978.

———. *Mythologies*. Trans. Richard Howard and Annette Lavers. New York: Hill and Wang, 2012.

———. *S/Z*. Trans. Richard Miller. New York: Hill and Wang, 1974.

Bartra, Roger. "Los hijos de la Malinche." *La Malinche, sus padres y sus hijos*. Ed. Margo Glantz. Mexico City: Taurus, 2001. 195–99.

Baudot, Georges. "Malintzin, imagen y discurso de mujer en el primer México virreinal." *La Malinche, sus padres y sus hijos*. Ed. Margo Glantz. Mexico City: Taurus, 2001. 55–89.

Bauzá, Hugo Francisco. *El mito del héroe. Morfología y semántica de la figura heroica*. Buenos Aires: Fondo de Cultura Económica, 2007.

Beard, Laura J. *Acts of Narrative Resistance. Women's Autobiographical Writings in the Americas*. Charlottesville: U of Virginia P, 2009.

Behar, Ruth. "Sexual Witchcraft, Colonialism, and Women's Powers: Views from the Mexican Inquisition." *Sexuality and Marriage in Colonial Latin America*. Ed. Asunción Lavrin. Lincoln: U of Nebraska P, 1989. 178–206.

Beltrán, Rosa. "La máquina fabuladora." *La novela según los novelistas*. Ed. Cristina Rivera Garza. Mexico City: Fondo de Cultura Económica y CONACULTA, 2007. 112–23.

Bencomo, Anadeli. *Voces y voceros de la megalópolis. La crónica periodística-literaria en México*. Madrid: Iberoamericana/Vervuert, 2002.

Benítez, Fernando. *Los demonios en el convento: Sexo y religión en la Nueva España.* Mexico City: Era, 2000.

———. *La ruta de Hernán Cortés.* Mexico City: Fondo de Cultura Económica, 1983.

Bergmann, Emilie. "Sor Juana's 'Silencio Sonoro': Musical Responses to Her Poetry." *Cuadernos de música, artes visuales y artes escénicas* 4.1–2 (2008–2009): 177–206.

Bolívar, Simón. *Carta de Jamaica.* 1815. Ed. Simón Andrés Sánchez. Trans. Amílcar Varela. Caracas: Comisión Presidencial para la Conmemoración del Bicentenario de la Carta de Jamaica, 2015.

———. "A Letter by Simón Bolívar." *Selected Writings of Bolivar.* Ed. Vicente Lecuna and Harold A. Bierck. Trans. Lewis Bertrand. New York: Colonial Press, 1951.

Boone, Elizabeth Hill. "*In Tlamatinime*: The Wise Men and Women of Aztec Mexico." *Painted Books and Indigenous Knowledge in Mesoamerica: Manuscript Studies in Honor of Mary Elizabeth Smith.* Ed. Elizabeth Hill Boone. New Orleans: Middle American Research Institute, Tulane University, 2005. 9–25.

———. "Writing and Recording Knowledge." *Writing without Words: Alternative Literacies in Mesoamerica and the Andes.* Ed. Elizabeth Hill Boone and Walter D. Mignolo. Durham, NC: Duke UP, 1994. 3–26.

Borton de Treviño, Elizabeth. *Leona: A Love Story.* New York: Farrar, Straus Giroux, 1994.

Bourdieu, Pierre. *La dominación masculina.* Trans. Joaquín Jordá. Barcelona: Anagrama, 2012.

Brotherston, Gordon. "La Malintzin de los códices." *La Malinche, sus padres y sus hijos.* Ed. Margo Glantz. Mexico City: Taurus, 2001. 19–37.

Brunner, José Joaquín. "Notes on Modernity and Postmodernity in Latin American Culture." *boundary 2* 20.3 (1993): 34–54.

Butler, Judith. *Gender Trouble: Feminism and the Subversion of Identity.* New York: Routledge, 1999.

Buxó, José Pascual. "De la historia a la literatura: Verdad o ficción." *Revista de la Universidad de México* 83 (2011): 14–20.

———. *Sor Juana Inés de la Cruz: amor y conocimiento.* Mexico City: Universidad Nacional Autónoma de México e Instituto Mexiquense de Cultura, 1996.

Calleja, Diego. *Vida de Sor Juana.* Ed. Ermilo Abreu Gómez. Mexico City: Instituto Mexiquense de Cultura, 1996.

Campobello, Nellie. *Obra reunida.* Mexico City: Fondo de Cultura Económica, 2007.

Cano, Gabriela. "¿Es posible hacer la historia de las mujeres en la Revolución Mexicana?" *Mexico's Unfinished Revolutions.* Ed. Charles B. Faulhaber. Berkeley: U of California P, 2011. 11–24.

———. "Inocultables realidades del deseo: Amelio Robles, masculinidad (transgénero) en la Revolución mexicana." *Género, poder y política en el México posrevolucionario*. Ed. Gabriela Cano, Mary Kay Vaughan, and Jocelyn Olcott. Mexico City: Fondo de Cultura Económica, Universidad Autónoma Metropolitana-Iztapalapa, 2009. 61–90.

———. "La invención de la Adelita." *Prensafondo.com*. 20 November 2010. Web. 30 November 2016.

———. "Las mujeres en el México del siglo XX: Una cronología mínima." *Miradas feministas sobre las mexicanas del siglo XX*. Ed. Marta Lamas. Mexico City: Fondo de Cultura Económica y CONACULTA, 2007. 21–75.

———. *Se llamaba Elena Arizmendi*. Mexico City: Tusquets, 2010.

Cantú, Irma. "Malinche as Cinderellatl: Sweeping Female Agency in Search of a Global Readership." *Colonial Itineraries of Contemporary Mexico*. Ed. Oswaldo Estrada and Anna M. Nogar: Tucson: U of Arizona P, 2014. 147–71.

Casasola, Gustavo. *Historia gráfica de la Revolución Mexicana: 1900–1970*. Vol. 2. Mexico City: Editorial Trillas, 1973.

Castellanos, Rosario. "La corrupción intelectual." *Mujer de palabras. Artículos rescatados de Rosario Castellanos*. Vol. 2. Ed. Andrea Reyes. Mexico City: Consejo Nacional para la Cultura y las Artes, 2006. 196–210.

———. *Declaración de fe: Reflexiones sobre la situación de la mujer en México*. Mexico City: Alfaguara, 1996.

———. "Esplendor y miseria del intelectual." *Mujer de palabra: Artículos rescatados de Rosario Castellanos*. Vol. 1. Ed. Andrea Reyes. Mexico City: Consejo Nacional para la Cultura y las Artes, 2004. 368–71.

———. *Mujer que sabe latín . . .* Mexico City: Fondo de Cultura Económica, 2007.

———. *Poesía no eres tú*. Mexico City: Fondo de Cultura Económica, 2004.

———. *Sobre cultura femenina*. Mexico City: Fondo de Cultura Económica, 2009.

Castillo, Debra A. "Coagulated Words: Gaspar de Alba's Malinche." *Feminism, Nation, and Myth: La Malinche*. Ed. Rolando Romero and Amanda Nolacea Harris. Houston: Arte Público Press, 2005. 67–80.

———. *Easy Women. Sex and Gender in Modern Mexican Fiction*. Minneapolis: U of Minnesota P, 1998.

Castro Ricalde, Maricruz. "Género." *Diccionario de estudios culturales latinoamericanos*. Ed. Mónica Szurmuk and Robert McKee Irwin. Mexico City: Instituto Mora y Siglo XXI, 2009. 112–19.

Cerda Muños, Alfredo. "Lo que faltaba decir de la Décima Musa en el siglo XXI: *Los indecibles pecados de Sor Juana*." *Mujeres novohispanas en la narrativa mexicana contemporánea*. Ed. Cecilia Eudave, Alberto Ortiz, and José Carlos Rovira. Alicante: Universidad de Alicante (Cuadernos de *América sin nombre* 33), 2014. 43–60.

Chandler, Brian T. "Signs from the Present: Víctor Hugo Rascón Banda's *La Malinche*." *Chasqui* 39.2 (2010): 3–16.

Chasteen, John Charles. *Americanos: Latin America's Struggle for Independence*. New York: Oxford UP, 2008.

———. *Born in Blood and Fire: A Concise History of Latin America*. New York: Norton, 2016.

Clavel, Ana. "Las dos Fridas." *CorazoNadas*. Mexico City: Posdata, 2014. 17.

Clifford, Katie. "Featuring *Frida*." *Art in America* 90.12 (2002): 61–63.

Coerver, Don M. "Religion." *Mexico: An Encyclopedia of Contemporary Culture and History*. Ed. Don M. Coerver, Suzanne B. Pasztor, and Robert M. Buffington. Santa Barbara, CA: ABC-CLIO, 2004. 429–32.

Corona, Ignacio and Beth E. Jörgensen, eds. *The Contemporary Mexican Chronicle: Theoretical Perspectives on the Liminal Genre*. Albany: State U of New York P, 2002.

Cross, Robin, and Rosalind Miles. *Warrior Women: 3000 Years of Courage and Heroism*. London: Quercus, 2011.

Cruz, Sor Juana Inés de la. *The Answer / La Respuesta: Including Sor Filotea's Letter and New Selected Poems*. Ed. and trans. Electa Arenal and Amanda Powell. New York: Feminist Press at the City University of New York, 2009.

———. *Obras completas*. Ed. Alfonso Méndez Plancarte and Alberto G. Salceda. 4 vols. Mexico City: Fondo de Cultura Económica, 1995.

———. *Poems, Protest, and a Dream*. Trans. Margaret Sayers Peden. New York: Penguin, 1997.

———. *Poesía, Teatro, Pensamiento*. Ed. Georgina Sabat de Rivers and Elias Rivers. Madrid: Espasa Calpe, 2004.

———. *A Sor Juana Anthology*. Trans. Alan S. Trueblood. Cambridge, MA: Harvard UP, 1988.

Curcio-Nagy, Linda A. "Faith and Morals in Colonial Mexico." *The Oxford History of Mexico*. Ed. Michael C. Meyer and William H. Beezley. New York: Oxford UP, 2000. 151–82.

Cypess Messinger, Sandra. *La Malinche in Mexican Literature: From History to Myth*. Austin: U of Texas P, 1991.

Day, Stuart A. *Staging Politics in Mexico: The Road to Neoliberalism*. Lewisburg, PA: Bucknell UP, 2004.

Del Palacio, Celia. *Adictas a la insurgencia: Mujeres en la guerra de Independencia*. Mexico City: Punto de Lectura, 2010.

———. *Leona*. Mexico City: Suma de Letras, 2010.

Del Río, Fanny. *La verdadera historia de Malinche*. Mexico City: Plaza Janés, 2010.

De Toro, Alfonso. "Las 'nuevas meninas' o 'bienvenido Foucault.' 'Performance'—'Escenificación'—'Transmedialidad'—'Percepción.' Frida Kahlo: Diario—Fotografía—Pintura." *Frida Kahlo 'revisitada.' Estrategias transme-*

diales—transculturales—transpicturales. Ed. Alfonso de Toro. Hildesheim: Georg Olms, 2014. 67–90.

De Toro, Alfonso, and René Ceballos. "Introducción." *Frida Kahlo "revisitada." Estrategias transmediales—transculturales—transpicturales*. Ed. Alfonso de Toro and René Ceballos. Hildesheim: Georg Olms, 2014. 7–23.

Díaz, Mónica. "The Establishment of Femenine Paradigms. Translators, Traitors, Nuns." *The Cambridge History of Latin American Women's Literature*. Ed. Ileana Rodríguez and Mónica Szurmuk. Cambridge: Cambridge UP, 2015. 52–65.

———. *Indigenous Writings from the Convent: Negotiating Ethnic Autonomy in Colonial Mexico*. Tucson: U of Arizona P, 2010.

Díaz del Castillo, Bernal. *The Conquest of New Spain*. Trans. J. M. Cohen. New York: Penguin, 1963.

———. *Historia verdadera de la conquista de la Nueva España*. Ed. Joaquín Ramírez Cabañas. Mexico City: Porrúa, 1998.

Doležel, Lubomír. *Possible Worlds of Fiction and History: The Postmodern Stage*. Baltimore: Johns Hopkins UP, 2010.

Echeverría, Bolívar. "Malintzin, la lengua." *La Malinche, sus padres y sus hijos*. Ed. Margo Glantz. Mexico City: Taurus, 2001. 171–82.

Eco, Umberto. *Serendipities: Language and Lunacy*. Trans. William Weaver. San Diego: Harvest, 1998.

Egan, Linda. *Carlos Monsiváis. Cultura y crónica en el México contemporáneo*. Trans. Isabel Vericat. Mexico City: Fondo de Cultura Económica, 2004.

———. *Diosas, demonios y debate: Las armas metafísicas de Sor Juana*. Salta: Editorial Biblioteca de Textos Universitarios, 1997.

Elias, Ana Sofia, Rosalind Gill, and Christina Scharff. "Aesthetic Labour: Beauty Politics in Neoliberalism." *Aesthetic Labour: Rethinking Beauty Politics in Neoliberalism*. Ed. Ana Sofia Elias, Rosalind Gill, and Christina Scharff. London: Palgrave Macmillan, 2017. 3–50.

Enrigue, Álvaro. *Muerte súbita*. Barcelona: Anagrama, 2013.

———. *Sudden Death*. Trans. Natasha Wimmer. New York: Riverhead Books, 2016.

Esquivel, Laura. *Malinche*. New York: Atria Books, 2006.

———. *Malinche*. Trans. Ernesto Mestre-Reed. New York: Atria Books, 2006.

Eudave, Cecilia, Alberto Ortiz, and José Carlos Rovira, eds. *Mujeres novohispanas en la narrativa mexicana contemporánea*. Alicante: Universidad de Alicante (Cuadernos de *América sin nombre* 33), 2014.

———. *Personajes históricos y controversias en la narrativa mexicana contemporánea*. Alicante: Universidad de Alicante (Cuadernos de *América sin nombre* 34), 2014.

Estrada, Oswaldo. "Crónica de un fracaso anunciado: Bernal Díaz y el viaje a las Hibueras." *Cuadernos Hispanoamericanos* 769/770 (2014): 104–18.

———. "Exploraciones del conocimiento místico en tres romances de Sor Juana Inés de la Cruz." *Calíope* 14.2 (2008): 69–86.

———. "Four Letters and a Funeral: Sor Juana's Writing in *Yo, la peor.*" *Colonial Itineraries of Contemporary Mexico: Literary and Cultural Inquiries*. Ed. Oswaldo Estrada and Anna M. Nogar. Tucson: U of Arizona P, 2014. 83–102.

———. *La imaginación novelesca: Bernal Díaz entre géneros y épocas*. Madrid: Iberoamericana/Vervuert, 2009.

———. *Ser mujer y estar presente: Disidencias de género en la literatura mexicana contemporánea*. Mexico City: Universidad Nacional Autónoma de México, 2014.

———. "Sor Juana's Gender Transgressions in the Works of Ana Clavel and Cristina Rivera Garza." *Cuadernos de música, artes visuales y artes escénicas* 4.1–2 (2008–2009): 53–81.

———. "Sor Juana y el ejercicio pedagógico en sus villancicos marianos." *Letras Femeninas* 32.2 (2006): 81–100.

———. "Sor Juana y San Bernardo: entre la fiesta religiosa y el disfraz literario." *Cuaderno Internacional de Estudios Humanísticos y Literatura* 7 (2007): 39–54.

———. "'Venid a la Escuela': Sor Juana y los santos en las aulas del conocimiento." *Anthropos* 243 (2015): 89–100.

Estrada, Oswaldo, and Anna M. Nogar, eds. *Colonial Itineraries of Contemporary Mexico: Literary and Cultural Inquiries*. Tucson: U of Arizona P, 2014.

Fernández de Lizardi, José Joaquín. *Heroínas Mexicanas: María Leona Vicario, M. Rodríguez Lazarín, María Fermina Rivera, Manuela Herrera y otras*. Mexico City: Editor Vargas Rea, 1955.

Flores Castillo, Adriana Y. "Leona Vicario: mujer, fuerza y compromiso en la independencia de México." *Juicios y causas procesales en la independencia Mexicana*. Ed. Francisco Ibarra Palafox. Mexico City: Universidad Nacional Autónoma de México, 2010. 149–73.

Foucault, Michel. *The History of Sexuality: An Introduction*. Trans. Robert Hurley. New York: Vintage Books, 1990.

Franco, Jean. *Las conspiradoras: La representación de la mujer en México*. Trans. Mercedes Córdoba. Mexico City: El Colegio de México y Fondo de Cultura Económica, 2004.

———. *Ensayos impertinentes*. Ed. Marta Lamas. Mexico City: Debate Feminista y Océano, 2013.

Fraser, Nancy. "Feminism, Capitalism and the Cunning of History." *New Left Review* 56 (2009): 97–117.

Fuentes, Carlos. *Los años con Laura Díaz*. Mexico City: Alfaguara, 1999.

———. "Introducción." *El Diario de Frida Kahlo: Un íntimo autorretrato*. New York: H. N. Abrams and La Vaca Independiente, 1995. 7–24.

———. "Introduction." *The Diary of Frida Kahlo: An Intimate Portrait*. Trans. Barbara Crow de Toledo and Ricardo Pohlenz. New York: H. N. Abrams and La Vaca Independiente, 1995. 7–24.

———. *El naranjo*. Mexico City: Alfaguara, 1993.

———. *Todos los gatos son pardos*. Mexico City: Joaquín Mortiz, 1970.

———. *The Years with Laura Díaz*. Trad. Alfred Mac Adam. New York: Farrar, Straus Giroux, 2000.

Galí Boadella, Montserrat. *Historias del bello sexo: La introducción del Romanticismo en México*. Mexico City: Universidad Nacional Autónoma de México, 2002.

Galván, Kyra. *Los indecibles pecados de Sor Juana*. Mexico City: Planeta, 2010.

Galván Gaytán, Columba Camelia. "José Joaquín Fernández de Lizardi y la educación de las mujeres: notas sobre las heroínas mexicanas." *Actas del XII Congreso de la Asociación Internacional de Hispanistas, 1995*. Vol. 6: *Estudios Hispanoamericanos*. Ed. Trevor J. Dadson. Birmingham: U of Birmingham P, 1998. 204–8.

García, Genaro. *Leona Vicario, heroína insurgente*. Mexico City: Editorial Innovación, 1979.

García Argüelles, Elsa Leticia. "La heroicidad femenina y la representación de Leona Vicario en dos novelas contemporáneas." *Revista de Literatura Mexicana Contemporánea* 50 (2011): 29–41.

———. "Leona Vicario en la novela histórica contemporánea." *Mujeres novohispanas en la narrativa mexicana contemporánea*. Ed. Cecilia Eudave, Alberto Ortiz, and José Carlos Rovira. Alicante: Universidad de Alicante (Cuadernos de *América sin nombre* 33), 2014. 115–28.

García Canclini, Néstor. *La globalización imaginada*. Buenos Aires: Paidós, 2005.

García Hernández, Arturo. "*Por debajo del agua* puede ser la primera novela gay de la Revolución." *La Jornada*. 21 May 2002. Web. 11 November 2014.

Gargallo, Francesca. *Ideas feministas latinoamericanas*. Mexico City: Universidad de la Ciudad de México, 2004.

Gaspar de Alba, Alicia. *[Un]Framing the Bad Woman: Sor Juana, Malinche, Coyolxauhqui and Other Rebels with a Cause*. Austin: U of Texas P, 2015.

Glantz, Margo. *Apariciones*. Mexico City: Alfaguara y Universidad del Claustro de Sor Juana, 1995.

———. "Diseminación y amplificación." *Revista de la Universidad de México* 104 (2012): 15–25.

———. "Doña Marina y el Capitán Malinche." *La Malinche, sus padres y sus hijos*. Ed. Margo Glantz. Mexico City: Taurus, 2001. 115–33.

———. "Letras de San Bernardo: la excelsa fábrica." *Calíope* 4 (1998): 173–88.

———. "La Malinche: la lengua en la mano." *La Malinche, sus padres y sus hijos*. Ed. Margo Glantz. Mexico City: Taurus, 2001. 91–113.

———. *Sor Juana: la comparación y la hipérbole*. Mexico City: Conaculta, 2000.

Gómez, José Luis. *El beso de la virreina*. Mexico: Planeta, 2008.

Gonzalbo Aizpuru, Pilar. *Historia de la educación en la época colonial: La educación de los criollos y la vida urbana*. Mexico City: El Colegio de México, 1999.

González Hernández, Cristina. *Doña Marina (La Malinche) y la formación de la identidad mexicana*. Madrid: Ediciones Encuentro, 2002.

Grossi, Verónica. "Hacia una revisión de la historia y cultura coloniales a través de una relectura de la obra (y de la crítica de la obra) de Sor Juana Inés de la Cruz." *Mujeres y re-presentación: entre muchas plumas andan*. Ed. Lucía Melgar. Mexico City: El Colegio de México, Programa Interdisciplinario de Estudios de la Mujer, 2007. 31–43.

———. *Sigilosos v(u)elos epistemológicos en Sor Juana Inés de la Cruz*. Madrid: Iberoamericana/Vervuert, 2007.

———. "*Sueño* de Ángeles Romero: una recreación multi-artística de la vida y obra de Sor Juana." *Cuadernos de música, artes visuales y artes escénicas* 4.1–2 (2008–2009): 111–53.

Gruzinski, Serge. *La guerra de las imágenes: De Cristóbal Colón a "Blade Runner" (1492–2019)*. Trans. Juan José Utrilla. Mexico City: Fondo de Cultura Económica, 2003.

Guerra, Lucía. *Mujer y escritura: Fundamentos teóricos de la crítica feminista*. Mexico City: Universidad Nacional Autónoma de México, 2007.

Guevara-Geer, Geoff. "The Final Silence of Sor Juana: The Abysmal Remove of Her Closing Night." *Approaches to Teaching the Works of Sor Juana Inés de la Cruz*. Ed. Emilie L. Bergmann and Stacey Schlau. New York: Modern Language Association of America, 2007. 201–8.

Guillén, Claudia. "Sor Juana en el centro de las miradas." *Revista de la Universidad de México* 64 (2009): 97–98.

Gutiérrez Mouat, Ricardo. "The Modern Novel, the Media, and Mass Culture in Latin America." *Latin American Literature and Mass Media*. Ed. Edmundo Paz-Soldán and Debra A. Castillo. New York: Garland, 2001. 71–101.

Habermas, Jürgen. *The Postnational Constellation: Political Essays*. Trans. and ed. Max Pensky. Cambridge, MA: MIT Press, 2001.

Haghenbeck, Francisco G. *El libro secreto de Frida Kahlo*. New York: Atria, 2012.

———. *The Secret Book of Frida Kahlo: A Novel*. Trans. Achy Abejas. New York: Atria, 2012.

———. *Sensacional de héroes*. Mexico City: Grupo Editorial Norma, 2010.

Harvey, David. *A Brief History of Neoliberalism*. Oxford: Oxford UP, 2007.

Herrera, Hayden. *Frida: A Biography of Frida Kahlo*. New York: Harper & Row, 1983.

Herrera-Sobek, María. *The Mexican Corrido: A Feminist Analysis*. Bloomington: Indiana UP, 1990.

Hind, Emily. *Femmenism and the Mexican Woman Intellectual from Sor Juana to Poniatowska: Boob Lit*. New York: Palgrave Macmillan, 2010.

———. "Sor Juana, an Official Habit: Twentieth-Century Mexican Culture." *Approaches to Teaching the Works of Sor Juana Inés de la Cruz*. Ed. Emilie L. Bergmann and Stacey Schlau. New York: Modern Language Association of America, 2007. 247–55.

———. "The Sor Juana Archetype in Recent Works by Mexican Women Writers." *Hispanófila* 141 (2004): 89–103.

Huyssen, Andreas. *After the Great Divide: Modernism, Mass Culture, Postmodernism*. Bloomington: Indiana UP, 1986.

Irwin, Robert McKee. *Bandits, Captives, Heroines, and Saints: Cultural Icons of Mexico's Northwest Borderlands*. Minneapolis: U of Minnesota P, 2007.

Jager, Rebecca K. *Malinche, Pocahontas, and Sacagawea: Indian Women as Cultural Intermediaries and National Symbols*. Norman: U of Oklahoma P, 2015.

Jehlen, Myra. "Gender." *Critical Terms for Literary Study*. Ed. Frank Lentricchia and Thomas McLaughlin. Chicago: U of Chicago P, 1995. 263–73.

Johnson, Julie Greer. *Women in Colonial Spanish American Literature: Literary Images*. Westport, CT: Greenwood Press, 1983.

Kahlo, Frida. *The Diary of Frida Kahlo: An Intimate Portrait*. Trans. Barbara Crow de Toledo and Ricardo Pohlenz. New York: H. N. Abrams and La Vaca Independiente, 1995.

———. *Escrituras*. Ed. Raquel Tibol. Mexico City: Universidad Nacional Autónoma de México, 1999.

Kaplan, Temma. "Género, caos y autoridad en tiempos revolucionarios." *Género, poder y política en el México posrevolucionario*. Ed. Gabriela Cano, Mary Kay Vaughan, and Jocelyn Olcott. Trans. Rossana Reyes. Mexico City: Fondo de Cultura Económica, UAM-Iztapalapa, 2009. 407–32.

Karttunen, Frances. "La Malinche and *Malinchismo*." *Concise Encyclopedia of Mexico*. Ed. Michael S. Werner. Chicago: Fitzroy Dearborn Publishers, 2001. 352–55.

Kirk, Stephanie. *Convent Life in Colonial Mexico: A Tale of Two Communities*. Gainsville: U of Florida P, 2007.

———. "Power and Resistance in the Colonial Mexican Convent." *Approaches to Teaching the Works of Sor Juana Inés de la Cruz*. Ed. Emilie L. Bergmann and Stacey Schlau. New York: Modern Language Association of America, 2007. 47–54.

———. "Women's Literacy and Masculine Authority: The Case of Sor Juana Inés de la Cruz and Antonio Núñez de Miranda." *Women's Literacy in Early Modern Spain and the New World*. Ed. Anne J. Cruz and Rosilie Hernández. Farnham: Ashgate, 2011. 139–57.

Lamas, Marta. *Cuerpo, sexo y política*. Mexico City: Océano y Debate Feminista, 2013.

Latorre, Guisela. "Agustín Víctor Casasola's *Soldaderas*: Malinchismo and the Chicana/o Artist." *Feminism, Nation and Myth: La Malinche*. Ed. Rolando Romero and Amanda Nolacea Harris. Houston: Arte Público Press, 2005. 98–110.

Lau Jaiven, Ana. "Las mujeres también fueron a la revolución." *Impacto de la Revolución Mexicana*. Ed. Patricia Galeana. Mexico City: Senado de la

República, Siglo XXI Editores y Universidad Nacional Autónoma de México, 2010. 91–112.

Lavín, Mónica. *La casa chica*. Mexico City: Planeta, 2016.

———. *Las rebeldes*. Mexico City: Debolsillo, 2013.

———. *Sor Juana en la cocina*. Recetas de Ana Luisa Benítez Muro. Mexico City: Editorial Clío, 2000.

———. *Yo, la peor*. Mexico City: Grijalbo, 2009.

Lavrin, Asunción. *Brides of Christ: Conventual Life in Colonial Mexico*. Stanford, CA: Stanford UP, 2008.

———. "*Lo femenino*: Women in Colonial Historical Sources." *Coded Encounters: Writing, Gender, and Ethnicity in Colonial Latin America*. Ed. Francisco Javier Cevallos-Candau, Jeffrey A. Cole, Nina M. Scott, and Nicomedes Suárez-Araúz. Amherst: U of Massachusetts P, 1994. 153–76.

———. "The Scenario, the Actors, and the Issues." *Sexuality and Marriage in Colonial Latin America*. Ed. Asunción Lavrin. Lincoln: U of Nebraska P, 1989. 1–43.

Leona Vicario. Dir. Luis Guillermo Basurto and Wilebaldo López. Mexico City: Televisa, 1982. Telenovela.

Leal, Luis. *Aztlán y México. Perfiles literarios e históricos*. Binghampton: Bilingual Press/Editorial Bilingüe, 1985.

———. "Female Archetypes in Mexican Literature." *Women in Hispanic Literature: Icons and Fallen Idols*. Ed. Beth Miller. Berkeley: U of California P, 1983. 227–42.

———. *A Luis Leal Reader*. Ed. Ilan Stavans. Evanston: Northwestern UP, 2007.

Lefere, Robin. *La novela histórica: (re)definición, caracterización, tipología*. Madrid: Visor Libros, 2013.

Leñero, Estela. *Soles en la sombra: Mujeres en la Revolución*. Mexico City: Editorial Jus y Compañía Nacional de Teatro, 2011.

Lévi-Strauss, Claude. *Look, Listen, Read*. Trans. Brian C. J. Singer. New York: Basic Books, 1997.

Lienhard, Martín. "La memoria popular y sus transformaciones." *La memoria popular y sus transformaciones: A memória popular e as suas tranformações: América Latina y/e países luso-africanos*. Ed. Martín Lienhard. Madrid: Iberoamericana/Vervuert, 2000. 13–24.

Lindauer, Margaret A. "Fetishizing Frida (excerpted from *Devouring Frida* [1999])." *Latin American Icons: Fame across Borders*. Ed. Dianna C. Niebylski and Patrick O'Connor. Nashville, TN: Vanderbilt UP, 2014. 173–85.

Linhard, Tabea Alexa. *Fearless Women in the Mexican Revolution and the Spanish Civil War*. Columbia: U of Missouri P, 2005.

Loaeza, Guadalupe. "El venado . . . (¡herido!)." *Revista de la Universidad de México* 43 (2007): 46–49.

Long, Ryan F. "Esquivel's Malinalli: Refusing the Last Word on *La Malinche*." *Laura Esquivel's Mexican Fictions*. Ed. Elizabeth Moore Willingham. Brighton: Sussex Academic Press, 2010. 197–207.

López de Mariscal, Blanca. *La figura femenina en los narradores testigos de la conquista*. Mexico City: El Colegio de México y Consejo para la Cultura de Nuevo León, 2004.

Lorenzano, Sandra. "*Hay que inventarnos*: Mujer y narrativa en el siglo XX." *Miradas feministas sobre las mexicanas del siglo XX*. Ed. Marta Lamas. Mexico City: Fondo de Cultura Económica y Consejo Nacional para la Cultura y las Artes, 2007. 349–85.

———. "Posmodernidad." *Diccionario de Estudios Culturales Latinoamericanos*. Ed. Mónica Szurmuk and Robert McKee Irwin. Mexico City: Siglo XXI e Instituto Mora, 2009. 228–34.

Luciani, Frederick. *Literary Self-Fashioning in Sor Juana Inés de la Cruz*. Lewisburg, PA: Bucknell UP, 2004.

Ludmer, Josefina. "Tricks of the Weak." Trans. Stephanie Merrim. *Feminist Perspectives on Sor Juana Inés de la Cruz*. Ed. Stephanie Merrim. Detroit: Wayne State UP, 1999. 86–93.

Macías, Anna. *Against All Odds: The Feminist Movement in Mexico to 1940*. Westport, CT: Greenwood Press, 1982.

———. *Contra viento y marea: El movimiento feminista en México hasta 1940*. Mexico City: Programa Universitario de Estudios de Género (Universidad Nacional Autónoma de México), 2002.

———. "Women and the Mexican Revolution, 1910–1920." *The Américas* 37.1 (1980): 53–82.

Madrid Moctezuma, Paola. "Sor Juana Inés de la Cruz y el barroco novohispano a través de los modelos narrativos de la ficción histórica y del *boom* hispánico femenino." *América sin nombre* 15 (2010): 93–106.

Manrique, Jorge Alberto. "Malinche." *La Malinche, sus padres y sus hijos*. Ed. Margo Glantz. Mexico City: Taurus, 2001. 247–49.

Marso, Lori Jo. *Feminist Thinkers and the Demands of Femininity: The Lives and Work of Intellectual Women*. New York: Routledge, 2006.

Martín del Campo, Marisol. *Amor y conquista: La novela de Malinalli mal llamada Malinche*. Mexico City: Planeta/Joaquín Mortiz, 1999.

Martínez Pichardo, José. *Leona Vicario: Grandeza de una mujer de su tiempo en la lucha por la Independencia*. Toluca: Gobierno del Estado de México, 2008.

Martínez-San Miguel, Yolanda. *Saberes americanos: subalternidad y epistemología en los escritos de Sor Juana*. Pittsburgh: Instituto Internacional de Literatura Iberoamericana, 1999.

Masiello, Francine. *Between Civilization and Barbarism: Women, Nation, and Literary Culture in Modern Argentina*. Lincoln: U of Nebraska P, 1992.

McDonough, Kelly S. *The Learned Ones: Nahua Intellectuals in Postconquest Mexico*. Tucson: U of Arizona P, 2014.

Mejía, Eduardo. "Presentación: La mujer en la visión de Rosario Castellanos." *Declaración de fe: Reflexiones sobre la situación de la mujer en México*. Rosario Castellanos. Mexico City: Alfaguara, 1996. 9–12.

Mendieta Alatorre, Ángeles. *La mujer en la Revolución Mexicana*. Mexico City: Talleres Gráficos de la Nación, 1961.

Menton, Seymour. *Latin America's New Historical Novel*. Austin: U of Texas P, 1993.

Merrim, Stephanie. *Early Modern Women's Writing and Sor Juana Inés de la Cruz*. Nashville, TN: Vanderbilt UP, 1999.

———, ed. *Feminist Perspectives on Sor Juana Inés de la Cruz*. Detroit: Wayne State UP, 1999.

———. "Toward a Feminist Reading of Sor Juana Inés de la Cruz: Past, Present, and Future Directions in Sor Juana's Criticism." *Feminist Perspectives on Sor Juana Inés de la Cruz*. Ed. Stephanie Merrim. Detroit: Wayne State UP, 1999. 11–37.

Miller, Beth. "Marina/Malinche: Masks and Shadows." *Women in Hispanic Literature: Icons and Fallen Idols*. Ed. Beth Miller. Berkeley: U of California P, 1983. 97–114.

Miller, Nicola. "Contesting the Cleric. The Intellectual as Icon in Modern Spanish America." *Contemporary Latin American Cultural Studies*. Ed. Stephen Hart and Richard Young. London: Arnold, 2003. 62–75.

Misemer, Sarah M. *Secular Saints: Performing Frida Kahlo, Carlos Gardel, Eva Perón and Selena*. Woodbridge: Tamesis, 2008.

Monsiváis, Carlos. *Aires de familia: Cultura y sociedad en América Latina*. Barcelona: Anagrama, 2006.

———. "De cuando los símbolos no dejaban ver el género (Las mujeres y la Revolución mexicana)." *Género, poder y política en el México posrevolucionario*. Ed. Gabriela Cano, Mary Kay Vaughan, and Jocelyn Olcott. Trans. Rossana Reyes. Mexico City: Fondo de Cultura Económica, UAM-Iztapalapa, 2009. 11–37.

———. "Frida Kahlo: de las etapas de su reconocimiento." *Misógino feminista*. Ed. Marta Lamas. Mexico City: Océano y Debate Feminista, 2013. 247–60.

———. *Las esencias viajeras: Hacia una crónica cultural del Bicentenario de la Independencia*. Mexico City: Fondo de Cultura Económica y Consejo Nacional para la Cultura y las Artes, 2012.

———. *El género epistolar: un homenaje a manera de carta abierta*. Mexico City: Miguel Ángel Porrúa, 1991.

———. *Las herencias ocultas de la Reforma liberal del siglo XIX*. Mexico City: Debate, 2007.

———. *Imágenes de la tradición viva*. Mexico City: Landucci, Universidad Nacional Autónoma de México y Fondo de Cultura Económica, 2006.

———. "La Malinche y el malinchismo." *La Malinche, sus padres y sus hijos*. Ed. Margo Glantz. Mexico City: Taurus, 2001. 183–93.

———. *Mexican Postcards*. Trans. John Kraniauskas. London: Verso, 1997.

———. *Misógino feminista*. Ed. Marta Lamas. Mexico City: Océano y Debate Feminista, 2013.

———. "La narrativa de la revolución." *Historia mínima de la cultura mexicana en el siglo XX*. Ed. Eugenia Huerta. Mexico City: El Colegio de México, 2010. 61–79.

———. "La Revolufia al borde del centenario." *La Revolución mexicana en la literatura y el cine*. Ed. Olivia C. Díaz Pérez Gräfe and Friedhelm Schmidt-Welle. Madrid: Iberoamericana/Vervuert/Bonilla Artigas, 2010. 9–31.

Montaño Garfias, Ericka. "Carlos Pascual gana el Premio Bicentenario de Novela Histórica convocado por Random House." *La Jornada*. 17 February 2010. Web. 2 August 2016.

Moraña, Mabel. "El afecto en la caja de herramientas." *El lenguaje de las emociones: Afecto y cultura en América Latina*. Ed. Mabel Moraña and Ignacio Sánchez Prado. Madrid: Iberoamericana/Vervuert, 2012. 313–37.

———. "Mujer y cultura en la colonia hispanoamericana." *Mujer y cultura en la colonia hispanoamericana*. Ed. Mabel Moraña. Pittsburgh: Instituto Internacional de Literatura Iberoamericana, 1996. 7–20.

———. "Pensar el cuerpo, politizar el género." *El salto de Minerva: Intelectuales, género y Estado en América Latina*. Ed. Mabel Moraña and María Rosa Olivera-Williams. Madrid: Iberoamericana/Vervuert, 2005. 329–42.

Muñoz, Rafael F. *Relatos de la Revolución: Antología de Rafael F. Muñoz*. Ed. Salvador Reyes Nevares. Mexico City: SepSetentas, 1974.

Myers, Kathleen Ann. *Neither Saints nor Sinners: Writing the Lives of Women in Spanish America*. New York: Oxford UP, 2003.

Navarro Salazar, María Teresa. "Mujer e identidad en la narrativa histórica femenina." *Reflexiones sobre la novela histórica*. Ed. José Jurado Morales. Cádiz: Fundación Fernando Quiñones y Universidad de Cádiz, 2006. 191–218.

Noemi Voionmaa, Daniel. "Efraim Medina Reyes: Literatura, ética y mercado." *Libro mercado: Literatura y neoliberalismo*. Ed. José Ramón Ruisánchez. Mexico City: Universidad Iberoamericana, 2015. 117–32.

Ochoa, John A. "Sor Juana, Food, and the Life of the Mind." *Approaches to Teaching the Works of Sor Juana Inés de la Cruz*. Ed. Emilie L. Bergmann and Stacey Schlau. New York: Modern Language Association of America, 2007. 229–37.

O'Connor, Patrick, and Dianna C. Niebylski. "The Afterlife of Icons and the Future of Iconology." *Latin American Icons: Fame across Borders*. Ed. Dianna C. Niebylski and Patrick O'Connor. Nashville, TN: Vanderbilt UP, 2014. 187–89.

———. "Reflections on Iconicity, Celebrity, and Cultural Crossings." *Latin American Icons. Fame across Borders*. Ed. Dianna C. Niebylski and Patrick O'Connor. Nashville, TN: Vanderbilt UP, 2014. 1–18.

Olivares, Cecilia. *Glosario de términos de crítica literaria feminista*. Mexico City: El Colegio de México, 1997.

Onasch, Konrad, and Annemarie Schnieper. *Icons: The Fascination and the Reality*. Trans. Daniel G. Conklin. New York: Riverside, 1997.

Ortiz, Alberto. "*No soy yo la que pensáis*: Variables contemporáneas del personaje Sor Juana Inés de la Cruz." *Mujeres novohispanas en la narrativa mexicana contemporánea*. Ed. Cecilia Eudave, Alberto Ortiz, and José Carlos Rovira. Alicante: Universidad de Alicante (Cuadernos de *América sin nombre* 33), 2014. 153–68.

Ortiz, Mario A. "Introducción: Representando a Sor Juana: no como es, sino como la imaginamos." *Cuadernos de música, artes visuales y artes escénicas* 4.1–2 (2008–2009): 12–26.

———. "Sor Juana en *El Niño* de John Adams y *Óyeme con los ojos* de Allison Sniffin." *Cuadernos de música, artes visuales y artes escénicas* 4.1–2 (2008–2009): 207–34.

Paden, Jeremy. "*Hunger's Brides*: obra, vida e imagen de Sor Juana." *Cuadernos de música, artes visuales y artes escénicas* 4.1–2 (2008–2009): 82–110.

Palapa Quijas, Fabiola. "Reconstruye experta la historia de una Leona Vicario 'apasionada.'" *La Jornada*. 21 July 2010. Web. 1 August 2016.

Palou, Pedro Ángel. *No me dejen morir así*. Mexico City: Planeta, 2014.

———. *Zapata*. Mexico City: Planeta, 2006.

Pascual, Carlos. *La insurgenta*. Mexico City: Grijalbo, 2010.

Paz, Octavio. *El laberinto de la soledad*. Mexico City: Fondo de Cultura Económica, 1994.

———. *The Labyrinth of Solitude and Other Writings*. Trans. Lysander Kemp, Yara Milos, and Rachel Phillips Belash. New York: Grove Press, 1985.

———. *Sor Juana Inés de la Cruz o las trampas de la fe*. Mexico City: Fondo de Cultura Económica, 1998.

Perelmuter, Rosa. *Los límites de la femineidad en Sor Juana Inés de la Cruz*. Madrid: Iberoamericana, 2004.

Pérez de Mendiola, Marina. *Gender and Identity Formation in Contemporary Mexican Literature*. New York: Garland, 1998.

Perkowska, Magdalena. *Historias híbridas: La nueva novela latinoamericana (1985–2000) ante las teorías posmodernas de la historia*. Madrid: Iberoamericana/Vervuert, 2008.

Pierce, Donna, Rogelio Ruiz Gomar, and Clara Bargellini. *Painting a New World: Mexican Art and Life, 1521–1821*. Denver: Frederick and Jan Mayer Center for Pre-Columbian and Spanish Colonial Art, Denver Art Museum, 2004.

Pizarro Cortés, Carolina. "Dos aplicaciones del modelo melodramático: Manuela Sáenz y Leona Vicario en el imaginario contemporáneo sobre las independencias." *Letras de Hoje* 49.4 (2014): 414–23.

Poniatowska, Elena. *Hasta no verte Jesús mío*. Mexico City: Era, 1997.

———. *Luz y luna, las lunitas*. Mexico City: Era, 1994.

———. *Las siete cabritas*. Mexico City: Era, 2000.

———. *Las soldaderas*. Mexico City: Ediciones Era y CONACULTA, 2009.

———. *Las Soldaderas: Women of the Mexican Revolution*. Trans. David Dorado Romo. El Paso, TX: Cinco Puntos Presss, 2006.

Poniatowska, Elena, and Fernando Robles. *La Adelita*. Mexico City: Ediciones Tecolote, 2006.

Poot Herrera, Sara. *Los guardaditos de Sor Juana*. Mexico City: Universidad Nacional Autónoma de México, 1999.

———, ed. *Sor Juana y su mundo: una mirada actual*. Mexico City: Universidad del Claustro de Sor Juana, 1995.

Portella, Eduardo. "Paradoxes of Memory: Foreword." *Diogenes* 201 (2004): 5–6.

Porzecanski, Teresa. "El silencio, la palabra y la construcción de lo femenino." *El salto de Minerva: Intelectuales, género y Estado en América Latina*. Ed. Mabel Moraña and María Rosa Olivera-Williams. Madrid: Iberoamericana/Vervuert, 2005. 47–57.

Price, Brian L. "Where History Ends and the Corrido Begins in Pedro Ángel Palou's *Zapata*." *Latin American Literary Review* 79 (2012): 45–60.

Rabasa, José. *Tell Me the Story of How I Conquered You: Elsewheres and Ethnosuicide in the Colonial Mesoamerican World*. Austin: U of Texas P, 2011.

Ramos Aguirre, Francisco. *Mujeres de armas tomar: Canciones y soldaderas de la Revolución mexicana*. Ciudad Victoria: Gobierno del Estado de Tamaulipas, 2010.

Ramos Escandón, Carmen. "Genaro García, historiador feminista de fin de siglo." *Signos históricos* 5 (2001): 87–107.

Rascón Banda, Víctor Hugo. *La Malinche*. Mexico City: Plaza Janés, 2000.

Reed, John. *Insurgent Mexico*. New York: International, 1969.

Reséndez Fuentes, Andrés. "Battleground Women: *Soldaderas* and Female Soldiers in the Mexican Revolution." *Warfare in Latin America*. Vol. 2. Ed. Miguel A. Centeno. Aldershot: Ashgate, 2007. 113–41.

Restall, Matthew. *Seven Myths of the Spanish Conquest*. New York: Oxford UP, 2003.

"Retrato de una Leona." *Gritos de muerte y libertad*. Dir. Mafer Suárez and Gerardo Tort. Mexico City: Televisa, 2010. DVD.

Richard, Nelly. "La crítica feminista como modelo de crítica cultural." *Debate Feminista* 40 (2009): 75–85.

———. "¿Tiene sexo la escritura?" *Debate Feminista* 9 (1994): 127–39.

Rieger, Angelica. "Naturaleza muerta 'Viva la vida.' Las fiestas de Frida Kahlo o la escenificación culinaria como autoestilización sensual." *Frida Kahlo 'revisitada.' Estrategias transmediales—transculturales—transpicturales*. Ed. Alfonso de Toro and René Ceballos. Hildesheim: Georg Olms, 2014. 25–51.

Rivera Garza, Cristina. *Los muertos indóciles: Necroescrituras y desapropiación*. Mexico City: Tusquets, 2013.

———. *Nadie me verá llorar*. Mexico City: Tusquets, 1999.

———. *No One Will See Me Cry*. Willimantic, CT: Curbstone Press, 2003.

Rivera Marín, Guadalupe, and Marie-Pierre Colle Corcuera. *Las fiestas de Frida y Diego: recuerdos y recetas*. New York: Clarkson Potter, 1994.

Rodríguez, Ileana, and Mónica Szurmuk. "Women Writers in Creole Societies: Nation Building Projects." *The Cambridge History of Latin American Women's Literature*. Ed. Ileana Rodríguez and Mónica Szurmuk. Cambridge: Cambridge UP, 2015. 97–101.

Rodríguez Freire, Raúl. *Sin retorno: Variaciones sobre archivo y narrativa latinoamericana*. Buenos Aires: Ediciones La Cebra, 2015.

Rojas González, Francisco. *La negra Angustias*. 1944. Mexico City: Fondo de Cultura Económica, 2012.

Romo, Tere. "La Malinche as Metaphor." *Feminism, Nation, and Myth: La Malinche*. Ed. Rolando Romero and Amanda Nolacea Harris. Houston: Arte Público Press, 2005. 139–52.

Rose de Fuggle, Sonia. "Bernal Díaz del Castillo cuentista: la historia de doña Marina." *Actas del X Congreso de la Asociación Internacional de Hispanistas*. Ed. Antonio Vilanova. Barcelona: Promociones y Publicaciones Universitarias, 1992. 939–46.

Rueda-Acedo, Alicia Rita. *Miradas transatlánticas: El periodismo literario de Elena Poniatowska y Rosa Montero*. West Lafayette, IN: Purdue UP, 2012.

———. "*Las Soldaderas* de Elena Poniatowska: estampas femeninas de la revolución." *Romance Notes* 51.3 (2011): 423–31.

Ruisánchez, José Ramón. *Historias que regresan: Topología y renarración en la segunda mitad del siglo XX mexicano*. Mexico City: Fondo de Cultura Económica y Universidad Iberoamericana, 2012.

———. "Introducción." *Libro mercado: Literatura y neoliberalismo*. Ed. José Ramón Ruisánchez. Mexico City: Universidad Iberoamericana, 2015. 7–11.

Sabat de Rivers, Georgina. *En busca de Sor Juana*. Mexico City: Universidad Nacional Autónoma de México, 1998.

Said, Edward W. *Representations of the Intellectual*. New York: Vintage, 1996.

Salas, Elizabeth. *Soldaderas in the Mexican Military: Myth and History*. Austin: U of Texas P, 1990.

Sánchez Prado, Ignacio M. *Screening Neoliberalism: Transforming Mexican Cinema, 1988–2012*. Nashville, TN: Vanderbilt UP, 2014.

Sánchez Robles, María Guadalupe. "Dos Leonas para el siglo XXI." *Mujeres novohispanas en la narrativa mexicana contemporánea*. Ed. Cecilia Eudave, Alberto Ortiz, and José Carlos Rovira. Alicante: Universidad de Alicante (Cuadernos de *América sin nombre* 33), 2014. 187–202.

Sarlo, Beatriz. "Cultural Studies and Literary Criticism at the Cross-Roads of Value." *Contemporary Latin American Cultural Studies*. Ed. Stephen Hart and Richard Young. London: Arnold, 2003. 24–36.

Schuchardt, Beatrice. "Collage entre resistencia y apropiación: transposiciones cinematográficas del cuadro *Allá cuelga mi vestido* de Frida Kahlo en el filme *Frida* de Julie Taymor." *Frida Kahlo 'revisitada.' Estrategias transmediales—transculturales—transpicturales*. Ed. Alfonso de Toro and René Ceballos. Hildesheim: Georg Olms, 2014. 91–113.

Seydel, Ute. *Narrar historia(s): La ficcionalización de temas históricos por las escritoras mexicanas Elena Garro, Rosa Beltrán y Carmen Boullosa*. Madrid: Iberoamericana/Vervuert, 2007.

Shattuck, Roger. *Forbidden Knowledge: From Prometheus to Pornography*. New York: St. Martin's, 1996.

Smith, Rachel Greenwald. *Affect and American Literature in the Age of Neoliberalism*. Cambridge: Cambridge UP, 2015.

Solares, Ignacio. *Ficciones de la Revolución Mexicana*. Mexico City: Alfaguara, 2009.

Sommer, Doris. *Foundational Fictions: The National Romances of Latin America*. Berkeley: U of California P, 1991.

Sontag, Susan. *Al mismo tiempo: Ensayos y conferencias*. Trans. Aurelio Major. Barcelona: Debolsillo, 2007.

———. *Styles of Radical Will*. London: Vintage, 2001.

Soriano Vallès, Alejandro. *La hora más bella de Sor Juana*. Mexico City: Consejo Nacional para la Cultura y las Artes, 2008.

Sotelo, César Antonio. "Ecos del Bicentenario: la nueva novela histórica mexicana y su revisión de la Guerra de Independencia." *Revista de Literatura Mexicana Contemporánea* 50 (2011): 7–20.

Soto, Shirlene Ann. *The Mexican Woman: A Study of Her Participation in the Revolution, 1910–1940*. Palo Alto: R&E Research Associates, 1979.

Taibo, Paco Ignacio II. *Pancho Villa: Una biografía narrativa*. Mexico City: Planeta, 2006.

Torres Sánchez, Rafael. *La bottega de la Revolución: Conflicto armado y creación artística*. Mexico City: Consejo Nacional para la Cultura y las Artes, 2008.

Townsend, Camilla. *Malintzin's Choices: An Indian Woman in the Conquest of Mexico*. Albuquerque: U of New Mexico P, 2006.

Twinam, Ann. *Public Lives, Private Secrets: Gender, Honor, Sexuality, and Illegitimacy in Colonial Spanish America*. Stanford, CA: Stanford UP, 1999.

Valdés, María Elena de. *The Shattered Mirror: Representations of Women in Mexican Literature*. Austin: U of Texas P, 1998.

Valero Juan, Eva. "Salir del blanco y negro: Sor Juana Inés de la Cruz, de la historia a la ficción." *Mujeres novohispanas en la narrativa mexicana contemporánea*. Ed. Cecilia Eudave, Alberto Ortiz, and José Carlos Rovira. Alicante: Universidad de Alicante (Cuadernos de *América sin nombre* 33), 2014. 225–42.

Vargas, Ángel. "Mónica Lavín desmitifica a Sor Juana Inés de la Cruz para hacerla más cercana." *La Jornada*. 2 May 2009. Web. 12 October 2015.

Vargas Llosa, Mario. *La civilización del espectáculo*. Madrid: Alfaguara, 2012.

———. *La tentación de lo imposible*. Mexico City: Alfaguara, 2004.

Villa, Rosa Helia. *Itinerario de una pasión: Los amores de mi general*. Mexico City: Plaza & Janés, 1999.

Villaneda, Alicia. *Justicia y Libertad: Juana Belén Gutiérrez de Mendoza, 1875–1942*. Mexico City: Documentación y Estudios de Mujeres, 2010.

Weisz, Gabriel. *Tinta del exotismo: Literatura de la Otredad*. Mexico City: Fondo de Cultura Económica, 2007.

Wood, Michael. *Conquistadors*. Berkeley: U of California P, 2000.

Wright, Amy. "Genaro García's *Leona Vicario, heroína insurgente* (1910): A Centennial Revision of the Mexican Woman's Place in the Public Sphere." *Iberoamericana* 39 (2010): 145–60.

Wright de Kleinhans, Laureana. *Mujeres notables mexicanas*. Mexico City: Secretaría de Instrucción Pública y Bellas Artes, 1910. *Biblioteca de México "José Vasconcelos."* CONACULTA. Web. 28 September 2016.

Zagal, Héctor. "La venganza de sor Juana." *YouTube*. 3 November 2009. Web. 15 October 2016.

Zagal, Mónica. *La venganza de Sor Juana*. Mexico City: Planeta, 2007.

Zaid, Gabriel. *El secreto de la fama*. Barcelona: Debolsillo, 2010.

Zamora, Fernando. *Por debajo del agua*. Mexico City: Plaza & Janés, 2002.

Zamora, Lois Parkinson. *The Inordinate Eye: New World Baroque and Latin American Fiction*. Chicago: U of Chicago P, 2006.

Zapata, Óscar. "*Yo, la peor*: Entrevista con Mónica Lavín." *Milmesetas*. 13 January 2011. Web. 4 November 2016.

Index